THE
OXYRHYNCHUS PAPYRI
VOLUME XLV

THE OXYRHYNCHUS PAPYRI

VOLUME XLV

EDITED WITH TRANSLATIONS AND NOTES BY

A. K. BOWMAN

M. W. HASLAM

S. A. STEPHENS

M. L. WEST

WITH CONTRIBUTIONS BY

M. A. H. EL-ABBADI

E. LOBEL

J. R. REA

M. E. WEINSTEIN

Graeco-Roman Memoirs, No. 63

———

PUBLISHED FOR

THE BRITISH ACADEMY

BY THE

EGYPT EXPLORATION SOCIETY

3 DOUGHTY MEWS, LONDON, WC1N 2PG

1977

PRINTED IN GREAT BRITAIN
AT THE UNIVERSITY PRESS, OXFORD, BY VIVIAN RIDLER
PRINTER TO THE UNIVERSITY

AND PUBLISHED FOR

THE BRITISH ACADEMY
BY THE EGYPT EXPLORATION SOCIETY
3 DOUGHTY MEWS, LONDON, WC1N 2PG

ISSN 0306–9222 and ISBN 0 85698 065 x

PREFACE

AMONG its literary texts this Part contains eleven not previously known. Of the literary and dramatic fragments four are by the hand of Mr. E. Lobel (**3211–13, 3215**), and four by Dr. M. W. Haslam (**3209–10, 3214, 3216**; preliminary copies of **3209–10** were made by Mr. Lobel). Two fragments of New Comedy (**3217–18**) have been contributed by Dr. Susan Stephens. The prose work of literary criticism entitled 'Treatise on Plato?' (**3219**) is a revised form of Dr. Haslam's edition of this text in *BICS* 19 (1972). Professor M. L. West has transcribed and commented on thirteen fragments of Hesiod's *Erga* and *Aspis* (**3220–32**). Drs. Haslam, Stephens, and Weinstein, respectively, have made themselves responsible for two rhetorical declamations (**3235–6**); a piece of Isocrates (**3233**) and two Homeric glossaries (**3237–8**); a fragment of Thucydides (**3234**) and an idiosyncratic alphabetic glossary (**3239**).

The same trio have undertaken a considerable bulk of the documentary publication. One group of texts (**3254–62**) may be specially singled out for notice. The work of Dr. Stephens, they not only introduce a new archive of the early fourth century, but they also illustrate the technique of growing and processing flax. Dr. M. A. H. El-Abbadi has worked on three documents (**3242, 3250, 3251**), and Dr. A. K. Bowman makes public a second instalment (the first being in Part XLIV) of the texts already used as sources in his book *The Town Councils of Roman Egypt*.

The general editors would like to thank the Oxford University Printer for his accustomed care. Mr. Parsons compiled the indexes for the literary sections, Dr. Rea those for the documents. Dr. W. E. H. Cockle has given help in cleaning some of the texts and in proof reading.

P. J. PARSONS
J. R. REA
E. G. TURNER
General Editors,
Graeco-Roman Memoirs

July 1976

CONTENTS

TABLE OF PAPYRI

I. NEW LITERARY TEXTS

† All dates are A.D.

AKB	= A. K. Bowman	EL	= E. Lobel	MEW	= M. E. Weinstein
MAHEA	= M. A. H. El-Abbadi	JRR	= J. R. Rea	MLW	= M. L. West
MWH	= M. W. Haslam	SS	= S. Stephens		

LIST OF PLATES

NUMBERS AND PLATES

NOTE ON THE METHOD OF PUBLICATION
AND ABBREVIATIONS

THE method of publication follows that adopted in Part XLIV. As there, the dots indicating letters unread and, within square brackets, the estimated number of letters lost are printed slightly below the line. The texts are printed in modern form, with accents and punctuation, the lectional signs occurring in the papyri being noted in the *apparatus criticus*, where also faults of orthography, etc., are corrected. Iota adscript is printed where written, otherwise iota subscript is used. Square brackets [ ] indicate a lacuna, round brackets ( ) the resolution of a symbol or abbreviation, angular brackets ⟨ ⟩ a mistaken omission in the original, braces { } a superfluous letter or letters, double square brackets ⟦ ⟧ a deletion, the signs ʻ ʼ an insertion above the line. Dots within brackets represent the estimated number of letters lost or deleted, dots outside brackets mutilated or otherwise illegible letters. Dots under letters indicate that the reading is doubtful. Lastly, heavy Arabic numerals refer to Oxyrhynchus papyri printed in this and preceding volumes, ordinary numerals to lines, small Roman numerals to columns.

The abbreviations used are in the main identical with those in E. G. Turner, *Greek Papyri: an Introduction* (1968). It is hoped that any new ones will be self-explanatory.

NOTE ON INVENTORY NUMBERS

The inventory numbers in general follow a set pattern, of the form 20 3B.37/D (3)a. Here ʻ20ʼ is the number of the present cardboard box; ʻ3Bʼ refers to Grenfell and Hunt's third campaign at Oxyrhynchus; ʻ37ʼ is the series number given within that year to the metal packing box; ʻDʼ indicates a layer of papyri inside that box. A few inventory numbers have the form A. B.3.2/A(6); these refer to a separate series of boxes.

NOTE ON THE TERMS
'RECTO' AND 'VERSO', 'FRONT' AND 'BACK'
AND THE USE OF ARROWS (→, ↓)

THE terms 'recto' and 'verso' are strictly applicable to papyrus only in those cases (which are in a minority) where a recognizable part of a roll is preserved. If there is doubt whether a roll can be recognized, the terms used here are 'front' and 'back', in conjunction with arrows placed beside the first line of the text to indicate the direction of the fibres in relation to the writing. A horizontal arrow (→) means that the fibres run in the same direction as the lines of writing; a vertical arrow (↓) means that the fibres run at right angles to the lines of writing.

To avoid confusion it must be stressed that an arrow of this sort refers always to the relationship of the writing to the surface on which it stands, that is, the vertical arrow is not used simply to indicate the back of papyrus which has on the front a text running parallel with the fibres. It means that the writing of the text on the side in question runs at right angles to the fibres. The addresses of letters and other endorsements are often written parallel with the fibres on the back, while the main text is written parallel with the fibres on the front. It will be readily understood that because of the method of manufacture of papyrus sheets this means that the endorsement runs at right angles to the text on the front. However, since an arrow refers only to a single surface, such an endorsement will be preceded by the note 'Back →'.

These signs can be applied to codices, since in them the writing is normally only horizontal across the page. The arrow in horizontal position → will therefore indicate a page of a codex in which the fibres run in the same direction as the writing, horizontally; an arrow in a vertical position will mean that the writing, if horizontal, crosses the fibres, which are by inference vertical. It is necessary to set this point out explicitly since the basis of use of the signs → ↓ is not that laid down in P. Antinoopolis III p. xii; and a theoretical defect of the new basis is that it cannot be used to describe a page of a codex which bears no writing.

When the terms 'recto' and 'verso' are applied to parchment codices, it is proposed to retain the time-honoured meanings 'recto' = a right-hand page, 'verso' = a left-hand page.

ADDITIONS AND CORRECTIONS TO PAPYRI
PUBLISHED BY THE
EGYPT EXPLORATION SOCIETY

I 32 (= Ch.L.A. IV 267) 28–30. Read and restore:
> *opto te felicissi[mum (domine?) mul-*
> *tis annis cum [tuis (omnibus?)]*
> (vac.) *ben[e valere.*   See *BASP* 13 (1976) 53–4.

50 3. Expand προπ(ρατικοῦ). See XLV **3241** 8 n (p. 103).

61 1–3. Restore:
> [Αὐρήλιος Cαραπίων ὁ καὶ Ἀπολλωνια-]
> ρ[ὸ]ς γεγό[με]νος [cτρα(τηγὸς) Ἀρcι(νοίτου)]
> νυνὶ cτρα[τ]ηγὸς Ἑ[ρμοπολίτου].   See *JEA* 38 (1952) 88 n. 6.

  19. Expand cύμβολ(ον). See XLV **3241** introd., p. 100.

103 2. For πρυτανε[ύ]οντει read πρυτανε[ύc]αντι. See XLIV **3188** introd., para. 2.

157 3. By τοιcφωβου understand τῆc Φοβώου. See *Festschrift z. 150jährigen Bestehen d. berl. äg. Museums (Staatl. Mus. Berl.: Mitteil. aus d. äg. Sammlung* VIII), 346, n. 17. Cf. BL VI 95.
    A photograph shows that for φωβου we should read Φωβ‘ώ’ου (= Φοβώου).   J. R. Rea.

170 (Description). Re-edited in *BASP* 13 (1976) 17–29.

II 276 (= CPJ II 422 = S. Daris, *Documenti per la storia dell'esercito*, No. 68) 12. For Δερμειθῶν read Μερμέρθων. Z. Borkowski; confirmed from a photograph. Delete Δερμειθαι from A. Calderini, *Dizionario dei nomi geografici*, ii 2, p. 97, and Δερμειθῶν κώμη from WB III p. 292.

289 2, 12, 15, etc. Expand the abbreviation λπ̄ more probably to Λ(υκίων) Π(αρεμβολῆc) than to λ(αύραc) Π(οιμενικῆc), cf. ibid. introd. See CPR V 1. 5 n.

304 (= SB X 10246) 12–13. For τὸ πᾶν προκείμενον κεφάλαιον read τὸ μὲν π. κ. See XLIV **3198** 14 ff. n.

305 (= SB X 10222) 18–19. Read ἀκύρων οὐcῶ[ν καὶ ὦν] ἐὰν ἐπενέγ[κ]ωcιν π[ί[cτεων παcῶ]ν. See *ZPE* 19 (1975) 268–9.

310 (Description = SB X 10247) 2. Between διαγ(εγράφηκεν) and γε(ρδιακοῦ) insert ὑπ(έρ). For (ἔτουc) a read a (ἔτουc).
    4. Between μαθ(ητήc) and διά insert a (ἔτουc).
    See *ZPE* 19 (1975) 265–6.

320. Re-edited in *ZPE* 16 (1975) 309–14.

III 413 162. For τῇ πλατ(ε)ίᾳ θύρᾳ read τῇ πλαγίᾳ θύρᾳ. See CPR V 17. 8 n.

IV 722 27. For Ἀχ[ιλλεῖ read and restore Ἡρ[ακλᾷ.
    30. For οὐδ' ἐπιε[read and restore οὐδὲ μέ[ρουc τρόπῳ οὐδενί. See *ZPE* 20 (1976) 59.

VI 891 11. The suggestion θέρ[μ]αc, made in a footnote to XXXI **2569** (pp. 117–18), is withdrawn. Closer inspection has shown that what was taken for the descender of *rho* is a riser from an extravagant flourish on the *xi* of ἐξηγητοῦ in 10, which descends to touch 12 and rises again almost to touch 11. J. R. Rea.

VII 1016. The *terminus post quem* for this manuscript of Plato, *Phaedrus*, has been raised to A.D. 235 by the re-dating of the *recto* (VII **1044**). See *ZPE* 21 (1976) 14.

1031 22. For ἡμιαρτάβῳ read ἡμιαρταβίῳ. This reference is given under μέτρον ἡμιαρτάβιον in WB III p. 362 col. ii, but the correction is not in BL I–VI or in W. *Chr.* 343. Delete ἡμιάρταβος from LSJ. J. R. Rea.

1044. Extensively corrected and re-dated to A.D. 235 in *ZPE* 21 (1976) 1–13.

VIII **1081.** See H. W. Attridge, *P. Oxy. 1081 and the Sophia Jesu Christi,* in *Enchoria* 5 (1975) 1–8.

1104 13–14. For τὸν τῶν πολειτικῶν [ἐπί-]/τρο̅π̅ο̅ν read τὸν τῶν πολειτικῶν / τραπεζ(ίτην).

21. For τ . .( ) read τρα(πεζίτης). See XLIV **3193** introd.

1116 5. For ἀμφόδου read φυλῆ[ς. See *HSCP* 79 (1975) 17 n. 50.

1127 15. Read τῷ τε (over, probably, δέ) τόπῳ καὶ τῷ περιστερέωνι. J. R. Rea.

IX **1204** 2. For Ζηνογένει read Ζηναγένει. See XLV **3246** introd.

25. See under XLIII **3105** 3–4.

X **1249.** See J. Vaio, *Babrius* 110. 3–4, in *Philologus* 117 (1973) 140–1.

XII **1405** 5. See under XLIII **3105** 3–4.

1496. Dated to 5 Probus = A.D. 279/80. See A. K. Bowman, *Town Councils,* 133 n. 9.

XIV **1631.** See under XL **2895** i 19–20.

XVI **1910** 24. For δικαίου τοῖς τεταρτομοι(ρίταις) read δικαίου τοῖς (= τῆς) τεταρτομοι(ρίας). See *Festschrift z. 150jährigen Bestehen d. berl. äg. Museums* (Staatl. Mus. Berl.: Mitteil. aus d. äg. Sammlung VIII), 345–6. Cf. BL VI 104.

1926. See H. C. Youtie, *Questions to a Christian Oracle,* in *ZPE* 18 (1975) 253–57, with Plate VIII.

4. For τραπέζ(ης?) read τραπεζ(ιτίας) or τραπεζ(ιτείας).

5. For ζυγοςταςίας the papyrus has ζυγοςταςείας. Ibid.

XVII **2108** 1. Read Cπα[ρτιάτης ὁ καὶ Χαι]ρήμων. See XXXI **2560** 2 n.

2121 2. For κωμάρχου restore κωμογραμματέως.

84. For κω(μάρχης) expand κω(μογραμματεύς). See *Le monde grec: Hommages à Claire Préaux* 782 n. Cf. BL VI 105.

XVIII **2162** fr. 1(a) i 3; 13–17; 34–6. See *ZPE* 19 (1975) 99–100.

XX **2256** fr. 3. See A. Deman, *Eschyle et les crues du Nil,* in *Le monde grec: Hommages à Claire Préaux* 115–26.

XXII **2333.** See T. J. Fleming, *Ancient Evidence for the Colometry of Aeschylus' Septem,* in *GRBS* 16 (1975) 141–8, with one plate.

2336. See F. Ferrari, *Euripide, Elena* 634–45, in *Riv. fil.* 103 (1975) 385–93.

2343 7. Restore [ἐξεκ]αλεσάμην.

8. Read and restore ἐ]νεγύηςα καὶ ἐδιδαξάμην . . . ῥήτορα, 'I put down a surety and instructed . . . an advocate.' See CPR V 5. 3 n. (p. 11 ftn. 1).

2347 15. For Ἀπίων read Ἀττίων (written ατ'τιων). Read the same name in P. Mert. I 36. 22, i.e. for Κ̣ατ̣τᾶς Εὐςταθίο(υ), sic, read Ἀ[ὐ]ρ(ήλιος) Ἀττίων (written ατ'τιων) Εὐποθίου. The same person occurs in PSI IX 1078. 32, as pointed out in *ZPE* 18 (1975) 213, but the name was doubtless Ἀττίων again, rather than Ἀπίων. J. R. Rea.

17. For ἐκ( ) read ἐγρ(άφη). See *ZPE* 18 (1975) 213–14.

XXIII **2380** 2. Read and restore κάλ]λιςτον τὸ [δικαιότατον, λῶιστον δ' ὑγιαίνειν. If correct, this means that the verse, Theognis 255, was deeply indented, and the indentation is probably to be connected with the beginning of a new section. See *ZPE* 19 (1975) 178–9.

XXIV **2384.** Two fragments possibly from the same codex of Matthew are published in *Prometheus* 1 (1975) 195–200.

XXVI **2438.** See I. Gallo, *Una nuova biografia di Pindaro* (P. Oxy. 2438), Salerno, 1968.

2450. See D. C. Kurtz, *The Man-eating Horses of Diomedes in Poetry and Painting*, in *JHS* 95 (1975) 171–2 and Pl. XVIII.

XXVII **2455.** Notes on fragments 5, 7, and 19 in *BASP* 13 (1976) 77–9.

2460 fr. 5 *recto*. For Δ[ι]οϲκούρ[ου read Δ[ι]οϲκουρ[-. The name Διόϲκουροϲ is exceedingly rare; Διοϲκουρίδηϲ is much more likely. J. R. Rea.

XXXII **2617.** See D. L. Page, *Stesichorus: The Geryoneis* (P. Oxy. 2617), in *JHS* 93 (1973) 138–54.

2619. See D. L. Page, *Stesichorus: 'The Sack of Troy' and 'The Wooden Horse'* (P. Oxy. 2619 and 2803), in *Proc. Camb. Phil. Soc.* NS 19 (1973) 47–65.

XXXIV **2715** 2. The first copy should have τοῦ λαμ(προτάτου) restored after Ε[ὐοδίου. The second copy actually has τοῦ λαμ(προτάτου), cramped and very faded. Suggested by J. C. Shelton; confirmed from the originals.

In 2 n. delete the vertical rule after Φλαουί[ου.

2729 6–7. For ϲαπρά cf. *JRS* 60 (1970) 47 and n. 72, referring to Arrian, *Epictet.* IV, 5, 17, where a coin is rejected as ϲαπρόϲ, because it is Nero's, though it is of greater value than one of Trajan which is accepted.

XXXVII **2803.** See under XXXII **2619.**

2820. See *GRBS* 16 (1975) 295–303 for a new assessment by N. Lewis, using the following new readings:

4. For .[. .]νων read ἱκανῶν. R. A. Coles. A very small trace to the left of]ν near the foot suits only a diagonal, e.g. of α. Most of the gap is occupied by the arms of κ and the main part of α.

10–11. For εξ/ηει.ε read ἐξήρτυε. J. R. Rea.

XXXVIII **2843** 25. For εἰ̈δ̣ουϲ(?) read μέρουϲ. See *ZPE* 20 (1976) 58–60.

2861 9–10 n. In the third sentence for 'former' read 'converse'. J. D. Thomas.

XXXIX **2878, 2879, 2881, 2883,** and **2891.** Notes by D. L. Page in *CQ* 23 (1973) 199–201.

XL Introd. p. 6. The wrong equation 5 *modii* = 1 *artaba* is based on bad arithmetic, see *ZPE* 13 (1974) 195–6. On the sizes of the various *modius* and *artaba* measures see now *ZPE* 21 (1976) 43–62.

2895 i 19–20. For Τ̣..κλ...ιων read Τι(βέριοϲ) Κλ(αύδιοϲ) Ὠρίων, who also appears in XIV **1631** 39. See *ZPE* 18 (1975) 215–16. (Note that, contrary to what is stated there, no papyrus has been lost. A piece was inadvertently folded under when Plate I was made. The remains are fully consistent with the suggested reading. J. R. Rea.)

Another reference to the same person in P. Gen. inv. 244. 54–5 (*ZPE* 12 (1973) 80) is pointed out in *ZPE* 21 (1976) 15.

2904 5. For Ταμόιτοϲ read Τααμόιτοϲ. See *CR* 26 (1976) 111.

2916 5. The suggestion οἰκῷ[ν for οἰκί[αν, made in *CR* 26 (1976) 111, is excluded by the traces of the doubtful letter which has a longish descender. J. R. Rea.

2925 1. Perhaps equate κανανικλαρίωι with Latin *canaliclarius/canalicularius*. See *BASP* 13 (1976) 49–52.

XLII **3006** 10. For parallels see *ZPE* 16 (1975) 76.

3028 introd. para. 3. The practice of keeping grain on the threshing-floor till government commitments were met is now attested by P. Petaus 53 of A.D. 184/5, over 100 years earlier than X **1255**. J. C. Shelton.

3030 3 n. (p. 94 para. 3). In the list of receipts after '131/2 P. Tebt. 361;' add '143/4 BGU I 299;'. J. C. Shelton.

3036–45 introd. Add PUG I 19 to the table of receipts for ἐπικεφάλαιον πόλεωϲ. See *Rev. hist. de droit franç. et étr.* 53 (1975) 511. (The plate (PUG Tav. XI) allows the possibility of reading the date in line 4 as θ′ [κ]αὶ ζ′ = A.D. 314/15 instead of ι̣γ̄ [καὶ] ᾱ

= A.D. 304/5. The Athenodorus who signed the receipt is presumably the systates of that name who appears in PSI V 462 of A.D. 314/15. J. R. Rea.)

3051 7. For Ϲενεκ[ι]ανῆϲ read Ϲενεκανῆϲ, cf. P. Hamb. I 3. 9 n. J. C. Shelton.

3068. Re-interpreted in *ZPE* 19 (1975) 280–1.

XLIII **3097** translation (p. 28). Before 'to undertake' insert 'immediately'. See *AJP* 97 (1976) 190.

3104 2 n. *ad fin.* For XX **2273** 1 read XXVII **2473** 1.

3105 3–4. For ελ./.[.].. read probably ἐλα/μ[ἐ]νῳ. So also in XII **1405** 5 restore probably ἐ[λα]μἐνῳ. See IX **1204** 25 with BL I 333 τῷ ἐλαμἐ[νῳ αὐτὸν εἰ]ϲ τὴν δεκαπρωτείαν. A photograph shows that the space requires the restoration of αὐτόν as Wilcken suggested. For εἰλάμην etc. see B. G. Mandilaras, *The Verb*, 154 (§ 318. 2). J. R. Rea.

3117 6. For τῷ . . . . . . .ῳ the suggestion τῷ ζερήνῳ, made in *AJP* 97 (1976) 190, does not appear to suit the traces. J. R. Rea.

18. Restore e.g. διακειμἐ]ναϲ. See *AJP* 97 (1976) 190.

19. Restore e.g. ἀξιοῦϲα]. Ibid.

3121 introd. Add to the table on p. 81 the price of gold in A.D. 301 found in the new fragments of Diocletian's price edict, 72,000 denarii. See R. and F. Naumann, *Der Rundbau in Aezani* (1973), 57; M. Giacchero, *Edictum Diocletiani*, 114–15. Cf. H. Temporini, etc., *Aufstieg u. Niedergang d. röm. Welt*, II ii, 593 addendum. T. C. Skeat.

3121 8 n. Add a reference to *ZPE* 18 (1975) 308, where attention is drawn to another occurrence of the title ὁ ἐπιφανέϲτατοϲ παῖϲ = *nobilissimus puer*, used this time of Flavius Honorius, consul A.D. 386 and future emperor.

3123 18. For τὸ β',] τοῖϲ μἐ[λλουϲι] ὑπάτοιϲ read probably τὸ β', μ]ἐλλ[ουϲιν] ὑπάτοιϲ. Dr. Dieter Hagedorn pointed out that none of the parallels, collected by him in *ZPE* 10 (1973) 131–4, has the article. The traces are very badly damaged, but the lack of space confirms that τοῖϲ did not appear here either. J. R. Rea.

3138. The word ὀρθογράφοϲ occurs also in *Archiv* 2 (1902–3) p. 219 l. 26 in a Christian subliterary text. C. H. Roberts.

8. For π.. (vac.) the suggestion πα(ρά), made in *AJP* 97 (1976) 190, does not appear to satisfy the traces. J. R. Rea.

3140. In the last line of the translation (p. 118) for 'Sarapion' read 'Serenus', see text line 12.

3150 7 n. Add a reference to Aurelia Tarilla daughter of Philadelphus in P. Merton III 124 of A.D. 520. She is clearly distinct from Tarilla d. of Praous in XVI **1995** of A.D. 542 and also not particularly likely to be identical with the Tarilla in **3150**. J. R. Rea.

XLIV **3169** 60, 92. For Πνεφερϲόιτοϲ read Τνεφερϲόιτοϲ, a woman's name. Correct translation and index accordingly. J. R. Rea.

P. Fay. 39. 1–2. For μιϲθωτῇ τέλουϲ ἱερο(ῦ) Βουκόλ(ων) read μιϲθωτῇ τέλουϲ ἱεροβουκόλ(ων). See *ZPE* 16 (1975) 77–9.

203 = P. Cair. Preisigke 1. Another scrap is now published in *JJP* 18 (1974) 187.

P. Hibeh II 205. On the date see *ZPE* 16 (1975) 292–4.

276 (= CPL 260). 5. Expand *leg(ati) n(ostri)* rather than *leg(ionis) n(ostrae)*. See *Le monde grec: Hommages à Claire Préaux* 773–4.

P. Tebt. II 304. 8–9. For μη[[.]]δένα λόγον ἀητίαν ϲυ⟨ν⟩ῆψαν read μὴ δὲ{ν} ἄλογον ἀητίαν ϲυ⟨ν⟩ῆψαν, equivalent to μοὶ δὲ ἄλογον ἀηδίαν ϲυ⟨ν⟩ῆψαν. See *ZPE* 18 (1975) 75–6.

371 (Description). Text in *ZPE* 16 (1975) 51–4.

392. 38. For Ἀγαθῆϲ read Ϲαγαθῆς. See *ZPE* 21 (1976) 16.

441 (Description). Text in *ZPE* 16 (1975) 55–8.

449 (Description). Text in *ZPE* 16 (1975) 47–50.

524 (Description). Text in *ZPE* 16 (1975) 59–62.

622 (Description). Text in *ZPE* 16 (1975) 54–5.

I. NEW LITERARY TEXTS

3209. ALCMAN, Μέλη vi

39 3B.78/L(1)a   Fr. 1, 8×16 cm.; fr. 2, 4·5×9·4 cm.   Second century

An end-title reveals these scraps to be remnants of a roll of bk. 6 of the μέλη of Alcman. The identification is due to Dr. Rea. An ambiguous notice in the Suda apart (see below), this is the first testimony of the sixth book of μέλη; on the basis of that notice, one supposes it to be the final such book. The papyrus gives us suggestive remains of the last few lines, most substantially of the last two, but their precise import is hidden.

The metre is of some interest. Five out of the last seven lines (fr. 1) have their first few syllables more or less intact:

$$
\begin{aligned}
&3\ \kappa\lambda\acute{\epsilon}o\varsigma\ \phi\epsilon\rho[&& \cup-\cup\ [\ (\text{or less likely } \cup--\ [) \\
&4\ \varsigma\kappa\alpha\acute{\iota}\rho o\iota\varsigma\alpha\ \tau[&& --\cup\ [\ (\text{or less likely } ---\ [) \\
&6\ \hat{o}\ \delta\ '\ \epsilon\mathring{v}\theta\grave{v}\varsigma\ .[&& \cup-\cup\ [\ (\text{or } \cup--\ [) \\
&8\ \mathring{\alpha}\chi\grave{\omega}\ \delta\ '\ \mathring{\alpha}\phi\ '\ \mathring{v}\psi\eta\lambda\hat{\omega}[&& --\cup---\ [\\
&9(ult.)\ \delta\acute{o}\mu\omega\nu\ \mathring{\alpha}\pi\ '\ \mathring{\alpha}\kappa\rho\omega[&& \cup-\cup--\ [
\end{aligned}
$$

We may synthesize as $\times-\cup-\underset{\times}{-}-$ [.[1] The uniformity is remarkable. The following citations may be compared:—

(1) A restoration of PMG 2 (iv) (**XXIV 2389** fr. 3(a)) 3–7 giving three and a half consecutive iambic tetrameters was suggested by Barrett (*Gnomon* 33 (1961) 685); the incorporated lemma is said by ps.-Herodian to have occurred ἐν τῇ δευτέρᾳ ᾠδῇ ('no doubt of Bk. 1' Lobel: this is supported by the context of the citation). PMG 15 (bk. 1?) may be a single such verse. Cf. PMG 92(d), PMG 79.

(2) PMG 59(a) consists of two consecutive iambic trimeters catalectic, $\underset{\times}{\cup}-\cup-\times\ |$ $-\cup-\cup--$ (ἔν τινι τῶν μελῶν, Archytas ὁ ἁρμονικός ap. Chamaeleon ap. Athen. xiii 600f). So does PMG 96 ($\underset{\times}{-}-\cup-\underset{\times}{-}\ |\ \underset{\cup}{\cup}\cup-\cup--$, Athen. xiv 648b); and PMG 30 is a single one ($\underset{\times}{-}-\cup-\underset{\times}{-}\ |-\cup-\cup--$, Aristid. *or.* 28. 51, II 158 Keil). PMG 19 is a sequence of three and a half lines of the same quantitative structure, $\times-\cup-\times-$ $\cup-\cup--$, but with caesura after the fifth element in only one of the verses (Athen. iii 110f): Ἀλκμὰν ἐν τῶι ιε cod. A (om. CE?), corr. to ε' Schweighaeuser. (Assigned to the same poem as PMG 96 by Wilamowitz.)

(3) PMG 14 has three otherwise unconnected lines of the form $\times-\cup-\cup\ |$ $-\times-\cup--$, analysed by Heliodorus as a catalectic iambic trimeter of a type admitting a spondee in the fourth foot. At least one of these lines occurred in company with

---

[1] $\underset{\times}{-}$ means presumed anceps element occupied in the given instance by a long syllable; similarly $\underset{\cup}{\cdot}$. × signifies that $\cup$ and $-$ are both attested.

B

dactylic cola; the fourth-foot alternation is attested '*in primo*' (sc. *libro*, one presumes; Priscian III 428 Keil). Cf. the lemma of the beginning of a poem at PMG 5 (XXIV **2390**) fr. 2 i 22–3 as supplemented by Page, cὲ Μῶ]ςα λίccομαι π[αντ]ῶν μάλιcτα.

(4) One of several lengths labelled 'alcmanicum' by Servius is the 'iambic trimeter brachycatalectic', $\overline{\underset{\times}{}} - \cup - \overline{\underset{\times}{}} \mid - \cup - \underset{\times}{\vee} -$, PMG 161(*c*); cf. PMG 174.

(5) PMG 20 consists of four and a half consecutive iambic dimeters, $\overline{\underset{\times}{}} - \cup - \times - \cup -$: ἐν τῷ ε′, Athen. x 416d. PMG 110 and 121 are single such lines. PMG 59(*b*) has another, with different but allied cola fore and aft.

(6) The metrical structure of PMG 89 is uncertain, but it contains several cola which begin with iambic movement, as well as several which do not. Cf. PMG 41, PMG 16.

For the iambo-trochaic (rather than κατὰ μέτρον iambic) nature of some of these lengths, see A. M. Dale, *CQ* 13 (1963) 48–9 (= *Collected Papers*, 117–18).

There is no proof that cola of different movement were not used in this final strophe or poem, but the papyrus gives strong presumptive evidence. The uniformity points in fact to composition κατὰ cτίχον. On the one hand we have the several sequences of identical iambic cola listed under (1), (2), and (5) above (PMG 2 (iv), 19, 59(*a*), 96, 20), on the other we have attestation of homogeneous composition in other metres, ὅλα ᾄcματα ἰωνικά (Heph. 12: PMG 46), ὅλαc cτροφάc of acatalectic dactylic tetrameters (Heph. 43: PMG 27), four consecutive dactylic hexameters (PMG 26), a pair of cretic hexameters (PMG 58), and the peculiar testimony of Heph. π. cημείων 4, p. 74 Consbr. (PMG 161(*a*)), of fourteen-stanza poems, the first seven stanzas being in one metre, the second seven in another. I do not know whether Hesychius' entry in κλεψίαμβοι (Ἀριcτόξενοc· μέλη τινὰ παρ' Ἀλκμᾶνι) is also relevant. It is a reasonable supposition, though in the present state of the evidence it can be no more than a tentative one, that we have here a stichic iambic composition: whether in tetrameters, catalectic trimeters, or dimeters, I cannot say, but if the end-title is centred, it will be one of the shorter lengths.

The statement in the Suda runs ἔγραψε βιβλία ϛ′ μέλη καὶ Κολυμβώcαc. It is now clear that this is to be taken as attesting six books of μέλη, and this is a welcome piece of clarification. But are we now to read ἔγραψε βιβλία ϛ′ μελ⟨ῶν⟩, καὶ Κολυμβώcαc, implying that the Κολυμβῶcαι are something apart from the six books of μέλη, or ἔγραψε βιβλία ϛ′, μέλη καὶ κολυμβώcαc, implying (despite the fact that the general title was simply μέλη, witness **3209** and XXIV **2392**) that κολυμβῶcαι along with μέλη are a constituent of the six books? The Κολυμβῶcαι remain as enigmatic as ever, and now that we are no longer free to adopt Mr. Lobel's hitherto phenomena-saving suggestion that there were five books of μέλη and one entitled Κολυμβῶcαι (*P. Oxy.* XXIV p. 8 n.), it is more likely than before that there is corruption (cf. J. A. Davison, *Proc. IX Int. Congr. Pap.* 35–8 = *From Archilochus to Pindar*, 179–83).[1]

---

[1] Might not κολυμβώcαc, by graphic error, be hiding μελιαμβικά or μελιαμβ(ικὰc) ᾠδάc? (But I will not conceal the principal objection to this, namely that the single certain attestation of the word

There is a bare possibility, raised by γαμ[at fr. 4. 3 and certainly not contradicted by the main fragment, that the pieces under this number are from a marriage-song.[1] (Leonidas of Tarentum calls Alcman τὸν ὑμνητῆρ᾽ ὑμεναίων.) If so, it is of interest that Sappho's final book appears to have been constituted mainly of epithalamia (see Lobel, *Cάπφους Μέλη*, xiii–xv, Page, *Sappho and Alcaeus*, 112–19, 126). It may be worth observing that all the Alcman quotations in catalectic trimeters (cited under (2) above) are compatible with their belonging to such a class of song.[2]

The text is written in a round and upright hand of fairly common type (comparable with, for example, the rather stiffer XXVIII **2494**), assigned a date within the first half of the second century. There is nothing remarkable about the lection signs. I find no trace of a second hand. The back is blank.

Fr. 1

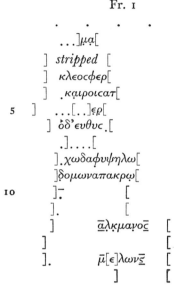

μελίαμβοι, Diog. Laert. 6. 76, is applied *not* to melic iambics such as we seem to have in **3209** but to one of Cercidas' dactylo-epitrite compositions. [Elsewhere the word is restored from μιμίαμβοι; VIII **1082** fr. 4. 17, Cercidas' end-title, may equally be με]λιάμβων or μι]μιάμβων.])

In the next sentence, πρῶτος δὲ εἰσήγαγε τὸ μὴ ἑξαμέτροις μελῳδεῖν, I would delete μή (cf. ps.-Plut. *de mus.* 3, of Terpander's prooemia, τοῖς ἔπεσι . . . μέλη περιτιθέντα ᾄδειν).

[1] In view of this possibility, it may be wondered whether Sappho fr. 117, †χαίροις ἀ νύμφα†, χαιρέτω δ᾽ ὁ γάμβρος, cited without attestation of authorship by Hephaestion *Ench.* iv 2 (p. 13 Consbr.), might find a better home in this poem or group of poems by Alcman: the metre is catalectic iambic trimeter. The only counter-indication that I see is that cod. U of Choeroboscus in Heph. iv (p. 220 Consbr.) transmits ἀνύμφα (with smooth breathing); but although this is the only relic of specifically aeolic prosody in the manuscripts at any of the three attestations, it is perhaps enough to uphold the traditional authorship.

[2] ϛ′ may be as likely a correction as ε′ for the attribution at PMG 19, in view of its special liability to corruption.

The papyrus continues for a further 6·5 cm., blank.

Fr. 1 4 ., possibly a flat-topped sigma   5 ..., scattered specks, extending into left margin
6 .[, trace just above letter-top level, close to ϲ, probably *apostrophe* or *diastole*, and medial speck to right
on isolated fibre   7 Mostly stripped; some ink on the lower layer suggests original damage   8].,
oblique trace coming in to foot of χ: α rather than ε   After δ, if an *apostrophe* was written it will have
been lost   11]., tail of *coronis*?   To the right of the name, a blot   14]., indeterminate
traces that I cannot account for

Fr. 2

]υκ.νεβρωι.[
].χυϲκατο[
]..ενκν[
]'..τα...[
5   ][
]απονα[
]καγερωχ[
]λενοιτ[
]ειϲα..[
10   ]εκϲπαρ[
]αιβ.[

· · · ·

Fr. 2 This fragment, badly abraded, was
found adhering to the back of the lower part
of fr. 1 (the other way up), and is in a fragile condition. The readings are unusually liable to be
erroneous.

Fr. 2 1 .[, low curve of e.g. ϲ, or bottom left
of δ   2].χυϲ, tops only   3].,
perhaps εϲ   4 *Apostrophe* uncertain   ...[,
traces anomalous: correction?   6 α, π,
and final α very doubtful, represented by scattered specks   9 ..[, κ or π, then rising curve,
e.g. λ

Fr. 3

·   ·   ·   ·   ·
]ακυν.[
]φοβω[
].τετρ[
].δητ[
·   ·   ·   ·

Fr. 3 1 The upper papyrus layer was defi-
cient when the text was written   α: a corner of
the papyrus is turned over and liable to become
detached, but α is certain   .[, medial trace,
apparently horizontal, perhaps ε   2 φ, represented by tail and part of right-hand side   β,
bottom half only   3]., confused with
offsets   4]., two specks, positions suggesting α

Fr. 4   Fr. 5   Fr. 6

```
     ·        ·           ·      ·              ·     ·     ·

   ].·.[              ].βεβ.[               ]ς [

   ]..[.].[           ]μειạ[                ]  [

   ]ϲ·γαμ[               ·        ·         ]οϲ[

   ]ατοϲτ.[                                 ]  [

5  ]κᾱλον[                              5   ]. [

   ].·.[                                    ]  [

     ·      ·      ·                        ]πν[

                                             ·     ·     ·
```

Fr. 4   1 Indeterminate traces on lower papyrus layer   2 Second letter, if a single letter, represented by a low curve, perhaps θ or ο   5 *Longum* not quite certain   Above ο, casual ink (rather than accent)?   6]., perhaps ε

Fr. 5   1]., oblique coming in to base of β, suggesting α   .[, traces on isolated fibre   2]μ, or λ, less good

Fr. 6   3 Perhaps line end   7 Or]π.ν[; π is on a displaced bit of papyrus

Remaining: (1) a scrap with indeterminate traces of perhaps three or four letters; (2) a piece (3·2 × 6·5 cm.) with horizontal fibres on both sides, probably therefore to be linked with fr. 2 and the lower half of fr. 1 (see at fr. 2): it has very slight traces of ink on either side; and (3) several small pieces, either blank or as near blank as makes no difference.

Fr. 1   3 Poets confer κλέοϲ on others, but it might be thought more likely that Alcman is concerned with his own κλέοϲ: does the Muse (or Muses) bring it?

κλέοϲ, not κλίοϲ, probably because of original intervocalic digamma: so Κλεηϲιϲήρα in the Louvre Partheneion 72, and Κλεο- regularly in the Laconian inscriptions. But πυλεῶν' at XXIV **2387** fr. 3 ii 5 (= PMG 3. 65) without such justification. Cf. on εὐθύϲ, line 6 below.

4 ϲκαίροιϲα is acceptable. Such behaviour is surely too undignified for a Muse; perhaps a παρθένοϲ? (I do not know if there is any relevance in the horse imagery at Alcm. 1. 50 ff. Anacreon has ϲκιρτᾶν in an extended girl–foal metaphor, PMG 417. 15.)

6 ὃ δ' εὐθύϲ rather than ὅδ' εὐθύϲ? Is the subject Alcman himself, or, if this is a wedding-song, the bridegroom? εὐθύϲ not εὖ θυϲ-, for ϲ appears to be followed by a *diastole*, clarifying the articulation (which otherwise might be ambiguous, εὐθύϲ or εὐθύ); for the high position of the sign see XLIV **3153** 563 n. Less probably εὐθύ ϲ', the sign being an *apostrophe* (Alcman has ϲε as well as τε attested for him by Apollonius Dyscolus, PMG 70). For the final letter, the location of the speck excludes only υ among vowels.

εὐϲύ(ϲ) would be the expected spelling. Lyric papyri often vary in the extent of dialectal thoroughness. Non-laconization again at line 8 below.

8 ἀχώ makes an acceptable reading, ἔχω and ὄχω are excluded. ἀχώ nominative or accusative? ἀφ' ὑψηλῶ[: singular or plural? ἀχώ (ἠχώ) appears in wedding-song context at Sappho 44. 27 (ἄειδον μέλος ἄγν[ον ἴκα]νε δ' ἐϲ αἴθ[ερα]| ἄχω θεϲπεϲία γελ[ ), [Hes.] *Scut.* 279 (περὶ δέ ϲφιϲιν ἄγνυτο ἠχώ), cf. Eurip. *IA* 1009 ('Υμέναιος . . . ἔϲταϲεν ἰαχάν), Theoc. 18. 8 (ὑπὸ δ' ἰαχε δῶμ' ὑμεναίῳ), and for ἀχώ Bacchyl. 23. 3, Alc. G 2. 34. But the word is of course not restricted to such context. Frequently of the sound of musical instruments. An alternative articulation would be ᾇ χ' ὦδ'.

ἀφ' ὑψηλῶ[: contrast]πιππωνεα[('presumably for]φ' ἱππ-' Lobel) at XXIV **2388** fr. 6. 9. This violates the principle stated by Ap. Dysc., PMG 87, unless ἀφ' ὑψ- is an alternative orthography for ἀπ' ὑψ-.

9 δόμων ἀπ' ἄκρω[: ἄκρω[ν, presumably. Ἄχω from the house-tops? The singing at the Athenian Adonis festival took place on the roof (A. *Lys.* 389 ff., and see Sandbach on Men. *Sam.* 39). Cf. further A. *Ach.* 262 (spectator of phallic procession), Callim. *Hy.* vi 1–4. Otherwise, δόμων may be qualified rather by ὑψηλῶ[ν, and ἀφ' ὑψηλῶ[ν . . .]| δόμων ἀπ' ἄκρω [τ(ε). . . becomes conceivable, however remotely. I suppose δόμω νάπα κρῳ[need not be considered.

The 'paragraphus' is presumably incorporated by a coronis, of which the remaining traces here and in line 11 will be remnants.

Fr. 2 1 νεβρῶ(ι), Ἔβρω(ι)?

7 If the reading is sound, part of ἀγέρωχος; again at PMG 5 fr. 1(*b*) 4 and 10(*b*) 15 (neither the present place), and attested for Alcman as meaning cεμνός by Eust. *Il.* 314. 43. If the metre is iambic, κἀγερωχ-.

10 ἐκ Cπάρ[τας, al.

Fr. 3 1 Part of κύων? But the verbs κυνῆν, μᾱκύνην are also available, *inter al.*

Fr. 4 3 γαμ[: μ is virtually certain: γαμῆν or cognate is highly probable (alternatives: γᾶ, γαμόροc, γαμφηλόc, γαμψῶνυξ or cognate). Reference to a famous marriage (Helen and Menelaus?), or to the present occasion, or neither?

5 κᾱλον: if the *longum* is (*a*) rightly read and (*b*) rightly placed, cf. κᾱλον (so marked in pap.) again at PMG 3 (**2387**) fr. 1. 5 and see note in ed. pr.

3210. COMMENTARY ON ALCMAN? (ADDENDUM TO XXIV 2389?)

No inventory no.   Fr. 1, 6·1 × 10·5 cm.   First century

The following fragments were referred to in the introduction to XXIV **2389**, a commentary on Alcman, where they were described by Mr. Lobel as 'a few very much tattered and rubbed prose fragments, perhaps also a commentary, in variant A'. I have been unable to elicit any coherent sense from them, but it is clear that the work represented is a commentary, and the internal evidence goes some way towards justifying a presumption that these are further fragments of the same manuscript as frr. 1–34 of **2389**. Sappho is twice mentioned (1. 9, 12), but a probable mention of Archidamus (2. 6) suggests that Alcman may be the poet under discussion.

Mr. Lobel, at **2389**, identifies other manuscripts that apparently proceed from the hand of the same scribe and isolates their various distinguishing features. XXXIV **2694** was claimed in *BICS* 7 (1960) 46 for the same man (wrongly, in my view), and I should have judged that he was responsible for XXV **2430**, a somewhat larger version of what Mr. Lobel designates variant A (the *coronides* of **2430** may be compared with that of **2389** fr. 4). Mr. Lobel assigns the hand to the second half of the first century.

Fr. 1

Col. i   Col. ii

·   ·   ·   ·   ·

(*a*)   ].[.]..τι   [

          ]ινα   .[

(*b*)   ].αρ.   ..[

          ].ιοδε [

5   ].νια   .[

(*c*)   ]φ[..]ωι   [

          ].[.]κα   .[

].φ[.]ελθ.[.].η   [

]..ϲαπφω[.]ιϲ   [

10   ]οτεδιαδυεινφ..ηεν   [

].......μφωνα`..´ληγει   .[

]ξειδ...ϲαπφωδια   [

]ερτωνε.ϲυμφωνον   [

]δον...α.[.].ενος..α   [

15   ]...ερ[.].ου.νιϲαρητεον   [

].....ηϲφηϲινοτιπαρατον   [

].[.]ν.....`.´[..]..οιειτηι   [

          ]κουρ[   ]α   [

          ]ωϲ.[

20   ]..[.]δοξε[

].[..]π[..]α.ου[

Foot (?)

Fr. 1 In many places the surface is so rubbed that the letters have almost completely or have completely disappeared. Where the damage is less severe and scattered traces survive I have reported those that represent a restricted choice of letters. Where no traces remain I have put square brackets, provided that there is reason for believing that letters once stood there. All supralineal additions and corrections are to be understood as being by the second hand unless otherwise stated.

Alignment of the verso and recto fibres establishes, I think, that the positions of (*a*) and (*b*) relative to each other and to (*c*) are as shown.

Col. i 3]., upright, perhaps π   ., oblique, compatible with α   4 οδ, a dot below is evidently accidental   ε, mid-stroke prolonged   6 φ, descender only   8 θ, or ο   .[, upright   ]., apex: δ or λ   9 [.]ι, or η   10 .., compatible with ων   11].., perhaps δε; the next three letters hardly ειϲ, not δυο; then ϲυ unverifiable   `..´, several traces, the last an upright   12 ιδ, or κ, less good   ..., a high and a middle speck; traces of a possible upright; upright and top bar (γ, τ); high speck of another letter: ειτο, ειτι, ητα, possible *inter alia*   13 ., apparent upright, followed by low trace: ν (ἐν) and ιϲ (εἰϲ) are possibilities   14]δ, or λ, μ   .[, perhaps κ   ..(*ad fin.*), anomalous: low trace suggesting upright followed by stroke sloping forwards and extending slightly below line: $\epsilon\rho$, $\epsilon\iota$?　　15 .(*ante* ϵ), compatible with π　　.(*ante* ν), upright, rubbed clean to right　　16 .(*tert.*), upright with hook or bar to right at top　　17 ...(*post* ν), specks, an upright, a low curve, two specks one low one above line　　.(*quart.*), γ, π, τ　　' . ', what remains appears to be a horizontal bar with an upward curl at right　At the end, some fainter traces that extend up to the previous line, possibly offsets　　20]., low horizontal, ξ?

　　Col. ii 3 ..[, either a lemma in ecthesis (perhaps $\epsilon\iota$[) or a marginal siglum (cf. e.g. **2389** fr. 9 ii)

Fr. 2

Top (?)

```
            ]η . . παν[
     ] . . . . [ . ] . . εκε[
     ] . . . . [ . ] . ν . . . ιδαν[
     ]τα . εκπ . . . . . . [
  5      ] . [ . . ] . [ . . . . . ]τα[
     ]αρχιδ[
        ] . . α . [ . ] . . [
        ] . ην . . [ . ] . [ . ] . [
     ]τη . . . . παρατηνγα[
 10  ]ατερτο .¯. ραφεεθαι ' . [ . ] . φ . οεεθαι ' [
     ]υθωεεετινγαιο[
        ] . ιεφαιρο ' τ . . ' μοι . . [
        ] . . οε . [
        ]ειεκαθα ' . ' . . [
 15       ]φατοετπ . [
          ] . α̅ι̅ε̅ι̅ε ' . . ' η̅[
          ] . ευντω[
        ] . [ . . . ]αιανδε[
          ] . δυναταιπα[
 20       ] . ανηγ . [
          ]ειδεε[
          ]υνθι[
          ] . ι . . . θειανμεν . [
          ] . ηεεεα . . εφω[
 25  ]ρχεεεωεεωεφ . [
     ]δ ' οι ' [ . ] . αλω[ . ] . [
     ]αρ ' ε ' ια . [ . . ] . ιν . . [
              *Foot* (?)
```

Fr. 2   3 .[, upright   After ν, perhaps α or ο; then scattered specks before ι, of which the most considerable is apparently oblique, running upwards from left to right: χ neither excluded nor particularly suggested   ν[, μ less good, for the left hasta is quite vertical   4 κ, or ν   After π, perhaps ε   7 Before α, two uprights   9 Before π, perhaps δι   10 .⁻., first, upright curving to right at top, second, upright, third, speck at letter-top level   11 ι, anomalous: extending below the line and sloping backwards; hardly ρ   12 ς, almost certain, ε just possible   14 ..[, πε possible   15 τ, or ιc   .[, α possible   16 '..', perhaps το   20]., seemingly two uprights, perhaps π   21 ς, or π   22 ι, or η   23 . (*ante* θ), high trace, perhaps top of oblique   .[, low curve: probably ο or ω   24]., a mere speck   η, represented by two apparent uprights with suggestion of mid-stroke   25 .[, a low curve: α, ε, ο, ω   26 'οι', apparently by 1st hand: the surface is stripped above the line, so that there is room for up to three letters after οι   ]., bottom of upright   ].[, several traces, one perhaps an upright; a sublinear speck may be accidental   27]., two strokes meeting at top to form an apex, the first more vertical than horizontal, the second more horizontal than vertical   ..[, first, upright with top bar to right (γ, c, π?), second, upright with hook to right at top (ε, c?)

Fr. 3

Col. i   Col. ii

a] ..ηρ[

b] εικαλο[

]θαιη   ..].εcτ[

].ατονα[..]'.'[   ] μενουπ[

]αυταμεν[   ]   αcκαλαφ[

]πε[.].ο....ο[   ]   cινα[

5   ]c   φηcε[

]γοντοc   [

]μαχεcθαι   [   ]α[

].β[   ]   ] ε[

.   .   .   .   .

Fr. 3 This fragment probably belongs above fr. 4, for in each fragment the script of the first column is rather small and cramped, whereas that of the second is larger than usual. They do not evidently join, however, and the distance between them cannot be determined.

a, b, in upper margin, in 2nd hand; apparently line beginnings.

Col. i 2]., high trace, compatible with τ   '.', probably a letter in suspension at the end of the line   4 π, or τ   ς, or ι   ]., upright   ...., four uprights, with mid- or high stroke between second and third:]ποιειτο[acceptable   8]., upright, probably ι or η

Col. ii 1 ..], or ...]   ]., upright   3 φ, or δ   4 ςι, better than τι, χι or π

Fr. 4

Col. i	Col. ii

.   .   .   .

]ημεις   [

]κεινοι   θ[

].ϛε   τα[

]ηοτ[ ]   το[

5]ψευδ[ ]   τ[

         ]   [

        ].   [

         ]   [

         ]   [

10   ]ρ   [

       ]ωι   ο[

        ]   .[

        ]   .[

            ].[

.   .   .   .   .

Fr. 5

.   .   .   .

]....[

]δ.[

]..[

].ωϛ[

5   ].[.]...[

].εορατ.[

]υλινδρο[

]..[

.   .   .   .   .

Fr. 6

.   .   .   .

].[

]φαιϛ.[

]ρητει[

].ονιϲα[

5   ]ιν.[

]..ο[

]δ..νν[

]..[

.   .   .   .

Fr. 7

Col. i	Col. ii

.   .   .   .

]ρ[   ]   [

]ν[.].[ ]   [

].ον   .[

].   [

5   ]π..   δ[

.   .   .   .

Fr. 8

. . .

]πε[

. . .

Fr. 9

. . .

]α[

]ικ.[

Fr. 10

. . .

]ιϛ[

. . .

Fr. 4 Col. i 5 ψ, or φ   δ, or λ, μ   10 ρ, descender only   ii 14 high curve, probably ρ or ϲ

Fr. 5 1 ..(*sec. et tert.*), uprights   2 .[, upright   6 ο, or θ   .[, low trace, perhaps of upright

Fr. 6 2 .[, low trace of upright or oblique   4 ι, perhaps ϊ, or τ   ϛ, or perhaps ε

Fr. 7 Col. i 3]., τ, γ

Fr. 1 10–13 Talk of vowels and consonants, but I cannot elicit the word or principle under discussion.

10–11 διὰ δυεῖν φωνήέν|[των, 'with two vowels', 11 σύμφωνα λήγει, 'ends [in *x*?] consonants'. Hephaestion, discussing 'lengthening by position', divides the phenomenon into five categories and quotes a verse supposedly from Alcman to illustrate the first, that represented by words that terminate in two consonants (λήξει εἰς δύο σύμφωνα): καὶ κῆνος ἐν cάλεccι πολλοῖc ἥμενοc μάκαρ ἀνήρ (*Ench.* i 3, p. 2 Consbruch, = *PMG* 15). But I am far from sure that there is relevance in this; it leaves διὰ δυεῖν φωνήέν[των unaccounted for. [The same goes for other doctrine on such words. No. 18 of Theodosius' *canones* of masculine declensions lays down the rule that nouns ending in two consonants keep two consonants in oblique cases (e.g. Τίρυνc, Τίρυνθοc), with the exception of ἅλc; also that the vocative of such nouns has the same form as the nominative (p. 17. 7–15 Hilgard). George Choeroboscus adds that all such nouns end either in c or in ξ (p. 256. 33 f. Hilgard).]

12 λή]ξει, λέ]ξει are two of many possibilities.

13 Presumably φωνη]έντων. The simple restoration διὰ |[δυεῖν φωνη]έντων should be too short, for the lines of XXVI 2389 whose lengths are guaranteed vary between 29 and 35 letters. Then ἐν cύμφωνον is a possible reading.

15 All is doubtful here. Possibly something on the lines of περ[ὶ] τοῦ κνῖcα ῥητέον [ὅτι (kappa is unverifiable), but ῥητέον is not a normal formula. The orthography of κνῖcα was treated by Herodian in his καθολικὴ προcῳδία. He stated (*a*) that it should be written with one sigma (κνιcα not κνιccα), and (*b*) that the iota is long (κνῖcα, not κνίcα or κνεῖcα); (*a*) on grounds of its derivation from the future of κνίζειν, (*b*) in accordance with the general rule regarding the quantity of the penultimate syllable of nouns and adjectives in -cα (Lentz i 266. 13–16, 445. 28 f., ii 536. 11 f.; i 533. 13–19, ii 12. 11–16; ii 455. 13–16). This whole line of inquiry is dubious in the extreme, and I see no way of controlling it. κνῖcα is not attested for Alcman or Sappho, and I have not found any other suitable word that is.

16 There is little hope of reading what precedes ηc; presumably this is the name of some authority. If τον is rightly read and the line ends here (faint traces hereabouts seem to be offsets), hardly the etymological formula παρὰ τό, 'derived from'.

Fr. 2 3 I have rejected the more suggestive alternatives to Αρχιδαμ[(Λεωτυχίδαν, Ἱπποκρατίδαν, παῖδα, etc.), but am not altogether convinced that Αρχιδαμ[is compatible with the traces.

6 A mention of Archidamus, apparently, but of no chronological importance, for in the Eurypontid succession given at Herod. 8. 131 Archidamus is two generations earlier than Leotychidas, who figures in the Alcman commentary XXIV 2390.

10 ἄτερ τοῦ ῑ (or η̄ or έ) γράφεcθαι? ἄτερ is found in late prose and in fact is used in two papyrus documents of the roman period with stylistic pretensions (VI **936** 18, P. Lond. 1171 verso *c* = W. *Chr.* 439. 3). If γαιο[is correctly read in the next line (iota is anomalous but less unsatisfactory than anything else), the orthography of some compound in γαι-/γᾱ- might be in question; cf. παρὰ τὴν γα[in 9. But I can make no progress along this speculative line. [(1) Two Spartan inscriptions: one, of the fifth century B.C., has Γαιάροχος (*IG* V i 213. 9 *alibi*), the other, probably second century A.D., has Γαάοχοι as the name of a contest (*IG* V i 296. 11). But since the papyrus has γαιο[, not γααο[or γαια[, I cannot see that this leads anywhere. (2) 16 could conceivably be referred to a discussion of γαῖα/γῆ, and 18 supplemented γ]αῖαν (or just αῖαν), but the possibility seems rather remote. Alcman has γαῖα at *PMG* 89. 3.]

11 (ἀν)ακολο]ύθωc?

15 -φατοc π.[, -φατο cπ.[, -φα τὸ Cπα[ρτ-, etc.

16 Apparently αι εἰc η̄ is the intention (the supralinear addition may be τό). If the reference is to Lesbian (it is surely not to Laconian) I should have expected rather η̄ εἰc αι. I doubt that the substitution of η for αι in Boeotian is of any relevance. Perhaps specifically on γαῖα > γῆ?

20 πανηγυ[ρ- is a possibility.

23 Unless simply θεῖαν, which is quite possible, probably εὐθεῖαν, perhaps with its grammatical meaning, 'nominative'. ορθειαν may not be ruled out, but the traces favour ευθειαν.

24 π is not to be read before φω, for in this hand the top bar of pi does not extend beyond the right hasta; so not Cάπφω.

25 How to articulate? It may be that one or other εωc is ἕωc in its function of bridging the first

and last words or phrases of a lemma. If it is the second such sequence that represents ἕως, I cannot suggest what the preceding word might be nor put forward plausible alternative readings. If it is the first, ἑωςφό[ρος suggests itself as the next word (and φω[ςφόρ- could be supplied in 24, and cf. 'Ορθείαν in 23?), but then the lemma is neither Lesbian nor Alcmanic.

26 Perhaps [α]παλω. If so, not in extant Sappho, Alcaeus, or Alcman.

27 It might be worth mentioning the possibility of β]αρεῖαν [τά]ϲιν, 'grave accent'.

Fr. 3 Col. i 6 Perhaps λέ]γοντος, but even so not necessarily introducing a lemma.

7 I see no connection with Alcm. 1. 63 (which is treated in **2389** 6 ii), or for that matter with Sappho 60. 7L–P.

Col. ii 3 Apparently a mention of Ascalaphus, whether as son of Ares and Astyoche (Homer) or as informer against Persephone in the underworld (Ovid, Apollodorus, late mythographers and commentators). A probability in favour of the former is established by the suspicion that Ascalaphus' name and place in the Persephone legend may not be prehellenistic and by the suggestion of a martial context in μάχεϲθαι at i 7. I would think that neither Άϲκάλ⟨ων⟩ nor ἄϲκαλα 'unhoed' (Theoc. x 14) need be considered.

Fr. 4 Col. i 1, 2 ἡμεῖς, [ἐ]κεῖνοι: presumably in paraphrase or explication, cf. ἡμᾶς at **2389** 6 ii 31.

Fr. 5 7 κ]υλινδρο[-: not a book reference, for they are not given according to the roll. I may say that I have attacked fr. 2. 12 with κύλινδρος in mind, without succeeding in extracting anything coherent from that line.

3211. LYRIC VERSES

Second century

The two scraps published under this number were not found together and there is nothing to show that they came from the same roll. The larger obviously contains verse and may reasonably be supposed to represent a lyrical verse text, what little survives of the other can be interpreted compatibly with lyric verse. But there is at present nothing useful, that I see, to be made of the text of the fragments. Their interest lies in the striking script. There is no doubt that the same hand wrote both, but fr. 1 is stiffer with a sharp-pointed α and a straight-backed ε, fr. 2 relaxed and rounded. Common to the two are an exceptional treatment of the right-hand apex of μ and the inordinate elongation of the stalks of stalked letters ρ, τ, υ, φ. I suppose that a comparison with such manuscripts as **1233** and **2307** and a dating in the second half of the second century will not be far astray.

Fr. 1

```
    ·      ·        ·
   ].εκ....[
   ]τεφαν.[
   ]δεκωμ[
      ]α  [
5     ]..[
      ·       ·
```

Fr. 2

```
    ·     ·    ·       ·
  ].ναλλαϲελπιδ[
  ].ρ...χα.ητ[]..[
  ]γαμιαιδα.ϲομ[
  ].ζυγιοιομακαρτ[
5 ]ρυϲεαναγκα.[
      ·          ·
```

Fr. 1 1]., the lower part of an upright descending below the line   After κ the lower part of an oval; not like ο of fr. 2, no θ for comparison. Near to this an upright descending below the line and having a speck to right just higher than its top (ρ or υ?), followed by another upright descending below the line at an interval suggesting τ   .[, the foot of an upright   2 .[, the lower part of an upright   5 On the edge of the break a flat stroke dipping at its right-hand end and having the start of a stroke descending from near its left-hand end

Fr. 2 1]., a slightly concave upright   2]., if one letter, the right-hand parts of η. Hardly π   After ρ a dot near the middle of its loop, followed by two slighter dots at the same level, below which is the lower part of an upright descending well below the line; something against τ or υ alone, and no room for both   Before χ a triangular letter, after α the lower end of a stroke descending from left   ]..[, on the line a short stroke rising to right to touch the left-hand end of the base of a circle   3 I think a letter (presumably ι) has almost completely vanished between α and ϲ   4]., the foot of an upright, above which a speck higher than the top of the letters   τ[, only the left-hand end of the cross-stroke   5 .[, a speck on the line and a speck vertically above it level with the top of the letters

Fr. 1 If lyric verses are represented—the short line, l. 4, supports the hypothesis—some part or derivative of ϲτέφανοϲ may be to be recognized in l. 2, some part or derivative of κῶμοϲ in l. 3. Cf. e.g. Pind. *Pyth.* viii 19 seq. . . . ἐϲτεφανωμένον . . . κώμωι.

Fr. 2 3 seq. -γαμιαι δαιϲομ[,].ζυγίοιο μακαρτ[, the prima facie likely articulations.
5 χ]ρυϲεαν ἀγκα.[. ἀναγκα.[not worth considering as an alternative.

3212. LYRIC VERSES

Second century

The following remains may reasonably be described as representing a lyric composition. There appear to be no dialectal peculiarities except α for η (and this is consistent with a source in dramatic lyrics), unless]κλεϊζ.[, l. 8, represents some form of κλεΐζω or εὐκλεΐζω (Pind. *Ol.* i 110, *Pyth.* ix 91; Bacchyl. vi 16).

Written slowly in a spaced, upright, rounded capital of average size by a hand which may be compared to those of **211, 220, 1249** and assigned to the second century.

. . . .

].τωνοιτυχον.εϲδεπ.[
].υδεθεωνατεραγνωγεδ[
]...χε.[]αιδαοιδακαι.[].ν.[
].οικαιδεδοικαθυμωμητ[
5   ].αιμονοϲ.[   ]ν[
]δεπιγαν[   ].ιχ[
τοδα.κα[   ].γεραϲ...[   ].μ[
φυλονε.[ ]ν[   ].ειν[   ]κλεϊζ.[

Rubbed; in some places the ink has completely disappeared. To judge by the margins to left of and below the text this was a copy of good quality.

1]., the end of a stroke from left touching the stalk of τ about the middle; α possible   Of ω opposite ends of the base; perhaps parts of separate letters   ọι of ọ only the top, but I think not ε   χ would certainly be taken for λ; there is no sign of the right-hand branch   Between ν and ε the foot of an upright; τ likely   Of π only the left-hand side   .[, the foot of a stroke hooked to right   2]., three disjointed traces of a partly circular or triangular letter   3]., a low upright, followed by the upper left-hand part of a circle, ϲ rather than ο   Before χ a short flat stroke level with the top of the letters   After ε, which is anomalous, a thick dot, level with the top of the letters, and a speck below and slightly to right on the line; ται not verifiable   .[]., a triangular letter and, after a blank, another; prima facie λ[]λ   .[, an upright with a small loop to left of its foot; if α, anomalous   4]., the right-hand end of a cross-stroke touching the top of ο   Of ν only the tip of the left-hand branch and the foot   5]., the top of a small circle or loop   .[, a dot above general level   6]., the lower part of a stroke curving down from left; λι or αι?   7 ạ and ạ[represented only by the bottom of the loops   ...[, on the line a small hook, open to right; the upper end of a stroke rising to right; the lower part of an upright   ]., the right-hand side of a circle   8 θ could not be ruled out for ε   ζ.[, on the line the base of a circle

3213. Lyric Verses in 'Doric'

Second century

The piece, of which parts of eight verses are preserved in this scrap of a roll copied by the same hand as **1092** (Hdt. ii),[1] was also copied by at least one other scribe, the writer of **2443**, the same verses being represented by **3213** 1 seq. and **2443** fr. 1, 11 seq. **2443** was tentatively attributed to Pindar (fr. dub. 345 Sn), but the text as now constituted has formal features that prima facie rule out all but Alcman of the known lyric poets that come into consideration as author. So far as I can judge from what

[1] Besides **1092** this copyist is recognized in PSI 1390 (Euphorion), PSI 1391 (commentary on lyric, now identifiable as **2622**, Pindar?), and other manuscripts as yet unpublished, both extant authors (Hdt. iii, Plato, *Phaedo*) and new text (commentary on *Odyssey* xxii). To these must be added both the text and the marginalia of the Alcaeus in **2297**, the text distinguished from all the rest by the employment of a shallow ('catena') -topped μ, instead of a deep v-centred μ, and of ω with a high central cusp, instead of ω with a nearly flat base.

A considerable number of small scraps, some susceptible to grouping, I have failed to identify either as from one of the identified rolls or from some other identifiable author.

survives I doubt whether I could have arrived at this conclusion on grounds of matter or style.

Of the additions (lection signs, and variants or corrections) that have been made, some it seems rather arbitrarily, to the text most look to me as if they might be due to one pen, and that the original hand's.

μα̣..ευκοθε̣α[	]ντεμενο[	μα. Λευκο⌊θεα[ν ἐρατὸ]ν τέμενο[ϲ⌋
εκτρυ.εᾶν̣α̣ν̣ι̣ω̣[	].ον [	ἐκ τρυ.εᾶν ἀ⌊νιώ[ν, ἔ]χον⌋
δεϲι̣δᾱϲδυ·ο·γλυκει̣ᾱϲ· [	δὲ ϲίδαϲ δύο γλυκείαϲ.
⸗τ̄αιδο̣.ϲδηποταμω[[ι]]καλλιροω[[ι]][	ταὶ δ' ο̣.ϲδη ποταμῶ(ι) καλλιρόω(ι)
5 ᾱρᾱϲαντ'ερατοντελεϲαιγαμον [	ἀ̄ρᾱϲαντ' ἐρατὸν τελέϲαι γάμον
καιταπαϲ·ει.ναγυναιξικαιανδρα[	καὶ τὰ παϲεῖν ἃ γυναιξὶ καὶ ἀνδρά[ϲι
].τακωριδιαϲτευνᾶ.[..]χῆν[	]ατα κωριδίαϲ τ' εὐνᾶϲ [τυ]χῆν κτλ.
].[.'].ο̣[		

The top of the column. The upper part of the piece is split and wrinkled and has a darkened area in which ink is sometimes only uncertainly distinguishable. There is also a sprinkling of black marks sometimes not distinguishable from ink. **2443** fr. 1, 11 seq. resolves some doubts in vv. 1 seq.

1 seq. The contribution of **2443** fr. 1, 11 seq. between half-brackets. In l. 12 υἷων is written.

1 λ is not verifiable; between α and ε there are only two or three dots level with the top of the letters   2 See note   3 The upper part of the *coronis* scored off, but clearly the middle of the *coronis* was not abreast of the *paragraphus*   Above ει the lower part of an upright   4 At an interval from δο the upper part of an upright   ε much distorted, but I see no likelier choice   8 Of ο̣[only the upper part; θ may be a possible alternative

1 μα. is preceded by a short line ending].οϲ, **2443** fr. 1, 10.

Λευκοθεᾶν: though it might be possible to devise a construction for the accusative singular, the prima facie likelihood is *Λευκοθεᾶν* .. *τέμενοϲ*. *Λευκοθέαι* by extension for Nereids is reported at *Et. Mag.* (Gen.) 561, 45 †*Μυρϲῖνοϲ* (*Μυρϲίλοϲ*) *δὲ οὐ μόνον τὴν Λευκοθέαν 'Ινὼ φηϲίν, ἀλλὰ καὶ τὰϲ Νηρηῒδαϲ Λευκοθέαϲ ὀνομάζει*, and Hesych. *Λευκοθέαι πᾶϲαι αἱ πόντιαι* is presumed to mean something of the same sort.

Pausanias says that there were many *τεμένη* of the Nereids (ii 1, 8), and mentions a particular one at Cardamyle in Messenia (iii 26, 7). Since there is no metrical reason for the choice, *Λευκοθεᾶν* for *Νηρεΐδων* might contain a clue.

Since -θ- is represented by -ϲ- in its only other occurrence, l. 6, -ϲιαν would have been consistent here. There can be no reasonable doubt that **2443** had nothing but -θεαν, but I am confident that ε in the present manuscript was converted (? by a different pen) from ι, and though I cannot affirm that θ was made from ϲ by closing the opening, it has an anomalous look and I am not sure whether it has been given its central stroke.

[νερατο], supplied by **2443**, looks too much for the space by not less than an average letter.

2 ἐκ .. ἀνιών: in phrases of this form (and the parallel, where the genitive precedes ἐξανιών however articulated), which are found in all kinds of hexameter verse, but as far as I can discover in no lyric verse but here, the genitive is usually a place-name, or something more or less equivalent, or the scene of an activity. Thus, e.g., *'Εφύρης Od.* i 159, Callim. *hy.* iv 43, *Τροίης Od.* x 332, *Αἰθιόπων*

Od. v 282, πομπῆς *Od.* viii 568, πολέμου *Il.* vi 480, περάτων Ap. Rhod. *Argon.* ii 165, βοτάνης Theoc. xxv 87, ἄγρης **2817** 20 (Ἑλλάδος Ap. Rhod. *Argon.* ii 459, γαίης Ὑλληῗδος iv 562, ἄγρης (corr.) *hy. Hom.* xix 15, θήρης Ap. Rhod. *Argon.* iii 69).

τρυ.εᾶν: the dotted letter must be read either as γ or as c, either anomalously formed and neither offering a recognizable meaning.

3 cίδας δύο γλυκείας: the ι of cίδη 'pomegranate' is long at Nicand. *Θηρ.* 72; 870, Ἀλεξ. 489; 609, short in Emped. 80 and in the derivatives cιδίων Aristoph. *Nub.* 881, cιδόεντος Ἀλεξ. 276. Pomegranates might be mentioned as significant in respect of the marriage envisaged in the next verses; *v.* Allen and Halliday's note on *hy. Hom.* ii 372.

-ᾰς: the shortening of the vowel in the accusative plural of words of the first declension is characterized as Doric in places where this scansion is requisite (e.g., *Il.* viii 378 schol. A ὁ δὲ Ζηνόδοτος . . . προφανείσας . . . cυcτέλλων τὴν τελευταίαν . . . . . ἔcτι δὲ ἄκρατον Δώριον, similarly scholl. B (Herodian) and T) and in places where it is an alternative not metrically determinable (e.g., Theoc. i 93 schol. K διχῶς τὸ μοίρας. εἰ μὲν γὰρ ἐκτεινόμενον, cημαίνει γενικήν, εἰ δὲ cυcτελλόμενον, αἰτιατικὴν ⟨τῶν⟩ πληθυντικῶν Δωρικῶς). Since there is here no ambiguity as between genitive singular and accusative plural and the quantity of ας is not metrically determinable, the 'shorts' have no critical function, but are themselves inferred from the doctrine, as being in a Doric text. The same appears to be true of].ειᾰcμυρ.ω̇ᵒᵘ., **2394** fr. 2(c) 5, the only other instance I have found.

(-ᾰς guaranteed by the metre is recognized in the Alcman quotation, fr. 17, 5; it seems to have been now dismissed from the Stesichorus quotation, fr. 7, 2. There appear to be no examples in the book-texts of Alcman, Stesichorus, Ibycus, or Simonides.)

δυ.ο̇.ᵂ: as far as I know δύω is not more Doric than δύο; indeed I find it only a couple of times, in compounds in Pindar (*Nem.* iv 28, *Ol.* ii 50). And ο would in any case be scanned as long before γλ.

γλυκείας: I can verify neither -ει-, in the line, nor η, if that was superscribed. Except for Pindar and Bacchylides, there is a nearly complete lack of evidence about the representation of this ending in the παράδοcιc of the relevant lyric poets. **2387** fr. 3 ii 3 (PMG 3) just fails to provide an instance for Alcman; -ηα may be elicited from the quotations Alcm. 6 (**2391** fr. 21(c) 2, a commentary), Alcm. 14, but the authority of quotations is slight. There is a reasonable likelihood that ἀδεî[testifies to -ει[α in the παράδοcιc of Simonides (**2430** fr. 44, 8, PMG 519). [The agreement of the quotations (Simon. 48, 1; 103 fr. 1, 29?, PMG 553; 608) can obviously have no significance in the case of the common form.]

].κειαν[at **2443** fr. 1, 4 may be relevant or not.

4 *seq.* I can give no account of what stands between δο and δη, which I can read only as πε, nor understand the construction of ποταμω[[ι]], if the cancellation of ι converting dative to genitive is to be accepted. [οτεδη, i.e. ταὶ δ' ὅτε δή, does not seem excluded as a decipherment (E. G. T.)]

There is no prima facie difficulty, if the dative is retained, in construing 'they . . prayed to the . . river', but there are obscurities left that I cannot resolve.

Genitives in -ω are characteristic of the παράδοcιc of Alcman. They are replaced by genitives in -ου in texts of Stesichorus, Simonides, Pindar, and Bacchylides, where -οιο also is admitted (and is preponderant in 'Ibycus', **1790**), but not ω except in 'Pindar' fr. 333, in which -ω is reported at (*a*) 6; 7 but -ου at (*d*) i 9; 17? **2394** has several examples of genitive or accusative in which ω has ου written above.

4 ταὶ δ':]φραcαμαν μονο̇c[(**2443** fr. 1, 8) and ἀνιών (**2443** fr. 1, 12 and **3213** 2) imply a single male speaker. On the prima facie natural assumption that ται is nominative plural, the first interpretation that would occur to me is: they (women previously mentioned) prayed that they might achieve . . . wedlock, etc., the construction as at *Il.* iv 143 seq. πολέες τέ μιν ἠρήcαντο ἱππῆες φορέειν, Hdt. viii 94, 3 νικῶcι ὅcον αὐτοὶ ἠρῶντο ἐπικρατῆcαι. I cannot reject this, but so far as I have been able to discover γάμον τελεῖν and comparable locutions are always used in reference to a man who obtains a wife, not a woman who obtains a husband, thus: Hes. *Cat.* 204 85 ἐλπόμενοι τελέειν γάμον, 211 5 seq. ὡς . . ἐτέλεccεν . . γάμον (Peleus), Callim. *hy. Apoll.* 14 εἰ τελέειν μέλλουcι γάμον (οἱ παῖδες), Ap. Rhod. *Argon.* iv 1161 οὐ . . . γάμον μενέαινε τελέccαι (Jason), *Od.* iv 7 τοῖcιν δὲ θεοὶ γάμον ἐξετέλειον, *hy. Hom.* xix 35 ἐκ δ' ἐτέλεccε γάμον (Hermes), Sapph. 112 1 seq. γάμβρε, coὶ μὲν δὴ γάμος . . . ἐκτετέλεcται. If this is not an imaginary difficulty, an alternative hypothesis might be to make the subject of the infinitive different

from the subject of the principal verb, the construction as in *hy. Hom.* vi 16 seq. ἠρήϲαντο ἕκαϲτοϲ εἶναι κουριδίην ἄλοχον. But in view of the multiple ambiguities and uncertainties of l. 4 I refrain from offering further speculations.

καλλιροω⟦ι⟧: if this and the next three verses are, as I suppose, dactylic tetrameters, καλλιρρόω(ι) must be recognized here and ends of lines at ἀνδρά[ϲι and -χῆν. They would be written in couplets, the last dactyl in each being replaced by a cretic. Examples of this substitution, theoretically justified διὰ τὴν ἐπὶ τέλουϲ ἀδιάφορον Heph. *Ench.* xv 8, are not easy to find. Besides Archil. fr. 115, quoted by Hephaestion, and Theocr. *epig.* xx 2 I have nothing but 'Ibycus' 1790 i 24 (PMG 282) εὖ Ἑλικωνίδεϲ ἐμβαίεν λογ[, where a final long seems inescapable.

6 seq. '. . . . experience those things that are . . . to women and men'.

παϲειν made into παϲ·ει̇.ν̇ (with η superscript): the representation in certain places of θ as ϲ is peculiar to texts of Alcman and is not found in any of the other lyric poets. It should by itself suffice to determine attribution.

-ειν is inconsistent with -ῆν, l. 7; it has been brought nearer by superscribing η as an alternative (or correction). In company with ϲ for θ what might be expected on the strength of the analogies in texts of Alcman is -εν (i.e. -έν), which represents -εῖν at Alcm. 1 17 (γαμεν), 43 (ἐπαινὲν), 6 fr. 4, 4 (φιλεν). But this apparent consistency may be fortuitous; -ειν is spelt both -εν (φάινεν sc. ἐν) and -ην (ἀνδάνην) in the same manuscript, 1 43, 88. Even wider divergences in the spelling of -εῖν are seen in what are taken to be manuscripts of Stesichorus, πολεμέ[ιν, 2617 fr. 4 i 8,]φυγην with ει written below η, fr. 7 i 2, γαμεν 2618 fr. 1 ii 9. The single available example from Simonides presents the spelling -έν (θορέν 2430 fr. 79, 12), from 'Ibycus' -ῆν (υμ]νῆν 1790 (a) 12). (There is apparently an instance of -έν for -εῖν in Pindar, ἀγαγέν *Pyth.* iv 56 not metrically protected; neither Pindar nor Bacchylides has any instances of -ῆν.)

]ατα: I suppose the general sense must be 'desirable'. χάρμ]ατα does not seem to me very attractive and I should say was too long, but I have nothing better to offer.

7 κουρίδιοϲ is the only vocalization of the first syllable found in any other place, except that in a fragment of a papyrus in Florence, published by Snell as Pind. fr. dub. 344, at col. ii 10 a verse begins κωριδ[, which may be a second instance of the same word and spelling.

κουριδίαν ἄλοχον is the only other instance of the word in a lyric poet (Stesich. 185 4, a quotation).

-ιδίαϲ τ' εὐνᾶϲ [τυ]χῆν seems clear enough; cf. (i) λέχοϲ . . . κουρίδιον *Il.* xv 39 seq., Ar. *Pax* 844 (κ.λ.), *Thesm.* 1122 (εὐνὴν καὶ γαμήλιον λέχοϲ); (ii) κουριδίων . . ἐκύρηϲε γάμων *Anth. Pal.* vi 133 (Archilochus), Pind. *Pyth.* ix 41 (ἀδείαϲ τυχεῖν . . εὐνᾶϲ). But the genitive singular κουριδιᾶϲ has been marked by means of a superscribed ⌣·, -ᾶϲ, as possibly a 'Doric' accusative plural. The same suggestion has not been made in regard to εὐνᾶϲ, and for that reason may be considered negligible. If in fact there was an ambiguity in a text presenting only -αϲ -ναϲ, it seems to point to [λα]χῆν, compatible with either case, and to rule out [τυ]χῆν, as the required supplement.

2394 (PMG 162) also contains fragments of lyric verses attributed to Alcman, like 3213, on the strength of dialectal characteristics. Between 2394 and 2443 there appears to be a correspondence of structure too marked to be dismissed as fortuitous but not exact enough to certify identity.

In the two tracts of text, one from either manuscript, shown below,

(a) two consecutive lines exhibit πε|εαν in the same vertical relation.

   (The evidential value of this fact may be, but is not necessarily, impaired by the fact that εαν is followed by κ in 2443, a different letter, prima facie τ, in 2394.)

(b) three consecutive lines exhibit αν|υ|εκ in the same vertical relation.

   In this apparent agreement there is some degree of illusion. 2443 has a whole line more than 2394, ending in another αν further to right by the breadth of a letter, or more, than αν in the preceding line, and consequently having υ|εκ in a different 'longitude' from 2394.

If there is anything in these observations, it must be supposed that the two manuscripts had different layouts or states of preservation.

2394 fr. 1 i (b) 4 is:

          ]φ[] .νϛτ'ουδειϲ⌀[,

and there are neither above nor below ends of lines extending as far to r.

2443 fr. 1, 7 is:

          ]εφ.[. . . .].υδειϲ.[,

and there are both above and below ends of lines extending as far as -ειϲ.[, or farther.

C

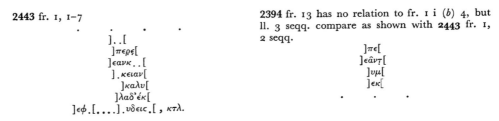

2443 fr. 1, 1–7

```
            .       .         .
         ]..[
        ]περε[
        ]εανκ..[
        ].κειαν[
         ]καλυ[
         ]λαδ'έκ[
   ]εφ.[....].υδεις.[ , κτλ.
```

2394 fr. 13 has no relation to fr. 1 i (*b*) 4, but
ll. 3 seqq. compare as shown with **2443** fr. 1,
2 seqq.

```
           ]πε[
          ]εᾶντ[
           ]υμ[
           ]εκ[
         .      .      .
```

3214. ANTHOLOGY (EURIPIDES)

45 5B.58/B(1–2)a   10×15 cm.   Second century

A fragment of papyrus from the lower part of a single column, broken at either side. The piece is unusual among papyrus anthologies in that it is a professionally executed manuscript. The text is written on the recto, in a largish round, upright, and ornamented book-hand, the type conventionally known as 'roman uncial'. This example does not have the lateral compression to which the style, like others, is prone: the letters are broad (omicron, for instance, has greater width than height), and the spacing between them is comparatively generous; not that the effect of distension is very marked, but it is an untypical palaeographical feature. P. Ryl. III 514 and P. Oxy. VIII **1084** are otherwise fairly similar; compare also XX **2260**, XXIII **2354**, XXXII **2634**. (On the style see G. Cavallo, *Annali della scuola normale superiore di Pisa*, serie II, xxxvi (1967), 209–20, E. G. Turner, *Greek Manuscripts, ad* no. 13.) The hand may be assigned with some confidence to the second century, and I would put it in the first half.

The calligraphic intent is reinforced by a curious feature of the layout. Each citation is headed by identification of its source: the script of this heading, which is centred, is reduced in size to almost half that adopted for the text of the quotations.

Five citations are represented. The first is unidentified, the remaining four are Euripidean: a pair of verses preserved in corrupt form by Stobaeus which now finds a home in either the Euripidean *Antigone* or the *Antiope*; a verse ascribed to the *Antiope*, also previously known from Stobaeus; what appears to be *Medea* 76, here attributed to the *Phoenix*; and a sequence of five verses from the *Protesilaus*, incorporating one quoted by Clement of Alexandria.

There are good grounds for thinking that the collection, or at least that section of it represented by the papyrus, was drawn exclusively from Euripides. The heading which identifies each extract takes the form of the title of the play in question, with ἐκ: e.g. ἐξ Ἀντιόπης. The papyrus is broken off to the left, but if the author as well as the play had been specified, the end of the dramatist's name would in some cases probably be visible. The inference from this apparent omission is perhaps not quite certain, for Euripides will invariably have been prominent in collections such as this, and one could conceive of a convention whereby the author was named only when he was someone other than Euripides. But the presumption is a strong one. Cf. XLII **3005**, an anthology which appears to be wholly Menandrean.

The selected passages (with the theoretical exception of the first) all have to do with marriage. Extracts on marriage were collected at least as early as the second century B.C.: witness P. Berol. 9772 and 9773 (BKT V 2. 123–8, 129–33). These latter two collections show a close affinity with Stobaeus iv 22, the chapter entitled περὶ γάμου; virtually all of their citations which are not new are found there. A similar affinity with Stobaeus, with the chapter περὶ δεσποτῶν καὶ δούλων (iv. 19), is to be seen in P. Schub. 28 (Pack² 1579), also of the second century B.C., and most strikingly in the third-century papyrus edited by H. Maehler in *Mus. Helv.* 24 (1967), 70–3. Cf. also the second- or third-century Florence papyrus previewed by V. Bartoletti in *Atti XI Congr. Pap.* 1966, 1–14. Of the present papyrus's five citations, two recur in Stobaeus' π. γάμου chapter. The papyrus anthologies generally follow a less elaborated system of arrangement than Stobaeus, and **3214** is no exception. The two passages in common, the second and third in **3214**, occur under Stobaeus' sections 5 and 4 respectively of the π. γάμου chapter. The bulk of Stobaeus' Euripidean extracts appears to have been taken from a compilation of Euripidean passages arranged in alphabetical order according to play title (see Stobaeus iii ed. Hense, *Prolegomena*, lv–lvii), but **3214**, while it does appear to be confined to Euripides, does not follow an alphabetic order.

The back is blank.

For the fragments of Euripides, I have referred both to Nauck and to Mette, *Lustrum* 12 (1967) [frr. 1–1181] and 13 (1968) [frr. 1182–1470].

```
. . . . .
]νδρωνηνμεναν[          × – ∪ – ]νδρῶν ἦν μεν ἀνδ[ × – ∪ –
] εξαντι·'οϲηϲ     [          ἐξ Ἀντιόπηϲ (vel Ἀντιγόνηϲ?)
]λεκτ.ατ..κα.ω.[          ἐγὼ γὰρ ἔξω] λέκτρα ἀτ.. καλῶϲ [ἔχειν
]ινοιϲιϲ.[..]ηραϲο[          δίκαιόν ἐϲτ]ιν οἷϲι ϲυ[γγ]ηράϲο[μαι
] εξαντιοπηϲ      [    5          ἐξ Ἀντιόπηϲ
]τοντονϲοφονκτ[          κῆδοϲ καθ' αὑ]τὸν τὸν ϲοφὸν κτ[ᾶϲθαι χρεών
] εκφοινεικοϲ     [          ἐκ Φοίνεικοϲ
]ωνλειπεταικηδ..[          × – ∪ – ]ων λείπεται κηδ..[ ∪ –
] εκπρωτεϲιλαου   [          ἐκ Πρωτεϲιλάου
]ουνμοιϲκα[]οϲ..[    10          × – ∪ ]ουν μοι ϲκα[ι]ὸϲ ..[ × – ∪ –
]αικοϲουνεκ'ανλ.[          × – γυν]αικὸϲ οὔνεκ' ἂν λ.[ – ∪ –
]του.ανδοκειτο.[          × – ∪ – ]του.ανδοκεῖ το.[ – ∪ –
]ειναιχρηνγυνα.[          κοινὸν γὰρ] εἶναι χρῆν γυναι[κεῖον λέχοϲ
]υτωϲευγενειατ[          × – ∪ ο]ὕτωϲ εὐγένεια τ[– ∪ –
```

1 .[, trace of base horizontal as of δ   2 `.', τ, see comm.   3 τ represented by cross-stroke and top of upright: compatible only with τ, ζ, ξ?, not π   .., a base trace seemingly oblique (downward from left) and a speck at letter top level, then equidistant between these and κ the top of an apparent upright, surface missing either side: οι acceptable   4 δ̔, breathing uncertain: anomalous

traces .[, foot of upright   8 ..[, traces on isolated fibre level with letter tops: oc or ɛv not suggested, but neither excluded   10 [], room only for ι   ..[, traces suggesting ɛ, then perhaps left-hand side of cup of υ   11 λ, remains of lower half, perhaps χ also possible   .[, base trace, of a serif or an oblique: of vowels, a, η, ι   12 ., surface thoroughly abraded: room for letter of medium size   ν represented by right hand hasta and rubbed traces of possible oblique   .[, mid-line trace perhaps of upright   13 .[upright

1 Apparently not extant. Presumably ἦν 'if', then either μ' ἐν (e.g. ἀ]νδρῶν ἦν μ' ἐν ἀνδ[ράϲιν τίθηϲ) or μέν (e.g. ἀ]νδρῶν ἦν μὲν ἀνδ[ρείαν ἔχῃ). The absence of an *apostrophe* (11, *scriptio plena* at 3) tells against the former, though in itself that is perhaps the likelier articulation.

2 Some high ink between ι and ο does not look accidental; the trace suggests the foot of an upright, and could be taken as part of a supralinear γ, added with the intention of converting Ἀντιόπηϲ to Ἀντιγόνηϲ. π is now damaged. There seems no doubt that π was written, but it seems possible that it was altered to ν: there is perhaps a trace of a downward oblique joining the foot of the second hasta. I do not know whether one would be justified in taking the fact that the next citation is headed ἐξ Ἀντιόπηϲ rather than, say, ἐκ τοῦ αὐτοῦ δράματοϲ as supporting intended ascription to the *Antigone*.

The papyrus's attribution is not necessarily the true one. Von Arnim (*Suppl. Eurip.* p. 17) has suggested that four citations ascribed in Stobaeus to the *Antiope* (among them the next in the papyrus) belong in fact to the *Antigone*. Similarly it is not easy to find accommodation for the present citation in the *Antiope*, whereas in the *Antigone* the lines could well be addressed to Creon by Haemon or by Antigone herself.

3–4 Eurip. fr. 1058N², 1291 Mette: hitherto *fabula incerta*. Preserved in corrupt form by Stobaeus in the section headed ὅτι ἐν τοῖϲ γάμοιϲ τὰϲ τῶν ϲυναπτομένων ἡλικίαϲ χρὴ ϲκοπεῖν (iv 22e. 113): ἐγὼ γὰρ ἔξω λέκτρ' αὐτοῖϲ καλῶϲ ἔχειν | δίκαιόν ἐϲτιν οἷϲι ϲυγγηράϲομαι.

The lines have defied emendation. It is clear that the papyrus does not have the impossible αὐτοῖϲ, and the presumption is that it has the truth, lurking in the damaged two or three letters between ἃ and καλῶϲ. Given the traces (which exclude παγκάλωϲ), I can suggest only ἅ τοι (so also E. G. Turner, J. R. Rea), 'I shall have a marriage which, let me tell you, it is right should be a good one—one in which I shall grow old' (sc. 'because I'll have married someone my own age'?—N.B. the Stobaean section which houses it). This is good as a reading and offers ready explanation of the Stobaean corruption, even if the particle does not seem to sit very comfortably. The Press reader suggests taking οἷϲι as a generalizing masc. and construing it with καλῶϲ ἔχειν: '. . . which it is fair should be good for those I shall grow old with'. Given that λέκτρα can approximate to 'spouse', however, I prefer the interpretation I have offered.

6 Eurip. fr. 214N², 266 Mette: Stob. iv 22d. 43, with attribution, as here, to the *Antiope*. Tentatively ascribed to the *Antigone* by von Arnim (loc. cit.), together with frr. 212, 213, 215N². The papyrus does not prove him wrong: the postulated corruption could have taken place at practically any stage.

Cf. Aesch. *PV* 890, τὸ κηδεῦϲαι καθ' ἑαυτὸν ἀριϲτεύει μακρῷ.

8 Almost certainly = *Med.* 76, παλαιὰ καιν]ῶν λείπεται κηδευ[μάτων. Either we have here a mis-attribution (due to omission of the *Phoenix* quotation: perhaps fr. 804N²?) or else the verse had been used in both plays, or had got interpolated in the *Phoenix* (on repeated lines in Euripides see P. W. Harsh, *Hermes* 72 (1937) 435–49). I consider the former the more likely.

10–14 Line 13 is Eurip. fr. 653N², 871 Mette. The papyrus confirms Nauck's emendation of ἄρα καί to χρῆν (implicitly rejected by Mette). Cited in isolation by Clement of Alexandria, *Strom.* vi 2. 24. 5 f. (p. 441. 13 Früchtel), it now acquires a context—or would do, if the tenor of the surrounding verses were intelligible. The speaker can hardly be anyone other than Acastus, but it is still not clear to me who (if anyone) is being addressed, nor what desirable thing would happen to εὐγένεια if monogamy were abandoned.

Obvious supplements for the beginnings of 10–11 are 10 ἐκεῖνοϲ] οὖν, 11 (almost certain) ὅϲτιϲ γυν]αικόϲ. There are many things one might do for a woman's sake. If Acastus has anyone particular in mind, it must be Protesilaus; but he may be generalizing. Of 12 E. G. Turner notes, 'must presumably be -]τοῦϲαν, fem. accusative present participle'. But we do expect a caesura. πανδοκεῖ, dat. of πανδοκεύϲ, would be apt enough in a gibe about Laodameia's supposed behaviour (see below—rather this, in the immediate setting, than in reference to Hades), though an adjective or feminine would be easier.

[πανδοκεύς unattested in tragedy, but I see no intrinsic objection to it in Euripides. πανδόκος ξενόςταςις Soph. fr. 274P = 252N², δόμοιςι πανδόκοις ξένων Aesch. *Cho.* 662, neither with innuendo; πανδόκον (so to be accented) . . . χέρςον (Hades) *Sept.* 860.] πανδοκεῖ as verb (Aesch. *Sept.* 18) is perhaps not out of the question either.

With the expression of 13 f., cf. *Med.* 573–5, χρῆν γὰρ . . . θῆλυ . . . οὐκ εἶναι γένος, χοὖτως ἂν οὐκ ἦν οὐδὲν ἀνθρώποις κακόν.

Any attempted reconstruction of the plot of the *Protesilaus* is bound to be fanciful; and the previously known line is perhaps the most enigmatic of the far from transpicuous fragments. (F. Jouan, *Euripide et les légendes des chants cypriens* (1966), 323, makes it an exasperated reaction by Acastus to Laodameia's refusal to remarry, after Protesilaus' death at Troy. This is clearly desperate, and a perversely literal reading of the line.) But the accession of something of its immediate context does I think make one thing clear: the passage must be considered in close relation to the four verses that constitute fr. 657N² (still *Protes.*). There the man who damns all women without exception is said to be ςκαιὸς κοὐ ςοφός. Some women admittedly are bad, but some—like Laodameia (αὐτή)—have a λῆμα εὐγενές. The verbal recurrences suggest strongly that that passage is in some sense a retort to the present one.[1] This helps define the speaker's attitude: we want a ψόγος γυναικῶν. Is Acastus speaking in moral indignation and disillusionment, occasioned by what he mistakenly thinks to be Laodameia's faithlessness to her newly wed newly dead husband? (Hyg. *fab.* 104. 2, *quod cum famulus matutino tempore poma ei* (sc. *Laodamiae*) *attulisset ad sacrificium, per rimam aspexit viditque eam †ab amplexu† Protesilai simulacrum tenentem et osculantem; aestimans eam adulterum habere Acasto patri nuntiavit.*) The point may then be sardonic, that if women are not to respect the institution of marriage, it would be better to abandon the futile attempt to maintain it: the resultant system being expressed in deliberately outrageous form. Cf. fr. 402N² (*Ino*). There the merit claimed for polygamy as against monogamy is that a man could throw out the κακή and keep the ἐςθλή. And here? What is the consequence for εὐγένεια (ηὐγένεια?)? Possibly that one's reputation as εὐγενής or δυςγενής would no longer depend upon birth (moral connotations of εὐγένεια played upon *passim* in Euripides, N.B. λῆμ' ἔχουςαν εὐγενές in fr. 657). We cannot be sure the quotation ends here: it may have continued in the next column.

3215. TRAGIC TRIMETERS

Second century

The hand of one and the same copyist is to be recognized in PSI XIII 1302 and **3215** frr. 1 and 2. **3215** fr. 1 and PSI 1302 resemble one another in size of writing, in number (20) of lines to the column, and, it is natural to infer, in lavishness of layout, though only the upper margin of **3215** fr. 1 now survives for comparison. In PSI 1302 a speaker ends a speech, 'any man who trusts a slave we count a great fool.' There is nothing to which this appears relevant in the preceding verses as preserved in PSI 1302. In the speech of which parts of 20 lines are preserved in **3215** fr. 1 a good proportion consists of references to slave and freeman.

It seemed reasonable on the basis of these congruences to suppose that **3215** fr. 1 represented the column immediately preceding that represented by PSI 1302, but the

---

[1] Not perhaps an immediate or direct retort, for the tone is mild and considered. It would be appropriate towards the end of the play: whether in the mouth of the chorus, or as the final comment of a messenger announcing Laodameia's suicide (the reference back to Acastus' outburst then being a piece of unconscious irony), or as a revelation *ex machina*, or as a retraction by Acastus himself, after learning (too late to save her?) of the unworthiness of his suspicions. On the other hand, fr. 654N² would make an admirably suitable comment by the chorus if the passages belong to either side of an *agon* (δυοῖν λεγόντοιν, θατέρου θυμουμένου, | ὁ μὴ ἀντιτείνων τοῖς λόγοις ςοφώτερος).

marginal note to right of l. 2 is not, so far as I can judge from PSI XIII tav. 3, in the same hand as the two marginal notes to left of 1302 ll. 1 and 3, or in the same relative position as either of them. If the two columns are not contiguous, there is no particular case for thinking them connected.

This copyist has been identified in a number of manuscripts produced on the same handsome scale and containing sometimes Sophocles, sometimes Euripides: PSI 1302, Eur. *Alcm.*, and 3215 fr. 1, having 20 lines to the column; 2077, Soph. *Scyrians*, 2452, Soph.? (Eur.?) *Theseus*, having more than 20 lines to the col.; 3215 fr. 2, Eur. *Hec.* 223–8 from the top of a column of indeterminate height; a number of scraps not as yet published of which the source is not ascertained. I should likewise incline to attribute to him Antiphon Soph., π. ἀληθ., in 1364, Aeschin. Socr., Μιλτιάδης, in 2889, though these have a different *v*.

Fr. 1

]˛νελευ[˛]ερω[] [	]˛ν ἐλευ[θ]έρω[˛]
]ματουνεανιου χρη˛[	]μα τοῦ νεανίου
]αντασυνκεινωιπονους	]αντα σὺν κείνωι πόνους
]˛δουλονενδομοισεχειν	]˛ δοῦλον ἐν δόμοις ἔχειν
5]ν·οῐδεσουκακειονες	]ν. οἱ δὲ σοῦ κακίονες
]˛αικρατουσιδωματων	]καὶ κρατοῦσι δωμάτων
]σι·συδετιπροσδοκῶνποτε	]σι· σὺ δὲ τί προσδοκῶν ποτέ
]νει·μημεθηῐς'ελευθερον	]νει· μὴ μεθῆῐ' ς' ἐλεύθερον.
]ολλακισδενουθετει	π]ολλάκις δὲ νουθετεῖ
10]οικοισιπολ[˛]μιωτατος	]οἴκοισι πολ[ε]μιώτατος
]δουλονοντελ[˛]υθερον	]δοῦλον ὄντ' ἐλ[ε]ύθερον
]...[]ανηγενοιτετι	]...[]αν η γένοιτ' ἔτι
]υμαρωσελευθερον	ε]ὐμαρῶς ἐλεύθερον
]...[ ]..[ ]ργοις· κεαρ	]...[ ]..[ ]ργοις·κέαρ
15]γωνουπαυομαι εὐλογῶν[	εὖ λέ]γων οὐ παύομαι
]˛[˛]τησπατηρμενουν [	δεσ]π[ό]της, πατὴρ μὲν οὖν
]μεδω	
]κασεισδομους [	μ' ἔδω]κας εἰς δόμους
]γιγνωσκεισαν˛ρ [	]γιγνώσκεις ἂν˛ρ
]..[˛]˛αξειετις [	]˛α[λ]λάξειέ τις
20]υθερον [ ]ημ[	ἐλε]ύθερον

1]., traces near the line, possibly the bottom right-hand curve of ω   2 *marg.* μ[not verifiable   4]., ν (represented by the lower end of the diagonal and the right-hand upright) sug-

gested   12]..., the top of a heavy upright, followed by the top of a stroke slightly hooked to right, and this by the upper end of a light stroke rising to right; if the last represented κ, a narrow letter might follow before α   14]..[, a slightly concave upright, perhaps the right-hand side of θ, followed by what now look like the right-hand side of a small loop and the upper end of a thick stroke descending to right, both level with the top of the letters   ]..[, a flat stroke, as of γ, with traces, apparently compatible with ε, at the right-hand end   18 αν.ρ, between ν and ρ faint traces not suggesting η   19]., a trace level with the top of the letters

I have found no identifiable quotation in these verses. PSI 1302 is identified as from Euripides Ἀλκμέων by the presence of fr. 86. The style of this speech is compatible with the same authorship.

7 i.e. τί ποτε προσδοκῶν . . .; and this is by far the commoner order in Euripides, and, I think, the other tragedians.

8 I suppose metaphorical, 'set free' a slave, but physical liberation is expressed by the same phrase, v. Eur. *Hec.* 551 seqq.

14 κέαρ is a much more noticeable feature of the vocabulary of Sophocles than of Euripides (only in *Medea*, twice).

15 The marginal entry looks like a variant not a comment. The supplement suggested might acceptably be accompanied by such a variant. But it should be said that in Euripides, at any rate, εὖ λέγειν much oftener means 'speak well' than 'speak well of' (e.g. *Alc.* 1070), and that εὐλογεῖν is much oftener employed than εὖ λέγειν when a word for 'praise' is wanted.

16 The supplement assumes that what was said came to 'more like a father than a master', cf. e.g. Eur. *Or.* 1520 seq. μὴ πέτρος γένηι δέδοικας . . .; μὴ μὲν οὖν νεκρός, Soph. *Aj.* 862 seq.

18 Presumably ἀνήρ, ε being insufficient for the space.

Fr. 2

Hecuba ll. 223–8

```
        ]ιναιθυματοσδεπιστα[
        ]πεστητουδεπαισαχιλλ[
                   . . c
225     ]|[ον·]|μηταποσπασθ.[
          '. . .]ιλλ[.]νεξελθ[
             ]α[.]πα[ ]...[
             ][
```

       .   .   .   .   .

This scrap is in the same hand as PSI XIII 1302 and **3215** fr. 1, but contains verses from a surviving play, to the text of which it contributes nothing.

224 ἐπέστη codd., Σ: ἐπέσται Nauck   225 δρᾶσον M, P, (τὰ καλὰ τῶν ἀντιγράφων Σ), δρασεις A, L, sscr. M¹ -σπάσῃς L   227 καὶ παρουσίαν cum codd. praeter L (καὶ κακῶν)

3216. TRAGEDY

5 1B.57/G   3 × 11 cm.   Second century

A fragment apparently of a tragedy, written in a small, round and upright hand, similar to **XXI 2294** except in so far as it is more freely serifed and in the case of ε and c less rounded. **XXI 2301** may also be compared. The hand may be assigned a date around the middle of the second century, or later rather than earlier. On the back there are illegible remains of one line, written across the fibres in a crude documentary hand.

Eistheses divide the remnant into three sections. The first two have their beginnings preserved and are evidently lyric; the latter of these is indented in relation to the former. Any restoration of the third section will project its beginnings further to the left than the first, so that there were two degrees of *eisthesis*. The doubly indented section is presumably an epode, and the unindented lines are likely to be trimeters, though trochaics are not excluded.

The evidence for authorship does not point in any one direction. ἀλίαcτον (7) is found among the tragedians only in Euripides, being used twice in the extant plays and attested for him as the *lexis* of fr. 1123 Nauck[2]. This hardly adequate ground for attribution to Euripides is made still less secure by ἴcχει (19), which is characteristically (though not only) Sophoclean. Of the subject-matter little can be said other than that mention is made of Apollo and of oracles and that there may be some connection with the Trojan war.

The lection signs appear to be by the first hand. There are four stops in middle position. A correction at 4 has been added in a thin pen, perhaps by the copyist; another hand seems to be responsible for the insertion of an iota adscript in 6. A corruption in 18 is uncorrected.

. . . . .

```
        ].[
     τονζο.[
     προϲφ[
         δ’
     λεγε·ει[
  5  φροντ[.]δι[
          ι
     λυηδεπονω[
     ειδ’αλιαϲτον[
     αλληϲβουλη[
     χρειανηκε.[
 10     αναξπ[
        πουκεκ[
        ϲονόμμ[
        κάιμοι[
    __.οιβουτ.[
 15     χρηϲμῶ.[
        καιφρυγω[
        δὸριχρηλα[
     >
     ]νεόποιϲδυϲτιν[
     ]νταϲιϲχειτᾱκ[
 20  ]γαρουχοιορτ’ερ[
        ].ϲμεν[
         ]ηϲφα[
         ]λῳταϲθ[
         ]μενουδ[
 25     ]γξαι·ϲυ.[
        ]δηπᾱϲ·λυ[
         ]ηγεμ[
```

2 .[, speck at line level   5 [.], room only for narrow letter   δ, base only, ζ perhaps not excluded   ι[, α possible, hardly ε or ο   7 ει, ink at foot of ι to left: offsets ? letter overwritten? 9 .[, trace at line level, perhaps of upright (e.g. ι)   14 ., trace apparently of descender on isolated fibre   .[, low trace of apparent curve   14/15 What is transcribed as a paragraphus appears not to be on the top layer of papyrus, and is in a lighter ink. Two further traces can be discerned at some distance to the left   15 .[, foot of upright   18 The first ο is open to the left, but no other reading is possible   21]., speck at mid-line level   23 θ[, or ε   25 .[, upper part of upright, with trace perhaps of horizontal leaving at top, e.g. γ

2 ζόφον, ζοφερόν.

5 As a reading, φροντ[ί]δι has the edge on φροντ[ί]ζ-.

7 ἀλίαϲτον: in tragedy at Eurip. *Hec.* 85, *Or.* 1479 (ἄλαϲτοc Wilamowitz), fr. 1123N² (a lexis in isolation, referred by Nauck to *Hec.* 85).

9/10, 17/18 Apparently the paragraphus is used to divide one choral section from the next, and the *diple obelismene* to mark the end of the lyrics. Dramatic papyri exemplify various systems of signs. Cf. Anecd. Paris., 'diple obelismene ad separandas in comoediis et tragoediis periodos', and the more comprehensive treatment of Hephaestion, π. ϲημείων 5–11.

10 In view of Φοίβου at 14, probably Π[ύθιοc or Π[ύθιε; ϲόν (12) suggests the vocative. Π[αιάν and Π[όϲειδον are other possibilities.

11 κεκ[: part of κρύπτειν?

14/15 The 'paragraphus' (see apparatus) is presumably without significance.

17 δὸρι: the accent distinguishes δορί from δόρει.

18–27 It seems reasonable to assume that these lines are iambics. I would suppose the first foot to be missing from 18, 19, and 20.

18 νεόπτοιϲ: the accent precludes correction to νεοττοῖϲ. The palaeographically closest word I can think of is νεόρτοιϲ (Π for PT); which would scan in iambics.

19]ντας ἴϲχει.
τᾱκ[: crasis is implied, τᾱκ-.

20] γὰρ οὐχ οἷόν τ' ἐρ[-.

23 ἁ]λώτας? But other articulations are open.

25 τέ]γξαι, ἐλέ]γξαι, κλά]γξαι, al. In this line and the following, the stop probably coincides with the caesura. The collocation δὴ πᾶϲ, however (26: but not necessarily δή), occupies the third foot at Soph. fr. 760N.

3217. MENANDER, *Sicyonius*

26 3B.51/D(1–2)b · · · · · · · · · · · · 2·7×4·8 cm. · · · · · · · · · · · Late first century

This scrap of dramatic dialogue is written in the same hand as X **1238** (now Kassel, *Sicy.* fr. 11), a rounded uncial dated by Grenfell and Hunt to the late first century A.D. Because of the marginal and interlinear addition of names of characters **1238** was identified as belonging to the *Sicyonius* of Menander (see *Recherches de Papyrologie* 3 (1964) 154), although its position in the play has never been established. An interlinear pi (line 3), presumably forming part of an abbreviation of the name Pyrrhias (but cf. Kassel ad *Sicy.* fr. 11), suggests strongly that this scrap belongs not only to the same play but to the same scene as **1238**. Attempts to align the two fragments have been unsuccessful. The back is blank.

→

```
                    ]νεαθ[
                    ]εαναυτο[
                         π[
                    ]τιν·  ..[
                    ]ποδων.[
              5        ].ερ[
                       ].ερουϲ[
                       ]με.[
```

1 θ[, top of the letter is broken off, but θ is more likely than ε.

3 Below and slightly to the right of π[, traces of 2 letters: a cross-stroke ligatured to an upright, then a trace of ink at foot level.

4 .[broad, round-bottomed letter with trace of ink below, φ or ψ possible, if the trace is part of the letter; if it is stray ink, ε, θ, ο, ω may be considered.

5]. perhaps feet of λ or χ, then ε or θ followed by traces like the ρ in line 6.

6 φέρουϲ[α or sim.? Cf. *Sicy.* 411 and fr. 11. 2 (**1238** 2). Only a dot of ink on a broken fibre remains of the initial letter.

7 .[, low trace, sloping up to right, foot of δ, λ or χ. α has too rounded a base.

3218. NEW COMEDY

41B.61/F(a)   Fr. 1 5 × 5 cm.   First century
                           Fr. 2 2·5 × 3 cm.

Two small fragments written along the fibres of a buff-coloured papyrus, so well made that while the horizontal fibres are stripped in several places the vertical fibres present an almost undamaged surface. Fr. 1, from the top of a column, contains ends of 7 lines of iambic trimeters; fr. 2 has parts of 6 lines.

Similar patterns of vertical fibres on the backs suggest that fr. 2 belongs below fr. 1 with its front right-hand edge in the same vertical alignment as the corresponding edge of fr. 1. It is even possible that fr. 1. 7 and fr. 2. 1 are parts of the same line, but attempts to place the fragments in that relationship have not proved completely satisfactory and it seems more likely that they were somewhat further apart.

The scribe wrote an informal round hand in which elegantly formed letters with serifs occur alongside forms much more cursively written. Compare E. G. Turner, *GMAW*, Pls. 37–8, which are dated to the early and late first century respectively. This hand exhibits characteristics found in both of these plates. A second hand has made the marginal correction at fr. 1. 2. The only lectional sign is a dicolon at fr. 1. 6.

The speaker of μὰ τοὺϲ θεούϲ (fr. 1. 4) is designated by $\bar{\Gamma}$, i.e. by an ordinal number standing for third actor. For dramatic texts with parts similarly designated see **XXVII 2458** (Eur., *Cresphontes*) and PSI X 1176 (New Comedy). The significance of this notation is discussed by E. G. Turner in **2458** introd. and by E. G. Jory, 'Algebraic Notation in Dramatic Texts', *BICS* 10 (1963) 65–78.

There is little of situation or language, in spite of the name Moschion (fr. 1. 5, fr. 2. 3), which suggests an identity for the fragments.

The back is occupied by writing in a serifed informal hand of the first or early second century; there is little to establish context beyond ἐπηρώθη (fr. 1. 4) and θεᾶϲ (fr. 2. 2), which might point to romance. A diplomatic transcript only is provided.

Fr. 1

→

]ριταυτηνιδων　　　　　　　　　]οι ταύτην ἰδών
　　　　λιθο[
]διαντεχωννεου　　　　　　　　　Λυ]δίαν τ' ἔχων λίθο[ν
]μαδικεισμαρτυρομα[ι　　　　　　]μ' ἀδικεῖc. μαρτύρομα[ι
]νοηγματους θεους　　　　　　　]νοη. Γ. μὰ τοὺc θεούc.
]κλαιωνμοσχιων　　　　　5　　　]κλαίων Μοcχίων
].ζ[...]ιcιθι: [[πευ]][　　　　　　　].ζ[　ε]ϊcιθι:
　　　].[　　　　　　　　　　　　　　　].[

.　　.　　.　　.　　.　　　　　　　　.　　.　　.

Fr. 2

.　　.　　.　　.　　.　　　　　　　　.　　.　　.

　].[　　　　　　　　　　　　　　　].[
]ροηcομα[　　　　　　　　　　π]ροήcομα[ι
]μοcχιων[　　　　　　　　　　] Μοcχίων [
]ατελιπον[　　　　　　　　　κ]ατέλιπον [
]ειcεγω βλ[　　　　　5　　　]ειc ἐγὼ βλ[
]μελλε[　　　　　　　　　　　]μελλε[

.　　.　　.　　.　　.　　　　　　　　.　　.　　.

Fr. 1　　2 νεου corrected to λιθον by m²　　　5]κ, stroke curving up to right, definitely suggesting κ　　　7].[, a rounded letter, c or ε rather than o

Fr. 2　1].[, a descender　　　6]μ, trace of upstroke and right descender

Fr. 1　2 The scribal error suggests that the copying was done by eye rather than dictation. E. W. Handley observes that in some writing styles the words νέου and λίθον might be easily confused.

Λυδία λίθοc: the touchstone used to distinguish false gold from true and, by extension, apparently a commonplace allusion to detecting the truth or falsity of a situation. No doubt entirely appropriate to New Comedy. See *Corp. Paroem. Gr.* ii on Λυδία λίθοc (Macar. v 75) and βάcανοc λίθοc (Greg. Cyp. i 64 and note). Compare Bacchylides, fr. 10: Λυδία μὲν γὰρ λίθοc μανύει | χρυcόν, Theocritus xii 37: Λυδίη ἴcον ἔχειν πέτρῃ cτόμα and Sophocles' *Alexander*: ἀλλ' οὐκ ἄτλαc γὰρ βάcανοc ἡ Λυδὴ λίθοc in H. Hunger, 'Palimpsest-fragmente aus Herodians καθολικὴ Προcῳδία', *J. OE. Byz.* 16 (1967) 7.

4]νοη: most probably part of a verb, κατα]νοῃ or sim. It might also be from a proper name, i.e. Χρυcονόη, Λευκονόη, but I find no such name in New Comedy.

Γ̄: the appearance of the text suggests that the scribe found the notation Γ̄ in his original for he has written it in continuously without separation or a break of any kind. It is unlikely that this text was ever used as a production copy, although it was probably copied from one.

6 πευ[deleted: probably the next line begun in error.

3218 Back

Fr. 1   Fr. 2

↓   ]τοτεπρωτονεπ[.   .   .

  ].τομοϲηνοπαρ[   ]..[.].[

  ]ντηναλεξανδ[   ]υθεαϲτ.[

  ]θυϲεπηρῳθη κα[   ]ετην α[

5]ερανου[...]ειδε[   ]ηϲουτη[

  ]..[5   ]λακα...[

    .   .   .   .

3219. TREATISE ON PLATO?

Second century

Of the following scraps, the two most considerable and some at least of the others have to do with the dialogues of Plato. The work appears to be a monograph, and the remains would be consistent with a work 'on Plato and the dialogue', but I cannot say whether this adequately reflects its scope. Fr. 1 describes Plato's indebtedness to Sophron as being 'in respect of the dramatic' (if the obvious emendation is correct), and, alleging βαϲκανία against Plato on Aristotle's part, repudiates the assertion made by Aristotle in the *De Poetis* (quoted by Athenaeus and alluded to by Diogenes Laertius) that Alexamenus of Teos (Tenos *apud* pap.) was the first to write dialogues—or dramatic dialogues, as the papyrus qualifies. Fr. 2 states that Plato uses the four characters Socrates, Timaeus, the Athenian Stranger, and the Eleatic Stranger as mouthpieces for his own doctrines, and asserts that the Strangers represent Plato and Parmenides. There is evidently a connection of some kind with Diogenes Laertius (DL) 3. 52, where a similar statement is made, except that there the identification of the Strangers with the two philosophers is expressly denied. Some scantier fragments seem to be concerned with the historical development of tragedy: conceivably in a comparison of the respective developments of philosophy and tragedy on a more elaborate scale than that found at DL 3. 56.

In *BICS* 19 (1972) 17–38, I have attempted to reach an understanding of the critical theory underlying the surviving text and have investigated, without positive result, the authorship of the work and its relationship with DL.

The hand is a rather small, rounded example of a not uncommon type, with a slight backward slant. Omicron, more variable than most letters, is usually small and often high, and the beginning of the 'mixed' style may be discerned in the broad kappa and delta. The hand may be assigned a date around the middle or the second half of the second century. XXI **2306** and XVIII **2159** are comparable in so far as most of the letters are made in the same movements, but the former is less well formed and shows more freedom with ligatures, while the latter is a more formal hand with a clear tendency to make all the letters the same size.

High stops are used, and *paragraphi* apparently mark off sentences. Apart from the occasional enlargement of the first letter of a word, there are no other lectional aids. The back is blank.

I am glad to have been able to consult partial transcripts by Mr. Lobel and by Professor Turner and a full transcript and some notes by Mr. Parsons.

Fr. 1

9·6 × 5·8 cm.

    ·   ·   ·   ·

```
     ....].[
  ..]ικιλον[ c. 6 ]φ[.]ρ[..].[....].νϲ
  .]ϝτουτωκ[...].φρον[.]μειμηϲαμε
  νοϲτονμιμογραφονκατοδραμα          ἐ]ν τούτῳ κ[αὶ Ϲ]ώφρον[α] μειμησάμε-
5 τικοντωνδιαλογωνουγαρπειϲ           νος τὸν μιμογράφον κα⟨τὰ⟩ τὸ δραμα-
  τ.οναριστοτελειυποτηϲπροϲπλα        τικὸν τῶν διαλόγων· οὐ γὰρ πεισ-
  τωναβασκανιαϲε[.]ποντιεντω          τέον Ἀριστοτέλει ὑπὸ τῆς πρὸς Πλά-
  πρωτωπεριποιητικηϲκαιπρο            τωνα βασκανίας ε[ἰ]πόντι ἐν τῷ
  πλατωνοϲγεγραφθαιδραματικουϲ        πρώτῳ περὶ Ποιητικῆς καὶ πρὸ
10 .....].[....]..[.]λεξαμενουτηνιου   Πλάτωνος γεγράφθαι δραματικοὺς
  c. 12      ].[...]φεικταιϲυν          διαλό]γ[ους] ὑπ' [Ἀ]λεξαμενοῦ Τηνίου
  c. 18      ]ετιϲ....
```

    ·   ·   ·   ·   ·

2 ϝ[, or ι; υ scarcely poss.   φ, ρ, tails only   ].[, bottom of upright: ρ, τ, ι?   ].νϲ, or].[.]νϲ
10].[,]..[, too slight for identification but compatible with 2nd transcript   11].[, minimal
12 ...., tops only: three upright or oblique strokes, high traces at end (poss. 'o')
There are negligible traces of a second column

Fr. 2

(*a*) 11·0 × 6·5 cm., (*b*) 5·3 × 5·3 cm.

Col. ii

.　　.　　.　　.

(*b*) ....]εγε[

διαπạντωγ[

τωνεϲτινῳ[

νικαδιατουτ[

5　τα ̇ποικιλλεινδε[

διαλογουϲπη[

πηδεδιατειμα[

ουτινοϲξενου[

αυτου.[

10　νι..[

επ[

Col. i

.　.　.

↑

8 lines

↓

(*a*)　].[

].ϲπρωταγορας.[...]ς..των

]χομενωνπαραυτω ̇ταδε

]ωδοκουντααποφαινεταιδια

5　]ροϲωπωνϲωκ...ουϲτειμαι

]ουαθηναιουξ[....]τουελεα

]ξενου ̇ειϲινδ[....]ατηϲξεν

]θηναιοϲξενο[....]τωνκαι

].ενιδηϲαλλαδιạδρạματι

10　]ϲποιουμενοϲτουϲδιαλογουϲ

]....[..].νακαιανειδωλο

]νυμạναθηναι

]μενοϲτογ...

π[

λη[

τεọ[

δε[

5　ονκαιτο.[

τιạαλληλọ[

ελεγχομ[

ουδεταϋπọ[

·γ̄·λοιπωνλεγ[

10　μ̣ẹ̄ταϋ[..]..[.].[

...]λε[

ἐλεγ]χομένων παρ' αὐτῷ· τὰ δὲ

αὐτ]ῷ δοκοῦντα ἀποφαίνεται διὰ

5　δ π]ροϲώπων, Cωκράτουϲ, Τειμαί-

ου, τ]οῦ Ἀθηναίου ξ[ένου,] τοῦ Ἐλεά-

του] ξένου· εἰϲὶν δ' [ὁ Ἐλε]άτηϲ ξένο(ϲ)

χὠ Ἀθηναῖοϲ ξένο[ϲ Πλά]των καὶ

Παρ]μενίδηϲ· ἀλλὰ

The distance between (*b*) and (*a*) may be calculated by alignment of the verso fibres. The estimate of a gap of eight lines has a margin of error of no more than a single line either way.

Col. i 2]., *a* or, better, *o* .[, *o*, *ω*, *c*　]ς, or *κ*; then seemingly anomalous letter, perhaps *α* or *o*; then low speck; perhaps another letter lost before *τ*　*τ*, or *ι* or *ρ*　　11]....[, slight traces on

loose fibre   ]. (*ante ν*), high trace suggesting ι, but ο, ω, α cannot be excluded   **13** cτ, or
c˙τ ..., tops only: αθη poss.

Col. ii (*b*) 3 ω̣[, ο less good   **9** .[, β better than δ, φ, μ?   **10** ..[, δε poss.   **11** π[,
or ι   (*a*) 3 ọ[, c less good   **5** .[, low speck   **6** ι̣α, η less good?   **10** ε̣, α less good
]..[.].[, three high specks

Fr. 3

```
            ]μ...[
         ]νδι̣ονυϲον[
          ]πιϲυποκρι
         ]ω[..].ϲενε
  5        ]να[.].
```

·   ·   ·   ·

Apparently, on external and internal evidence alike, from the same vicinity as fr. 4. J. R.
Rea suggests combining the fragments so as to
make 3. 3 ff. the line-ends of 4. 1 ff.; this is possible
but I cannot confirm it. The fibres on the back
point, though not definitively, to another combination: ω at 3. 4 in alignment above ν 4. 2.

1 Perhaps μο̣ν̣.[**4**]., low curve:
c, ε, η, α?   **5**]., high trace, possibly end of
a final alpha

Fr. 5

·   ·   ·   ·

```
           ]ωντρ[
          ].ντο.[
        ]ωδ[...]ενφ[
         ]ατραγωδιαν[
  5       ].απολλωκ.[
       ]αλεγοντων‵προ̣′[
        ]πηγαγεν.[
            ]ν̣τ..[.].[
            ]πτω[
```

·   ·   ·   ·

2]., anomalous ο?   .[, θ, τ?   **5** α and
κ enlarged   ]., η, ν, .ι   .[, ν, α?   **6** ‵ο̣′, or ω, α
7]τ, or τ, ε

Fr. 4

·   ·   ·   ·

```
        ]δ̣[.].λθ.[
      ]ε̣[.]αδετουτον.[
        ].υτερονυποκ.[
        ]φοκληϲδ[
```

·   ·   ·   ·

1 θ, or ε   **3**]., ε poss.

Fr. 6

·   ·   ·   ·

```
          ]δραμ[
          ]πονυ[
```

·   ·   ·   ·

2]π, or]απ

Fr. 7

·   ·   ·   ·

```
          ]νορα[
          ]ηιδρ[
          ]λε̣[
          ]φερο[
  5       ].[.]ηιαι[
          ]ειπνοι.[
          ].[.].[
```

·   ·   ·   ·

4 ọ[, or ε   **6** .[, minimal (Postscript:
The papyrus has suffered damage and the latter
part of 5 now reads ηια[.)

Fr. 8

```
        ]..[
        ].αιον[
      ]ειδηκα.[
      ]υδοκουν[
   5  ]ιτωντεϲϲ[
      ]ωναυταγ.[
```

2]., ι or ν best, μ just poss., not β   3 .[,
high trace: κ, τ, ι, ρ, al.   5]ι, or ν   6 .[,
high speck

Fr. 9

```
      ]τεεκ[
      ]νηνυπο.[
      ]εριτωνπ[
      ]τωδειξ[
   5  ]...[
```

2 ν enlarged   3 π[, τ less good

Fr. 10

```
        ].[
      ]περ[
      ]υρο[
     ]λογοϲ[
   5  ]κ[.]κρι.[
      ].[...]φ[
     ]αλληλο.[
     __].ναε.[
       ]κε[
```

3]ν, perhaps]αι   7 .[, ι, ν poss.
8 .[, ϲ, θ, o?

Fr. 11
Top (?)

```
   ]ορι[ c. 6 ].φ[
   ]ϲτ.[...]λαρυθ[
   ]δεπ[.]ατ[.]ντηντ[
   ]οφιανιϲταπρωτα[
5  ]ηδιαλεκτικον[
    ]τικονωνκυρι[
   ]οϲτοδιαλεκτικ[
   ].τωνπολειτικ[
    ]ϲτηνθεωριαν[
10  ]ϲυν[.]χ..αϲλε.[
```

2 .[, η, ι?   6]τ, or ε; θ less good
10 .., or .[.]: ε[.] poss.   ϲ, perhaps ι· .[, ν suggested, perhaps λ

Fr. 12

```
   ]α..[.].[ c. 5 ]ρ[
   ]οϲοφιαϲαλλε[
     ]κατεπ[
     ]κτονα[
5     ]ωρη.[
      ]εν[
```

4 α enlarged   5]ω, or o   .[, τ poss.

Fr. 13

```
   ].τω[
   ]οϲτ[
```

1]., ι, ν

D

Fr. 14

```
]ωνα.[
]τερον.[
]..[.]ο[
```

.   .   .

1 α enlarged

Fr. 15

```
         .     .     .     .     .
           ]..[
         ]ηνμε[
         ]νωναλ[
         ]ηθ[
5        ]τω[
         .     .     .     .
```

Fr. 16

```
   .        .        .
        ].[
     ]ινεπανορθου[
     ]ικονομικ[
     ]καιθοκα.[
5    ]τεεστινβε[
     ]εριπαντας[
     ]λειπ.[
     ]ολην[
     ]ζειτο.[
10   ]τρια.[
     ]νοκ[
   .     .     .     .
```

Fr. 17

```
   .     .     .     .
        ].[
     ]τον.[
     ]τοδ[
     ]λειτικ[
   .     .     .
```

Fr. 18

```
   .     .     .     .
        ]νυ[
        ]οε..[
     ]ςμεθοδους
     ]ξεωσκαιπα
5    ].[.].[.]..υ
     ].εαποδε[
     ].ε.[
   .     .     .     .
```

Fr. 19

```
   .     .     .     .
..]φ[...].α..[.]λεκ[
εξουρουςατηω[
δουςατημαθημ[
ποθετο[.]εςτι.[
5   ..]εςις..[.]οντ[
   .     .     .     .
```

1 φ, tip of descender   δι[α]λεκ[poss.   2 ω[,
or ς, less good   4 .[, prob. ν or γ   5 ..],
or ...]   ..[, rubbed   [.], or [..]

Fr. 20

．　　　　　．　　　　　．

]θετ[．．．]τασα[
]ξεωϲμεθοδουϲ[
]．ιαλεκτικ[
]μενητοι[
5　]ωκενεπε[
]ταιαγ．[
]．ικοϲκ[
]νηλ．[
]．．[

．　　　　　．　　　　　．

6 χ, or π　　8 .[, θ or ε suggested

Fr. 21

．　　．　　．　　．

λαβειν．[
δειχθη[
．ητικον[
．ικονμω．[

．　　．　　．　　．

3 ., θ or ρ　　4 ω., or ϱν

Fr. 22

Col. i　　Col. ii

．　　．　　．　　．

　　　　τε[
]λαι　　κε．[
]．　　　γουμ[
　　　　εϲτ[
5　　　ε．．[
　　　　．[

．　　．　　．　　．

Fr. 23

Col. i　　Col. ii

．　　．　　．　　．

]ε[
]ψομε[
]καιταϲ[
]δυνα　[
5　]νεφα　　τ[
]　　　　αυ[
]υ　　　　δε[
　　　　κη．[

．　　．　　．　　．

Fr. 24

．　　．　　．　　．

．[
λαμ[
τικ[

．　　．　　．　　．

Fr. 25

．　　．　　．　　．

]ωϲκ．[
]　　　τ̄[
]εινακ[
]．ιϲητο[

．　　．　　．　　．

Fr. 1 'meanwhile(?) imitating Sophron the mimewriter too in respect of the dramatic element of the dialogues; for Aristotle is not to be believed when he says in his malice against Plato, in 'On Poetry' (*vult* 'On Poets') bk. 1, that dramatic dialogues had been written even before Plato by Alexamenus of Tenus.'

2 πο]ικίλον, cf. ποικίλλειν 2 ii 5.

3–5 Comparable statements are made by (1) DL 3. 18, δοκεῖ δὲ Πλάτων καὶ τὰ Cώφρονος τοῦ μιμογράφου βιβλία ἠμελημένα πρῶτος εἰς Ἀθήνας διακομίcαι καὶ ἠθοποιῆσαι πρὸς αὐτόν,

(2) Olympiodorus, *Vita Platonis*, 3, ἔχαιρε δὲ πάνυ καὶ Ἀριστοφάνει τῷ κωμικῷ καὶ Cώφρονι, παρ' ὧν καὶ τὴν μίμηcιν τῶν προcώπων ἐν τοῖς διαλόγοις ὠφελήθη· κτλ.,

(3) Anon., *Prolegomena in Platonis dialogos*, 3, ἐζήλωcεν δὲ καὶ Cώφρονα τὸν γελωτοποιόν, τὴν μιμητικὴν ὥcπερ κατορθῶcαι βουλόμενος· ὁ γὰρ διαλόγους γράφων μίμηcιν προcώπων εἰcάγει, and

(4) Tzetzes, *Chil*. 10. 806–10, which is vaguer but important for the authority cited, ... ἀφ' οὗπερ (sc. τοῦ Cώφρονος βιβλίου) ἐμιμήcατο γράφειν τοὺς διαλόγους, | ὡς ἐν τοῖς Cίλλοις φαίνεται ὁ Τίμων διαγράφων, cf. ibid. 11. 8–10, ἐκ μίμων δὲ τοῦ Cώφρονος μιμεῖται διαλόγους. | ὁ Cώφρων ὅcα γράφει γάρ εἰcι τῶν ἀμοιβαίων, | ἐρώτηcιν, ἀπόκριcιν, cύμπαντα κεκτημένα.

Our author is unique among ancient writers in describing Plato's debt to Sophron expressly in terms of 'the dramatic'.

8 π. ποιητικῆc: in error for π. ποιητῶν, the less well known work, as in frr. 75, 76, 77 Rose. The passage in question is quoted by Athenaeus, 11. 505c, and alluded to by DL 3. 48, the matter under discussion being in either case the εὕρεcιc of the dialogue form: fr. 72 Rose, F17 E. Mensching, *Favorin* I.

Athen. 11. 505c: ἐγκώμια αὐτοῦ (τοῦ Μένωνος) διεξέρχεται ὁ τοὺς ἄλλους ἀπαξαπλῶς κακολογήσας (Πλάτων), ἐν μὲν τῇ πολιτείᾳ Ὅμηρον ἐκβάλλων καὶ τὴν μιμητικὴν ποίηcιν, αὐτὸς δὲ τοὺς διαλόγους μιμητικῶς γράψας, ὧν τῆς ἰδέας οὐδ' αὐτὸς εὑρετής ἐcτι. πρὸ γὰρ αὐτοῦ τοῦθ' εὗρε τὸ εἶδος τῶν λόγων ὁ Τήιος Ἀλεξαμενός, ὡς Νικίας ὁ Νικαεὺς ἱcτορεῖ καὶ Cωτίων. Ἀριcτοτέλης δὲ ἐν τῷ περὶ ποιητῶν οὕτως γράφει "οὐκοῦν οὐδὲ ἐμμέτρους τοὺς καλουμένους Cώφρονος μίμους μὴ φῶμεν εἶναι λόγους καὶ μιμήσεις, ἢ τοὺς Ἀλεξαμενοῦ τοῦ Τηίου τοὺς πρώτους γραφέντας τῶν Cωκρατικῶν διαλόγων;" ἀντικρὺς φάcκων ὁ πολυμαθέcτατος Ἀριcτοτέλης πρὸ Πλάτωνος διαλόγους γεγραφέναι τὸν Ἀλεξαμενόν.

(The papyrus does not settle the vexed question of the soundness of Athenaeus' text of the quotation, for πρὸ 11ιʹ ἵτωνος is an equally legitimate paraphrase whether Aristotle said that Alexamenus' dialogues were the first of the Socratic dialogues or—as the various emendations would have it—that he wrote dialogues before the Socratics.)

DL 3. 48 διαλόγους τοίνυν φαcὶ πρῶτον γράψαι Ζήνωνα τὸν Ἐλεάτην· Ἀριcτοτέλης δὲ ἐν πρώτῳ Περὶ ποιητῶν Ἀλεξαμενὸν Cτυρέα ἢ Τήιον, ὡς καὶ Φαβωρῖνος ἐν Ἀπομνημονεύμαcι (*FHG* iii 579). δοκεῖ δέ μοι Πλάτων ἀκριβώcας τὸ εἶδος καὶ τὰ πρωτεῖα δικαίως ἂν ὥcπερ τοῦ κάλλους οὕτω καὶ τῆς εὑρέcεως ἀποφέρεcθαι.

The only other mention of Alexamenus extant in ancient literature, the present passage excluded, is at Eustathius, in *Il*. 21. 142 (cited for the accentuation), Ἀλεξαμενός, Τήιος ἀνήρ, εὑρετής φαcι τοῦ μιμητικῶς γράφειν. This is manifestly dependent on Athenaeus.

It is remarkable that the papyrus specifies *dramatic* dialogues. I have elsewhere (*BICS* 19 (1972) 19–22) given reasons for thinking that 'dramatic' is not an arbitrary qualification but is tantamount to 'mimetic', and that what our author is concerned to repudiate is Aristotle's assertion that Alexamenus' *logoi* are to be accounted *mimeseis*. Briefly, I take his position to be: Plato got the dramatic element of his dialogues not from Alexamenus but from Sophron.

10 Τηνίου: Τηίου Aristotle *ap*. Athen. loc. cit.: Τήιος Athen. ibid.: Cτυρέα ἢ Τήιον DL loc. cit.: Τήιος Eustath. loc. cit. The chances are that of Τήνιος and Τήιος, one is the corrupt version of the other.

I find nothing to determine the choice other than the weight of authority in favour of *Τήιος*. The *De Poetis* quotation utilized by Athenaeus, and DL's source, each had 'Tean', for the mutual agreement of these authors is enough to protect either of them from suspicion of subsequent corruption. More generally, the papyrus' other mistakes or corruptions in this section (*κατοδραματικον* and *περὶ ποιητικῆς*) do not encourage faith in it.

11]*φ* is virtually certain. I do not know how *ἀφεῖκται* (or *ἐφ-*) would relate to what precedes. The only alternative is *ἐφεικταί* or compound, which does not look attractive.

12 Possibly *τις ἄλλο(ς)*.

Fr. 2 Col. i 'Protagoras . . . refuted in him. His own doctrines are represented (*or* he represents his own doctrines) through four characters, Socrates, Timaeus, the Athenian Stranger, and the Eleatic Stranger; and the Eleatic and Athenian Strangers are Parmenides and Plato, but in making the dialogues out-and-out dramatic(?). . .'

2–9 Cf. DL 3. 52, *τούτων δὲ τὸ μὲν δοξαζόμενον πρότασίς ἐστιν, ἡ δὲ δόξα ὑπόληψις. ὁ τοίνυν Πλάτων περὶ μὲν ὧν κατείληφεν ἀποφαίνεται, τὰ δὲ ψευδῆ διελέγχει, περὶ δὲ τῶν ἀδήλων ἐπέχει. καὶ περὶ μὲν τῶν αὐτῷ δοκούντων ἀποφαίνεται διὰ τεττάρων προσώπων, Σωκράτους, Τιμαίου, τοῦ Ἀθηναίου ξένου, τοῦ Ἐλεάτου ξένου· εἰσὶ δ' οἱ ξένοι οὐχ, ὥς τινες ὑπέλαβον, Πλάτων καὶ Παρμενίδης, ἀλλὰ πλάσματά ἐστιν ἀνώνυμα· ἐπεὶ καὶ τὰ Σωκράτους καὶ τὰ Τιμαίου λέγων Πλάτων δογματίζει. περὶ δὲ τῶν ψευδῶν ἐλεγχομένους εἰσάγει οἷον Θρασύμαχον καὶ Καλλικλέα καὶ Πῶλον Γοργίαν τε καὶ Πρωταγόραν, ἔτι δ' Ἱππίαν καὶ Εὐθύδημον καὶ δὴ καὶ τοὺς ὁμοίους.*

The immediate points of difference are (1) the order of the treatment of *τὰ ψευδῆ* and *τὰ αὐτῷ δοκοῦντα*, and (2) whether or not Plato and Parmenides are to be recognized in the Strangers.

3 *παρ' αὐτῷ* : as we would say, 'in Plato'.

9–10 *διὰ δραματι[κῆ]ς* or *διαδραματι[κού]ς* ? Either restoration will introduce a novelty. *δραματική* is to the best of my knowledge nowhere used as a substantive, but there are of course numerous analogies, *μιμητική* among them : *διαδραματικός* would be a new word, but the formation is unobjectionable (*δια-*intensive). Palaeographically there is nothing to choose.

If *διὰ δραματι[κῆ]ς*, line 11 will contain a predicate (e.g. *ποικίλους*) and continue *ἵνα καὶ ἀνειδωλο-[ποιῇ τὸν ἀνώ]νυμον Ἀθηναῖ[ον κτλ.* But it is nearly nonsense to say that Plato made the dialogues *ποικίλους*—or whatever—'*in order to* image-make the unnamed Athenian'.

With *διαδραματι[κού]ς*, 11 ff. could be thought to have read *ὡς ἄλλον τινά* (or *οὐχ ὡς Πλάτωνα) καὶ ἀνειδωλοποιεῖ τὸν ἀνώνυμον Ἀθηναῖον*, 'he represents the unnamed Athenian as someone other than himself.' For the construction cf. Philo iv 87. 17 C–W, *μόνον ἀναζωγραφούσης καὶ ἀνειδωλοποιούσης τὰ μὴ ὄντα ὡς ὄντα*, and *Σ* Aristoph. *Acharn.* 198, *ὡς γυναῖκας εἰδωλοποιεῖ τὰς σπονδάς.* Against this is the apparent redundance of *καί* and the near tautology of the expression. An alternative and in my view preferable restoration would be *ἀλλὰ διαδραματικοὺς ποιούμενος τοὺς διαλόγους εἰσάγει εἰκόνα καὶ ἀνειδωλο-ποιεῖ τὸν ἀνώνυμον Ἀθηναῖον*, 'but in making the dialogues out-and-out dramatic he introduces an image (*sc.* of himself) and conjures up (makes an imaginary character of) the unnamed Athenian.' (For this use of the verb cf. Didymus' note on *Λαμίας ὄρχεις ἀπλύτους*, Aristoph. *Pax* 758, *ap. Σ ad loc.*: *εἰδωλο-ποιεῖ τινας ὄρχεις Λαμίας· θῆλυ γάρ.*)

Dr. Rea points out the possibility of articulating *δια* as *δι' ἅ*, tentatively suggesting a text on the lines of *δι' ἃ δραματικοὺς ποιούμενος τοὺς διαλόγους ἔχει πεπλασμένα καὶ κτλ.*, 'because of the figments which he has constructed in making the dialogues dramatic, he also . . .'. (I cannot quite rule out *ε* as a reading before *να* in 11.)

13 Possibly *τὸν Ἀθη|[ναῖον*.

Col. ii. (*b*) 4 *Πλατω]]νικά?*

5–9 e.g. *ποικίλλειν δὲ [αὐτῷ δοκεῖ τοὺς] διαλόγους πῇ [μὲν διὰ Σωκράτους,] πῇ δὲ διὰ Τειμα[ίου ἢ δι' Ἀθηναί]ου τινὸς ξένου [ἢ Ἐλεάτου τινὸς τὰ] αὐτοῦ δ[όγματα ἀποφαινομένῳ. (πῇ [μὲν . . .] πῇ δέ* J. R. Rea. I had read *πι[* in 6.) Plato's adoption of a number of different characters as mouthpieces for his own views is in the interests of diversification, *ἡ ποικιλία*.

10 In view of the *paragraphus*, *Πλάτω]]νι δέ* has some probability.

(*a*) 6 *ἐναν]]τία ἀλλήλο[ις?*

9 *γ̄* = *τριῶν*: cf. [*δ*] 2 i 5. If *οὐδὲ τὰ ὑπὸ [Σωκράτους καὶ τῶν] γ̄ λοιπῶν λεγ[όμενα*, I do not know why *λοιπῶν*, not *ἄλλων*, is used.

Frr. 3–5. These fragments have to do with tragedy, specifically, it seems, with the introduction and increase in number of actors. They add nothing to our historical knowledge. Fr. 3 evidently belongs closely before fr. 4, but I cannot exactly fix their physical relationship (see apparatus).

There is no necessity to assume that the discussion has any bearing on the Platonic dialogues, but it is possible to find the connection in a comparison of the stages of development through which tragedy and philosophy respectively passed, such as is made at DL 3. 56: ὥσπερ δὲ τὸ παλαιὸν ἐν τῇ τραγῳδίᾳ πρότερον μὲν μόνος ὁ χορὸς διεδραμάτιζεν, ὕστερον δὲ Θέσπις ἕνα ὑποκριτὴν ἐξεῦρεν ὑπὲρ τοῦ διαναπαύεσθαι τὸν χορὸν καὶ δεύτερον Αἰσχύλος, τὸν δὲ τρίτον Σοφοκλῆς καὶ συνεπλήρωσεν τὴν τραγῳδίαν, οὕτως καὶ τῆς φιλοσοφίας ὁ λόγος πρότερον μὲν ἦν μονοειδὴς ὡς ὁ φυσικός, δεύτερον δὲ Σωκράτης προσέθηκε τὸν ἠθικόν, τρίτον δὲ Πλάτων τὸν διαλεκτικὸν καὶ ἐτελεσιούργησε τὴν φιλοσοφίαν. Another possibility, given our author's view of Plato *qua* dramatist, is a comparison of some kind between the number of actors in tragedy and the number of participant characters introduced in dialogue.

Fr. 3   3 Θές]πις ὑποκρι[τὴν εὗρεν τὸν πρῶτον, *v. sim.*, seems secure.
4 τραγ]ῳ[δί]ας ἕνε|[κα? ἐτραγ]ῴ[δ]ησεν? But there are other possibilities.

Fr. 4   1 δ[ι]ελθ-?
2 μ]ε[τ]ὰ δὲ τοῦτον (unless, as Dr. Rea cautions, τοῦτο): *sc.* Thespis, probably.
3 δ]εύτερον ὑποκρ[ιτήν, 4 Σο]φοκλῆς. The introduction of the second actor is presumably attributed to Aeschylus, as in DL, for it seems clear enough that the papyrus does not credit Aeschylus with the introduction of the third.
4 Σο]φοκλῆς δ[ὲ τρίτον *v. sim.*?

Fr. 5   1 τρ[αγῳδία, τρ[ιῶν, *al.*
3 τραγ]ῳδ[ία? Perhaps I should not venture to proffer ἐτραγ]ῴδ[ης]εν φ[ιλοσοφίαν.
5 Articulation as Ἀπόλλω is practically enforced by the enlarged alpha, which rules out -α πολλῷ and discourages ἃ πολλῷ. If this fragment is part of a comparison of tragedy and philosophy, perhaps Apollo stands as the representative of philosophy, as Dionysus (3. 2) of tragedy.
6 προ: or πρῳ (πρῶτος?) or πρᾳ (Πρατίνας?).

Fr. 6   2 In view of δραμ[, perhaps πρόςω]πον.

Fr. 7   2 τ]ῆι δρ[αματικῆι? Iota adscript is not written in the other fragments (1. 3, 7, 8; 2 i 3, 4; 19. 3), but should probably be recognized at line 5 of this fragment.
5 Since ἰαίνειν seems out of the question, the articulation is presumably]ηι αι[(or]ηι Αι[ ).
6 (-)δ]είπνοις or -δ]είπνοι. It is conceivable that the *Symposium*, or symposiac literature generally, is under discussion.

Fr. 8   The appearance of this fragment is consistent with its belonging to col. ii of fr. 2, but I cannot place it. The following restorations then suggest themselves:
2 Ἀθη]ναῖον (palaeographically better than Τί]μαιον).
3 Παρμεν]είδη (spelt -νίδης in fr. 2, but cf. the inconsistency of μειμησάμενος and μιμογράφον in fr. 1).
5 περ]ὶ τῶν τεσσ[άρων (προσώπων).

Fr. 9   3 π]ερὶ τῶν π[ροσώπων?
4 οὕ]τω, αὑ]τῷ, *al.*

Fr. 10   4/5 Apparently a *diple obelismene* (to mark a new section?), but it may be an ordinary *paragraphus*.
5 Not υ]π[ο]κριτ[.

Fr. 11   3 Π[λ]άτ[ω]ν.
4 Apparently φιλοσ]οφίαν ἰς (*l.* εἰς) τὰ πρῶτα.
5 Dialectic again in line 7. DL, in his analogy between tragedy and philosophy (3. 56: see on frr. 3–5 above), says that Plato perfected philosophy by the introduction of dialectic, but I cannot offer any plausible reconstruction of the fragment using that passage as a model.

6 ὦν (κύριος) or ὦν (κυριώτατον or κυριεύει).

9 I do not know whether the subdivisions of the 'practical' and 'theoretical' sciences have any relevance for the fragment.

Fr. 12 4 μει]κτόν, *al.* The enlarged alpha enforces this articulation.

5 Possibly θε]ωρητ[ικ-.

Fr. 15 2 Conceivably μέ[θοδον, cf. 18. 3, 20. 2.

Fr. 16 2 ἐπανορθου[calls to mind the three forms of government distinguished by the commentators as ἐξ ἐπανορθώσεως (διορθ- Albinus), ἐξ ὑποθέσεως, and ἀνυπόθετος (Albinus *didasc.* xxxiv 118 Hermann vi, Anon. *Proleg.* xxvi *sub fin.*, Proclus *in remp.* ii 8. 15–21 Kroll). Cf. ἀνυπόθετος at 19. 4. But the use of the verb rather than the noun is against interpretation on these lines, and the rest of the fragment does not naturally fall in with it.

3 ο]ἰκονομικ[- or -]ικὸν ὁ μικ[τός (or μικ[ρός). Against the latter is the papyrus' regular spelling of ῑ as ει (the ratio is 7 or 8 to 1).

4 The only possible articulation seems to be to isolate θ as a numeral, but it is strange that it should have no special designation as such, contrast the elaborate ·γ̄· at 2 ii(*a*) 9. ἐν τοῖς η] καὶ θ is then the obvious restoration ('in books 8 and 9'), but neither the *Republic*, nor the *Laws*, nor the *Letters*, is an obviously suitable reference, nor do any *Oeconomica* bring light. In view of the twofold difficulty, κα{ι}θὸ καί might be considered.

5 βέ[λτιον (or βέ[λτιστον) or βέ[βαιον probable.

Fr. 17 4 πο]λειτικ[-.

Fr. 18 3–4 Cf. 20. 2, which perhaps makes 4 πρά]ξεως καὶ πα|[θήματος (or πά|[θους) a less likely suggestion than it would be otherwise.

Fr. 19 This fragment is likely to have some relationship with the ἀνυπόθετος ἀρχή discussion of Pl. *Rep.* vi 510 c–11 a and vii 533 b–d, but I cannot get at the sense of it. The relation of ἡ διαλεκτικὴ (μέθοδος) to τὰ μαθήματα is treated by Albinus, *didasc.* vii *ad fin.* (162 Herm. vi), but there is no close affinity with the papyrus. Cf. also Proclus *in remp.* i 283 Kroll, *in Alcib.* i 128 and 246.

1 Perhaps δι[α]λεκ[τική, as the subject of the following participles.

2 ἐξουροῦσα is not credible, ἐξ οὗ ῥοῦσα scarcely more so. I would emend to ἐξευροῦσα. The trace above the first omicron, transcribed as if it were the tail of a phi, may in fact be a supralinear correction.

3 δοῦσα τῇ μαθημ[ατικῇ.

3–4 No doubt ἀνυ]|πόθετο[ς] (or -ο[ν]). 4–5 ὑ|πόθ]εσις is less secure.

Fr. 20 1 ἀνυπο]θέτ[ους] τὰς ἀ[ρχάς (cf. 19. 4–5) is perhaps a rather far-fetched suggestion.

2 'Methods' in the vicinity of -ξεως also at 18. 3. The fragments are unlikely to belong close to each other, for the writing there is smaller.

Fr. 21 2–3 θεω]|ρητικόν?

Fr. 23 i 2 Probably λημ]ψομε[ν-.

Fr. 25 2 A heading?

II. EXTANT CLASSICAL TEXTS

3220. Hesiod, *Erga* and *Aspis*

Second century

Π_{39}. On these fragments see the introduction to **2495**. Under that number were published others, apparently in the same hand, from at least two lost works of the Hesiodic corpus. The fragments of *Erga* and *Aspis* published here might have belonged to two different rolls, but it is equally possible that both poems were contained in one. In *Erga* the column-height was 38–9 verses, about 22 cm. The *Aspis* fragments are at least compatible with this format; a column may perhaps have ended at v. 194.

ERGA

· · · · ·

15   ]ιλει.[

      ]ἐριν̣τ̣[

       ]μεν[*interlinear*

· · · ·

          · · · · ·

        ]κγ[

        ]ο̣ν̣εχο̣[

        ]ιωϲονο̣[

        ]ονιω[

260   ]απο̣τ̣[

        ]ρανοϲ̣[

        ]νεπ[

· · · · ·

     · · ·

308   ]εργω[

309   ]ιτεργα[

311?   ].[

· · ·

Erga 17 μὲν had perhaps been accidentally omitted   309 Π agrees with other sources in having τ' before ἐργ-   311 The trace does not suit the letters of 310 (omitted in four other papyri and CD): probably]ε[

Top of column

γ ω

]καιμεταδοιη[

]τα . . νκαταθυμον[

]δειηφιπιθησας,[

360   ]χνωϲενφιλονη[

]κρωικαταθειϙ[

]μεγακαιτο[]γεν[

]αιθοπαλιμ[

]ανερα[. .]δ[

365   ]ντοθυρη̣ι̣[

. . . .

381   ] . αιεν[

]γωερ[

]νεπιτ[

. . . .

]ρονεχ[

]γεριϲαν[   ]ακικ . [

440   ]δεεργον[   ] . ναυθιλι[

]εϲϲαραϙ[   ]έ̆τηϲαιζη[

ϲ[

]νηϲατ[   ]υφονοκ[

] . . .   ]οϲ[. . .   ]νκαυλακ[]ελ[

]μηϙ[   ]θομηλικα[

445   ]θυμ[   ]ντου . [   ] . ωτεροϲαλ[

]ϲπε[   ]ϲϲαϲθαι[   ]ϲποριην[

]κϙ . [   ]αρανηρμ[. . .

]φραζε . [   ]υτανγερ[

]ψοθεν[. . .

450   ] . ροτ[

. . .

357 μετα was a slip, but δοίη is a variant known from $Π_5$, Proclus, and the Φ manuscripts except E
358 not τέρπεθ' ἐὸν as Φ   361 καταθεῖο as $Π_5Π_{19}$ codd., Plutarch, etc.; Philoponus and cod.
M of Stobaeus give the active (cf. Plato, *Crat.* 428 a)   365 Apparently θυρηι[φι as in C; contrast
-ηφι in 359   383 επιτ[ελλ- as codd. and many quotations: περιτελλ- Max. Tyr.   441]έτηϲ:
the accent appears to be in a different ink. $Π_{46}$ and the medieval tradition give -ετὴϲ. Cf. Kühner–Blass
i 545 n. 11; Chandler, *Greek Accentuation*, 2nd edn., para. 703   442 The interlinear sigma is crude
and heavy. Below it the top of τ[ετρατρ]   443 κ' αὔλακ': the κ', omitted in most codd., was given by
Laur. 32. 16, Par. 2707, Vat. gr. 57, but suspected of being a Byzantine conjecture. It is also found in
$Π_{47}$ below

```
                  .           .
            ]ηιδιον[
            ]ηιδιον[
455         ]ηcὶδαν[
            ]ηπιοc[

                  .           .
                                      .        .        .
                  .    .    .      ]ωρμη[
460         ].[]ν.[            ]διερ.[
            ]πρωϊμα[           ]πε[
            ]εαριπολ[                .        .        .
        ]   νειονδ.[
        ]   νειοcαλ[
                    ..[
465     ]   ε[
        ]   ε[
        ]   αρ.[
        ]   χε[
              .        .        .

              .        .        .
            ]αρδ[
            ]ωρηιχ[
495         ]cχανε[
498         ]πολλαδ[
            ]χρηιζω[
500         ]ελπιcδ[
            ]ημε.[
            ]εικ[
              .        .        .

              .        .        .
536         ]καιτ[
            ]χλα.[
            ]τημ[
              .        .        .
```

459 ἐφορμηθῆναι codd.   462 ἔαρι as Pollux. One cod. gives ἦρι, the rest εἴαρι   465 sscr.
perhaps κα[496–7 omitted, as in Ω, schol. vet., Et. Gen., and Tzetzes. Plutarch and Proclus
knew the lines, but not necessarily in just this place; Schoemann suggested that they belonged after 492
538 If c]τημ[ονι was written, the margin was not straight

. . .

575   ]εναμ[

        ].τοϲϲ.[

        ]ανιϲταμε[

        ]αρτεργοιοτ[

        ]ριπροφερειμ[

580   ]ητεφανειϲαπ[

          ]πολλ[

. . . . . .

            ]τ'αν[

           ]οϲλ.[

     . . . .]υγω[

585   ]οτατ[   ]ιγεϲ[

       ]αιδεγ[ ]ναικε[

       ]κεφαλ[]ηνκα[

       ]χρωϲ[]υποκ[

        ]εϲ[]κιη[

590   . . .].ηιγαλατ[

End of column

Top of column

        ]περκαπ[

630   ]εινπ[

. . .

. . .

        ]ταδεπαντ[

689   ]υϲιναπα.[

691   ]ποντουμετ[

        ]παμαξ[

. . .

578 γάρ τ' as codd. (cf. 309)   588 The space available indicates ἀυαλέος δὲ] (Hermann) rather than ἀυαλέος δέ τε (codd.), though the omission might be a mere accident   590 False iota adscript   689 ἄπαγ[τα as codd.: παντ[α Π_{49} below   690 omitted, as in Π_{49}; homoeo-teleuton will be responsible   692 ἐπ' ἄμαξαν as Π_{49}, not ἐφ' as part of the medieval tradition

```
                    ·   ·   ·
698              ]η[
699(?)           ]πα[
700?        ]   τ[
702        ]   ουμ[
           ]   τηϲ[
           ]   δ[
                    ·   ·   ·
```

```
                                        ·     ·     ·
705                          ]..[
                             ]αγμ[
                             ]ρο[
                                  ·       ·       ·
```

```
                                        ·   ·   ·
736                          ].αλλαθανα.[
737                          ]αμωνκαλλι.[
                             ]η`ι´ιδωνεϲκα[
                             ]υηρατωιυδατ[
740                          ].τητιδεχει[
742                          ]ωνενδα[
                             ].ναιθωνι[
                             ]μενκρητ.[
             ·   ·   ·
745      ]πι[                ].μ[..]ατ[
         ]  μη[              ]εϲτ[.]νκ[
         ]μη[                ]ξηλακερυ.[
         ]μη[                ]νεπιρρεκτ[
```

End of column

699 f. Prima facie, πα[is 699 παρθενικὴν ..., τ[is 700 τὴν δὲ μάλιϲτα γαμεῖν ..., and 701 πάντα μάλ' ἀμφὶϲ ἰδών ... is missing; or 699 is missing and 700–1 are transposed. But the line one might expect to be absent is 700, which is omitted by two other papyri ($\Pi_5\Pi_{49}$) and Stobaeus, ignored by Proclus, and marginal in Vat. gr. 57. It is not impossible that the τ[was a π (= 701), though the horizontal would be abnormally prolonged to the left   705 Perhaps]α[.]δ[, i.e. γήρ]α[ϊ] δ[ῶκεν. An ancient variant had θῆκεν, see below on Π_{49} 736a (= 758) is absent, as in Π_5, Proclus, Moschopulus, Triclinius, and Vat. gr. 904   738 Insertion and trema by a second hand   740 Aristarchus athetized the line. This scribe is very sparing with tremas and elision-marks, so their absence here does not necessarily imply the articulation κακότητι δέ. Codd. are divided between this and κακότητ' ἰδὲ; the schol. vet. mentions also readings κακότητ' ἴδε and κακότητ' ἔπι. The omission of 741, if it is anything but an accident, would imply ἴδε   742 ἐν as quotations and most codd.: ἐνὶ Vat. gr. 57 and 904   746 ἀνεπίξ]εϲτ[ο]ν as codd., quotations, Proclus, schol. vet.: ἔνιοι δὲ ἀνεπίρρεκτον γράφουϲι schol. (cf. 748)   747 κρώ]ξη as $\Pi_5\Pi_{49}$ C, etc. Other sources give κρώζῃ

Top of column

]˳μηδελ[

750   ]κινητ[

. . .

. . .

775   ]καρποναμ[

]μεγαμεινω[

]ότητοσαραχν[

]αμᾶται [

]οιτοτεεργον[

780   ]ην[. . .]cθ˳[

]ψαc˳[

. . .

. . .

]cμεν[

800   ]ονακο[

. . .   ]ουτωια˳[

]μπ[   ]ιτεκαι[

]πε[   ]φ[

]κο˳[. . .

805 . . .

. . .   ]ωη[

]υυλοτομου[   ]ιαδ[

]τεξυλαπολλατ[   ]ελοντ[

]ιδαρχ[. .]θαινη[⟦ϵ̣ξτ⟧αc[

810   ]ηεπιδ[   ]ρ· [

]πα[   ]ρωπ[

]εφ[   ]ενε[

. . .   . . .

807 βάλλει]ν as Π_5 codd., not βαλλέμε]ν (Rzach)   809 αρετας was written instead of ἀραιάc, **and** corrected with an ϵ (for αι). The correction was made with a blunter pen

Uncertain location (314–15?)

.   .   .

]ωιερ.[
]...ν[

.   .   .

Fragment of uncertain location, 2: a flat dot at letter-top height is closely followed by the upper left part of a round letter; then a pointed top before ν. Compatible with κ]τ̣ε̣α̣ν̣[ων (315), but if so, Π had τ]ωι for τό in 314. This has figured in several conjectures. I cannot find any alternative location for the scrap in *Erga* or *Aspis*. (*Erga* 382–3 and 443–4 are excluded by the presence of other fragments.)

ASPIS

.   .   .

     ]ετο̣δ[
    ] ο̣[.]ραμι̣[
85   ] ηδικη[
    ] ζωεδαγα[
    ] η̇αλοχω[
    ] γει̣νομ[
     ]co[.]τεπ[
90   ].[

.   .   .

             .   .   .
             ]αχιϲϲ̣[
             ]γρετοϲ[
             ]πετειλ[
95   ]φοιν[
             ]εϲιθα[

             .   .   .

    ]τεϲ̣υναϊγδ[
190   ]εϲινηδελατ[
    ]αρεοϲβλοσυ[
    ]ϲεοι˙ενδεκ[

.   .   .

Asp. 85 ἦ not ἦι is correct   87 The ι is a later addition   92 -ϲτον- or -ϲτεν-]αχιϲϲ[ατ' is a new reading; codd. have -ίζετ'   94 ἐ]πετειλ[ατ' (as Vat. gr. 1825, *s.* xiv) or ἐ]πετειλ[εν (as Tricl.). Most codd. have ἐπετέλλετ' (cf. *Od.* 11. 622) or ἐπέτελλεν (cf. [Hes.] fr. 190. 12)   95 φοιν[ι-κόεντα as most codd.: ϲιγαλόεντα (cf. *Il.* 5. 226) F   189 The space indicates και] (*b*J, etc.) not οι] (B)   ϲυναῖγδην as BJ, Et. Gen./Magn.: ϲυναῖκτην *b* schol.

(.   .   .?)
195   ]αραδεδε[
]ιπολεμονκατα.[
]αγελειητριτογε[
]μαχηνε[.]ελο[
].[.].[.]ϛϵ[.]ηντετρ[
200   ]τοφυλο[
]οϛ˙ενδαρ[
]ητουϲυ[

.   .   .

195 δὲ as BJ: δὴ *m* (om. RLS)   197 ἀγελείη as *b*J: ολοὴ B, which led Peppmüller to conjecture ὀλοὴ ἦν   199 Apparently χ[ρυ]ϛϵ[ι]ην as Vat. gr. 1825 and *m*: χρυϲέην the rest. Preceding it,
χει]ρ[ι] (BFS) rather than χερ]ϛ[ι] (*b*J)   202 διοϲκαιλ]ητουϲυ[ιοϲ as BS: λητοῦϲ καὶ διὸϲ υἱόϲ *b*J

3221. HESIOD, *Erga,* 93?–108

93/Dec. 18/H3   3·0 × 8·4 cm.   Second/third century

*Π*₄₁. Written on the back of a list containing words beginning χα, χϵ, χη, etc.
Most of these words are covered up by a strip of papyrus stuck over them for strengthen-
ing. On ↓ the Hesiod text is copied in an ugly informal upright rounded capital, leaning
slightly backwards, to be assigned to the latter part of the second or the early third
century.

.   .

↓   ].[.]..[
]ωμαφϵ.[
95   ]τοκηδϵα.[
]τοιϲιδομοι[
]νουδϵθυρα[
]ωμαπιθο[
]ρϵταο[
100   ]ουϲαλαλ[
]ηδϵθαλ[
]αιδ᾿ϵπ.ν[
]οιϲιφϵρ.[
]ητιϵτα[
105   ]ξϵλααϛ[
]νϵκκο[
]ρϵϲιβα[
]ανθρ[

.   .

The traces of the first line are not sufficient to show whether it was 93 (unknown to Origen, Proclus, and part of the medieval tradition) or 92   94 There may have been an elision-mark as well as the smooth breathing   96 Π disagrees with Seleucus, who read $\mu\nu\chi o\hat{\iota}c\iota$ for $\delta\acute{o}\mu o\iota c\iota$ 99 is present, as in all manuscripts; it is omitted in one quotation, while two others end with 98   102 Π supports quotations and most manuscripts against Φ's $\mathring{\eta}\delta$' $\dot{\epsilon}\pi\dot{\iota}$ 104 was athetized, according to the scholia   105 $\epsilon]\xi\epsilon\lambda\alpha\alpha c[\theta\alpha\iota$ by error for $\epsilon\xi\alpha\lambda\epsilon\alpha c\theta\alpha\iota$

3222. HESIOD, *Erga*, 144–56

30 4B.41/D(2–3)a   2·6 × 8·2 cm.   Third century

Π_{42}. A competent but ugly example of the mixed style, with a slight lean to the left, probably to be assigned to the third century.

.   .

$]\nu\delta\epsilon\nu[$

145    $]\iota\mu o\nu\cdot\acute{o}[$

$]\acute{c}\cdot o\nu\delta\acute{\epsilon}\tau[$

$]\nu\kappa\rho\alpha[.]\epsilon\rho o\phi[$

$].\iota\rho\epsilon[.].'\alpha\pi[$

$]\beta\alpha\rho[\ldots]\iota\mu[$

150    $]\alpha\lambda\kappa\epsilon o\iota\delta\acute{\epsilon}\tau[$

$]\nu\kappa\acute{\epsilon}c\kappa\epsilon c\iota[$

$]\tau\epsilon\rho\eta\iota c\iota\delta\alpha.[$

$\overset{\mu[\ ]}{]\tau\epsilon.[.]\alpha\ddot{\iota}\delta[}$

$]\alpha\gamma\lambda o\nu c\pi\epsilon[$

155    $]\alpha o c\eta\epsilon\lambda\iota[$

$]\gamma\hat{\alpha}\iota\alpha\kappa\alpha\lambda[$

.   .

146 Above c·o, the right-hand end of a stroke resembling a grave accent (not expected here) followed by a small semicircle open to the lower right and a dot   152 .[: a spot above the line, possibly the right-hand end of an acute accent, which would have been on the alpha. As this is the wrong accent for $\delta\alpha\mu\acute{\epsilon}\nu\tau\epsilon c$, it might conceivably point to a variant $\delta\acute{\alpha}\mu\eta c\alpha\nu$ 153 Perhaps $\kappa\rho\alpha]\tau\epsilon\rho o\nu$ was written for $\kappa\rho\nu\epsilon\rho o\hat{\nu}$ (P. Berol. 21107 and codd.); the trace after ϵ can be taken as ρ, but there hardly seems room for $o\nu$. I cannot explain the suprascript, which is in the same hand as the text. It might be read as ρ.   156 Π agrees with P. Berol. and all codd. in unaugmented $\kappa\acute{\alpha}\lambda\nu\psi\epsilon\nu$

3223. HESIOD, *Erga*, 172–215, 228–45

21 3B.29/C(11–12)a   13·0 × 22·5 cm.   Second century

Π_{43}. Upright, small, quickly made hand of the type in which hypomnemata are written (cf. VI **853**, XXXI **2536**, and PSI XII 1285). Probably a working copy, to be assigned to the early second century. Written on the back of a register containing

18 lines mentioning names, arouras, and small sums of money, in a regularly clerkly hand of the later first century.

Part of two columns; 2.5 cm. of the upper margin remains. The space between columns is about 4 cm., the column itself being about 9 cm. in width. The height of the first column was 56 verses, 25 cm., if no verses were missing, but in col. ii the writing is slightly bigger. The earlier part of *Erga* must have occupied the three preceding columns, but the number of verses present in this text cannot be calculated exactly.

Top of column

172	]τοις[	]δεα[..]ρπον		ε[..]ήν[
	]θαλλονταφ[	]ζειδωροσαρου[.]α[ ]		αργαλ[
	]τ'ωφελλον[	]πεμπτοισιμετειναι[ ]	230	ουδέπ[
175	]ληπροσθεθ[	]νηεπειταγενεςθαι		ουδάτ[
	].ο.εστιςιδ[	]ονουδέποτ'ημαρ		τοιςι.[
	]αματουκα[	]ζυοςουδετιννυκτωρ		άκρη[
	]οιχαλεπαςδε[	]εοιδωςουςιμεριμνας		.[.]ροπ[
	]καιτοιςιμεμιξ[]εταιεςθλακακο[ι]ςι		235	τικτου[
180	]εικαιτουτογεγοςμεροπωνανθρωπων[ ]			θαλλο[
	]ομενοιπολιοκρόταφοιτελεθωςιν			νείςο[
				δ'
	]ρπαιδεςςινομοιϊοςουδετιπαιδ..			όιςυβρ[
	].ςξε[]νοδοχωκαιεταιροςεταιρω			τοῖςδ[
	]νη[[ς]]τοςφιλοςεςςεταιωςτοπα[.]οςπερ		240	πολλάκ[
185	]αςκονταςατε[ι]μηςουςιτοκηας[ ]			ὄςτιςα[
	]αιδαρατουςχαλεποιςβαζοντε[..]επεςςι			τοιςιν[
	].δεθεωνοπινειδοτεςουδεμ..οιδε			καιλε[
	].ιτοκευςι[]αποθρεπτηριαδοιεν			ουδεγ[
	]ετεροςδετερουπολινεξαλαπαξει		245	ζηνο[
190	].ρκουχα[...]εςςεταιουδεδικα[..]υ		[	
	]μαλλονδεκακωνρεκτηρακαιυβριν			
	].ςουςιδικηδενχερςικαιαιδ[.]ς			
	]λαψειδοκακοςτοναρειοναφωτα			
	]κολιο[..]ενεπωνεπιδ'ορκονομειται			
195	]νθρωποιςινοϊζυροιςιναπαςι			
	]οςκακοχαρτ[.]ςομαρτηςειςτυγε[.]ωπης			
	]προςολυμ[ ].οχθονοςευ[..]οδειη[.]			
	]φαρε[]ςςικαλ[ ]ενωχροακαλ[.]ν			

E

```
        ]νμεταφυλον[              ]ρολιποντ[]ανθρωπους
200     ]νεμεϲιϲ·ταδ[             ]εταιαλγεαλυγρα
                                        ουκ
        ]νθρωπ[                   ]δεϲϲεταιαλκη
        ]ονβαϲ[                   ]ονεουϲικαιαυτοιϲ        νοεουσι
        ]προε[                    ]οικιλοδειρον
        ]ενεφ[                    ]χ[.]ϲϲιμεμαρπωϲ
205     ]ν[                       ]ηαμφ[]ονυ[..]ϲϲι
                                  ]μυθονεει[.]ϲ
                                  ]ολλοναρϲ[..]ν·
                                  ]ϲ[
                                  ]ϲω
210                               ]εριζειν
                                  ]χει
                                  ]νιϲ
                                  ].
                                  ]θλοϲ
215                               ]αυτηϲ
```

.   .   .

173 Π does not give the additional lines after 173 attested by Π₈ and Π₃₈ and in part by the scholia   174 Π agrees with Π₈ against ὤφειλον given by many of the manuscripts and the scholia   177 κ]αματοιο was at first written, as in Φ, but it was corrected before the next words were added, ιο being made into υκ   179 Π agrees with Π₈ and all manuscripts in the spelling μεμιξεται not μεμειξεται   183 -δοχω, banalization of the Ionic -δόκωι. Similarly cod. Riccard. 71   The scribe began to write ετερος, but corrected himself before completing the second ε   186 αρατους: Marcus Aurelius 11. 32 gives ἀρετήν. Π agrees with the direct tradition   βάζοντες ἔπεσι CΦ, Marcus: βάζοντες ἐπέεϲ(ϲ)ι or βάζοντ' ἐπέεϲϲι the majority of the other manuscripts   187 ο]ὐδε is superior to the οὔτε of the medieval tradition, and it has been printed by editors since Aldus   For οὐδὲ μὲν Brunck conjectured οὐδέ κεν. The critical letter in Π might have been κ, but it looks more like μ   At the end, the codd. have οἵ γε, but Et. Gen. (cod. A) s.v. γηράντεϲϲιν gives οἷδεϲ, which points to the reading given by Π   188 Apparently not τοκευϲι[ν]   190 ουδε: so CDΦ; a number of manuscripts have ουτε   198 There is not room for φαρε[ε]ϲϲι given by manuscripts and testimonia. φάρεϲϲι had been restored from the close imitation in Kaibel, *Epigr. Gr.* 1110. 2. The inscription has καλυψαμένα; Π agrees with the other sources   202 The marginal variant, νοέουϲι for φρονέουϲι, was known from ps.-Ammonius π. ὁμοίων καὶ διαφόρων λέξεων and related works, and P. Berol. 21107 has it in the text   203 προε[ειπε by mistake for προϲέειπε   204 Apparently ενεφ[εεϲϲι for εννεφεεϲϲι   207 Π agreed with most manuscripts in ἀρείων (ἀμείνων Ambr. G 32 sup.)   210–11, athetized by Aristarchus, are present, as in the three other papyri which cover the passage (Π₅Π₈Π₃₈)   215 Π₈ has αυτον, which is impossible   237 Or perhaps νείϲϲ[. Both spellings are found among medieval manuscripts (the second being commended by Moschopulus), besides νίϲ-, νίϲϲ-, νήϲ-   241 Π agrees with the manuscripts against ὅϲ κεν (Aeschines)   243 Manuscripts, Aeschines, and other quotations agree on λιμὸν ὁμοῦ καὶ λοιμόν (λ]ι[μον]ομου[Π₅). Π probably had και λε[ιμον και λοιμον, or unmetrically και λε[ιμον ομου και λοιμον   244–5, omitted by Aeschines and either omitted or condemned by Plutarch in his commentary (Proclus ad loc.), are present here, as also in Π₅Π₉Π₅₂

3224. Hesiod, *Erga*, 179–95

8   1B.199/F(2)a   Second century

Π_{44}. Upright, informal capitals, not unlike the mixed style, and probably to be assigned to the later second century. *υ* has a long tail curving to the left.

```
              ]εμπ.[.]κα[
180           ]υςδ.λεςεικα[
         ] — εν[..]υγειν...[
         ] >    ⁙ ουδεπατηρπα[
         ]         ουδεξειν[
         ] ⟩    ⁙ ουδεκα[
185      ] ⁙  — α[..]α[
         ]  ×  μ[          ].δ[
                          ]ε[
              ]ν[.]εςςιτ[
              ]οδικαι·ετε[
190           ]δετιςευορκου[
              ]γαθου,μαλ[
              ]ατιμηςου[
              ]ται·βλαψε[
              ]ςι'ςκολιο[
195           ]ςδα..[
```

The interest of these scraps lies almost entirely in the critical signs visible in the margin. They include the obelos, the diple, the asteriskos, of which the cross has the form of a χ, and perhaps a bare χ in 186, but it may have been a diple or another asteriskos. It is known that Aristophanes and Aristarchus used critical signs at least in the *Theogony*; and for the *Works and Days* critical signs in an ancient edition are implied by schol. 276 b τὸ ϲημεῖον ὅτι οὐδέποτε Ὅμηροϲ νόμον εἶπε (an Aristarchean observation) and 649 a ϲημειοῦται ὁ ϲτίχοϲ οὗτοϲ κτλ. The scholia on 181–6, however, contain nothing corresponding to the signs in the papyrus. Obeli also occur in certain papyri of the *Catalogue of Women* (**2075** fr. 1 = fr. 25. 26–33 M.–W.; **2478** fr. 1 ii = fr. 129. 47–50 M.–W.).

181 The obelos implies athetesis, unless it was preceded by an asteriskos as in 185. γειν- as Π_8 DψΦ: γιν- Ω (but ε superscr. C m¹). The manuscripts of Aristides, who quotes the line, are divided 182–5 The asteriskos, according to the *Anecdotum Romanum*, p. 3 Osann, was used by Aristarchus in his edition of Homer ὡϲ καλῶϲ εἰρημένων τῶν ἐπῶν ἐν αὐτῷ τῷ τόπῳ ἔνθα ἐϲτὶν ἀϲτερίϲκοϲ μόνοϲ. It is the correlative of the ἀϲτερίϲκοϲ μετὰ ὀβελοῦ, which signifies ὡϲ ὄντα μὲν τὰ ἔπη τοῦ ποιητοῦ, μὴ καλῶϲ δὲ κείμενα ἐν αὐτῷ τῷ τόπῳ ἀλλ' ἐν ἄλλῳ. (Cf. sch. Dion. Thr. p. 737. 15; sch. *Il.* 6. 490–3.) In other words, the signs were used where a line or passage occurred more than once and was judged to be more appropriate in one context than in another. ⁙— is found in this sense in P. Tebt. 4 (second century B.C.) at *Il.* 2. 141 and 164, and in PSI 8 (first century A.D.) at *Od.* 5. 110; ⁙ in P. Lit. Lond. 27 (first century A.D.) at *Il.* 23. 657, in III **445** (second/third century A.D.) at *Il.* 6. 490–2, and also in codd. Vat. gr. 30

(*s.* xiv) and Par. 1805 (*s.* xv) at *Il.* 5. 891. The Hesiodic lines, however, are not known to have occurred anywhere else. I presume that a diple preceding an asteriskos has its usual function of calling attention to something in the line worthy of remark, though I have not found other instances of the conjunction 185–6 are closer together than normal　　　186 The χ, a general-purpose symbol, is one of the commonest critical signs in papyri (cf. E. G. Turner, *Greek Papyri*, pp. 116 f.), though it seems not to be found in Homer papyri, and it is absent from the list in the *Anecdotum Romanum*. The papyrus is not well enough preserved here to rule out the possibility that this was a diple or another asteriskos

3225. HESIOD, *Erga*, 265–79

21 3B.27/C(1–2)c　　　　　　　　　　　　　　　　　　　　　　　　　　Second century

Π_{45}. Written in well-formed, medium-sized rounded formal capitals, bilinear, some letters having serifs. Probably to be assigned to the middle of the second century. The back is blank.

```
                    .           .
265          ]ατ[
             ]ουλη[
             ]δωνδιοσοφθαλμ[
             ]άδ᾽αικεθεληιεπ[.].ε[      .        .        .
               ]τηνδε[.]ικην.[        ]ϲεε[
270          ]γωμῆτ᾽αυτοϲεν[          ]ϲιδ.[
             ]τ᾽εμοϲυι.[.]επε.[        ]δίκα[
             ]ειμειζωγεδικ[            ]ωτερο[
             ]᾽υπωέολπατε[.]ε̇.[        ]ητιόε[
             ]ϲυδεταυτα·μ[.]τ[.]φ[     .        .        .
275          ]᾽κηϲεπακουεβ.[
             ]γαρανθρωποιϲ[.]ν[
             ]ιμενκα[.]θηρϲικαι[
             ]ναλληλ[
             ]..ϲιδ[
                    .           .
```

267–73 were condemned by Plutarch, but there is no evidence that they were ever omitted by a manuscript　　　268 εθελη ι as **1090** (Π_{10}), against (ἐ)θέλης᾽ of the codd.　　　270 μῆτ᾽: the accent is anomalous. A minute trace below the circumflex may represent an acute　　　271 The space between the two fragments calculated from the other lines suggests επει[κακοναρα] (ᾱρα instead of ἄνδρα) as in Π_{10}　　　273 After]ε prima facie ϛ, sc. εει written for metrical ει as in Archilochus, **2310** fr. 1 i 14, **2313** fr. 8(*a*) 14, (*b*) 3, **2319** fr. 4. 13; Anacreon, **2321** fr. 1. 4. But it might be a large serif at the foot of ι running into the corner of ν. Above, a dot (perhaps casual) followed by what may either be a circumflex (which would be anomalous with the spelling τελεειν; cf. δοκέει in Anacreon loc. cit.) or a suprascript correction (ϛ[?)　　　μ]ητιόε[ντα as Π_{10}, Proclus, CΦ, and some of the ψ manuscripts, against τερπικέραυνον (D, Tzetzes, *al.*)　　　278 εσθει]ν (Π_{10} to judge by the space, most quotations, and all codd.), not εσθεμε]ν (Clement)　　　279 ἀνθρώπ]οιϲι δ[᾽ ἔδωκε as codd. and most quotations, not ἀνθρώποιϲ δὲ δέδωκε as Porphyry on *Od.* 9. 106 ff.

3226. Hesiod, *Erga,* 311–16, 345 53, 414–19, 421–2, 432–6, 441–3

27 3B.39/E(1)a and 41/G(4–6)b   Fr. 2 3·0×6·3 cm.   Second/third century

Π_{46}. Five fragments in fair-sized upright flowing capitals; many verticals have a right-pointing tail at their foot. Only roughly bilinear, β above, ρ below line, deep μ. Same general type but not same hand as VIII **1090** (*Erga*), XVII **2090** (*Theogony*), and PSI 847 (New Comedy). Probably falls within the second century but could be second/third. There were 33 or 50 lines to the column. The back is blank.

Fr. 1

Top of column

$\qquad\qquad\qquad\overset{\nu}{}$
→   311   ]εργο⟦ϲ⟧δ[
        ]ειδεκε[
        ]πλουτε[
        ]δαιμον[
                 $\overset{\alpha}{}$
  315   ]εικεν⟦ε⟧⟦[
    …]εργον[

· · ·

Fr. 2

· · ·

345   γειτο[
      πῆμα[
      εμμο[
      ουδαν[
      ευμεν[
350   αυτωιτ[
      ωϲα῾ν᾿χρ[
      μηκακ[
      τ[.]νφιλ[

· · ·

Fr. 3

]π[.]ορθοιοτελη[421
]νμεμνημενο.[422

Top of column

]μένοϲοξέοϲ.[
415   ]᾿μουμετ᾿ọπ.[
            $\overset{\delta\epsilon}{}$
   ]᾿[ ]·ẹταδρέπετα[
   ]δηγαρτότεϲιρι[
   ]ηριτρεφε[
     ].᾿τενụ[

· · ·

Fr. 4

· · ·

].ηϲάμε[
]ειπολυλω[
      $\overset{\kappa\epsilon\ \iota}{}$
].υποβὸυϲιβ[
435   ]κịώτατοιϊϲτ[
    ]ν·βόεδ᾿ε[

· · ·

Fr. 5

· · ·

].[
441   ]νταετήϲα[
    ]ετρατρυφον[
   ]…[..].[.].[

· · ·

314–16 As codd. and four other papyri; Π_{19} had eight unidentifiable verses here   315 ϵ[π before correction: the same slip in Vat. gr. 38 (corr. m²)   316 ϵιϲ] as Π_5, codd., Et. Gen., not ϵϲ]   353–5 were condemned by Plutarch 421–2 are added in a different hand. They were presumably omitted lower down as a result of homoearchon, 420 and 422 both beginning with τῆμοϲ (but 420 ἧμοϲ Athous Iviron 209 a.c. and Tricl., πῆμοϲ Par. 2774)   415 Or perhaps ὅπ or ὅπ   416 μεταδρέπεται was apparently written instead of μεταδετρέπεται. Above the first alpha is a small delta, followed at a much lower level by what looks like an epsilon perched on the delta   417 ϲείριοϲ Π_{38}, codd.   434 The codd. have ἐπὶ βουϲὶ preceded by κ', γ', δ', or directly by ἕτερον. In Π, υπο is preceded by a trace of a vertical, so presumably ετερο]ν. The correction introduces two separate changes, suggesting collation with a different copy rather than simple rectification of a slip   435 α]κιώτατοι as codd., Proclus, Hesychius. Et. Magn. attests a variant ἀκιρώτατοι   436 γυη]ν as Ωb D ψ and grammatical citations, against γύηϲ of Tzetzes and Φ   441 Above the second tau, traces of a suprascript   443 The first trace is the top of a round letter

3227. Hesiod, *Erga*, 415, 421–35, 440–53

16 2B.47/D(d)   Fr. 1 9 × 10·5 cm.   Second/third century

Π_{47}. Two fragments of a roll written in a large-sized roughly made 'Biblical majuscule', reminiscent of but not the same as XXVIII 2486. Not so regular as XVII 2075 or XXII 2334. Bilinear, υ and ρ scarcely reaching below the line. There is a just perceptible contrast in thickness of stroke in some horizontals. Should probably be assigned to late second or early third century. On the back is part of two columns of a money account of the third century (↓).

The column had 34 lines. Its height was about 17 cm., its width much the same. 2·5 cm. of the upper margin is preserved, and 4 cm. of the lower; the height of the roll must have been about 25 cm.

Fr. 1

Top of column

→   415   ]οπωριονομβρησαντος ⌢

421   ]θδιότελησει

]ημενοςωριονε[.]γον ·

]ινυπερονδετριπηχυ .

]ρνυτοιαρμενονουτω ·

425   ]φυρανκεταμοιο .

]εκαδωρωαμαξη ·

]νδεγυηνοτανευρης

]οςηκαταρουραν [ ]

]χυρωτατοςεςτι [ ]

430   ]ματιπηξας

]ηρ[[ε]]ταϊςτοβοῇ̣ι̣ ᵃ

]ηςαμενοςκαταοικον [

]πολυλωιονουτω[ ]

].βουςιβαλοι̣ο[

435   ].[

•   •   •

Fr. 2   440   ]..ν ·[

]ζηοςεποιτο[ᵉ

]φονοκτάβλ.[

]κ'αυλακελα[

]ήλικας·αλλεπιε̣[

445   ]ροςαλλοςαμει[

]πορίην[...]α[

]ικαςεπτο[

]νηνεςακου[

]κλαγγυιης·[

450   ]ματοςωρ[

]δὰκ'α.[

]αςεν[

]αιαμα[

End of column

415 μετ]οπωριον by mistake for -ινον. Π agrees with Π₃₈, codd., Et. Sym. in the accusative; Et. Gen. has the genitive. The marks above and below the last letter of the line may represent a bracket (περιγραφή). Dr. Rea suggests that 415 was repeated by mistake after 420 because of the similar beginnings of 414 and 420 (see the note on the passage in **3226** above)   421 πτορ]θοῖο: the accent is

anomalous, but perhaps serves to distinguish the sense 'sprouting' from the usual sense 'a shoot'. Cf. ps.-Ammonius p. 12. 3 Nickau on ἄμητος and ἀμητός   422 ὥριον ἔργον as Π₃₈, sch. vet., Proclus' lemma, ΩDψ, Tzetzes, sch. Eur. *Andr.* 1164: ὥρια ἔργα Φ, editors   423 τρίπηχυ as D and Laur. 32. 16: -νν the rest. ὕπερον is elsewhere neuter   424 οὕτω as most codd.; a few give οὕτως 425 κε τάμοιο as Π₃₈ and most codd., against τετάμοιο EN   429 ὀχυρώτατος most codd.: -τερος Vat. gr. 44 and 121, Ambr. C 222 inf.   431 The correction is mistaken   441 I cannot account for the suprascript   443 κ': see above (p. 41) on Π₃₉   448 φω]νην as most codd.: -ῆς Vat. gr. 121, sch. Arat. 1012 cod. A   ἐσακ- Ωb, Vat. gr. 1825: ἐπακ- the rest with sch. Arat. 449 κεκληγυίης codd., sch. Arat. The form κέκλαγγα is used by Stesichorus and Attic writers 452 βό]ας as most codd.: βοῦς Vat. gr. 2383, Cantab. Trin. O. 9. 27

3228. HESIOD, *Erga*, 511–29

12 1B.137/L(a)   4·7 × 14·6 cm.   Second century

*Π*₄₈. Informally made, medium-sized upright round capitals, fairly tall. Probably early second century rather than first. The back is blank.

```
              .     .     .

511      ]μπ[..].[
                              ςϲ
         ]θηρεϲδεφρι[[ζ]]ου[
                  ιλ
         ]τωνκα[[ιλ]]άχνη‘δ[
         ]ψυχροϲεωνδιάη[
515      ]κάιτεδιαρεινου[
                      ι   ą
         ]κάιτεδιαγα’ιηϲιτ[
         ]οννεκεπὴἐτὰ.[
         ι]ϲανεμουβορεω[
         .[].
         ]καιδιαπαρθεν[
520      .]τεδομωνεντ[
         ]όυπωεργ’ειδυια[
         ]ἐυτελοεϲϲαμε[
         ]χριϲαμενημ[
         ].ματιχει.[
525      .]νταπυρω[
           ]οιηε[
           ]ικυα[
           ]φατα.[
           ]τεδὴ[
                ].[ interlinear

              .     .     .
```

513 The suprascript is in a different hand. The corrector supposed a mistake to have been made because he misread καιλ as καμ   516 Corrected by the first hand   518 βορεω confirms Rzach's correction of codd. βορέου   519 Above και perhaps κ[.].   521 εργ'ειδυια as codd. Some editors call for ἔργα ἰδυῖα   523 Apparently μ[υχίη as Proclus and some Φ manuscripts, not νυχίη   526 It cannot be determined from the space whether οἱ was preceded by οὐ γάρ (codd., Et. Gen.) or by οὐδέ (Hermann)   Above 530, interlinear ink; possibly λι relating to μυλιόωντες (μυλλιόωντες some manuscripts; μαλκιόωντες Crates)

3229. Hesiod, *Erga*, 670–4, 686–716, 743–56

28 4B.61/B(2–4)a and 62/B(1–2)a   Fr. 2 13·5×23 cm.   Second century

Π_{49}. Four fragments of a generously laid out manuscript. There were 18 verses to the column, which measures 14 cm.; 3·8 cm. of the upper margin is preserved, and 5·5 of the lower. The large formal round calligraphic letters (each 5–6 mm. high) are as large in size as in any papyrus manuscript. The type is that of the Hawara Homer, not of XVII 2075 (note the deep μ); but the scribe's work lacks the delicacy of the Hawara manuscript. Probably to be assigned to the middle or later second century. The back is blank except for a column of figures.

Fr. 1

.   .   .

670   ].[
            ]θοη[
            ]ν·φρ[
            ]ιϲτ[
            ]τε[

.   .   .

Fr. 2

Top of column

]ιλοις[

]αν[   ]υμαςι[

]αδεπαντ[   ]φρεϲιν[

689   ]ηυϲινπαντ[   ]κοιληι[

691   ]ποντουμε[   ]μαϲιπη[

]κ᾽επαμαξα[   ]ρβιοναχ[

].αιϲκαιφορτ[..]μαυρωθα[

]ϲεϲθαικαιροϲδεπιπαϲι[

695   ]να[ι]κατἐονποτι[..]κονα[

]οντωνετεωνμ[...]πολ[

]ϲμαλαπολλα·γαμ[....]το[

]ετορ᾽ηβῶοι·μ̄εμπ[....]εγ[

699   ]νδεγαμεινῶϲκ[....]κ[

701   ]αμφιϲιδωνμηγε[

]τιγ.ναικοϲανηρλ[

]τηϲδ᾽αυτεκακηϲο[

]ηϲἠτ᾽ανδ[..]κ[

705   ].[[ο]]διοκαιω[

End of column

Fr. 3

Top of column

]υλαγμ[

]ταιρον[

]ονε[

]εγ᾽α[

710   ]αϲ:[

]ϲεγ᾽α[

]αρα[

]ἐτ᾽α[

]ωει[

715   ]εϲ[

]κ[

.   .

Fr. 4   .   .   .

```
              ]αμνϛι[
              ]ντιθέμ[
745           ]γαρεπαυ[
              ]ν[.].επ[
              ].ηκρωξ[
              ]όδωναν[
              ]λοϵϲθαιεπϵ[
750           ]ητοιϲικαθι[
              ]καταιονοτα[
              ]καμηνονι.[
              ]ϵιωιλ[.]υτρ[
              ]ϛη.αρεπιχ[
755           ]νεπαι[
              ]λαθϛοϲ[
```

                          .   .   .

689 παντ[α: ἄπαντα codd., Π₃₉   690 omitted; see on Π₃₉ above (p. 43)   692 ἐπ᾿ ἄμαξαν: see on Π₃₉   693 καί is the better-attested reading (sch. lemma, CDΦ, al.); some manuscripts give τὰ δὲ   θα[: or perhaps θι[, θη[; anyway not θε[ιη   695 ποτι as Π₅, quotations, sch. lemma, and some ψ manuscripts: ἐπὶ CDΦ, al.   696 τριηκ]οντων as Π₅, quotations and most codd. Tzetzes 'corrected' to -κοντα, which influenced some copyists   698 ἡβώοι as Π₅, quotations (except Pollux 1. 58 v.l. and Et. Sym. s.v. τέτορε), and most manuscripts, against ἡβώη   The first π of πεμπ[τωι is corrected from μ; the correction consists simply of a horizontal line resting on the apexes   699 ὡς κ᾿ as Π₅, Stobaeus, codd. (except for one or two giving ὥϲτ᾿), against ἵνα (ps.-Aristotle *Oecon.* and Aristides)   700 is omitted, as in some other sources. See on Π₃₉   704 δειπνολοχ]ηϲ as Gregory of Nazianzus, Π₅, Proclus, sch. lemma, codd., Et. Gen./Magn., Eustathius: -χου Stobaeus, ps.-Zonaras   705 Only Stobaeus has δαλοῖο. Other sources all give δαλοῦ, whether followed by καὶ ἐν ὠμῷ γήραι θῆκεν (Plut. *Mor.* 527 a, Stob., Π₅ (καιενω[........]κεν)), καὶ ὠμῷ γήραι δῶκεν (Plut. *Mor.* 100 e, Et. Gen., ΩDψ, Tzetzes, Eustathius), or καὶ ὠμῷ γήραι θῆκεν (Φ)   709 ϲ]ε γ᾿ as Π₅, Proclus᾿ lemma, Et. Gen., CDψΦ, Tzetzes: ϲ᾿ ὅ γ᾿ Vat. gr. 57, al.: κεν Et. Gud., N², Moschopulus, Triclinius   711 ϲε γ᾿ again, here only with D: κεν the other codd. with Proclus᾿ lemma and Etymologica   713 αλλοτ]έ τ᾿ a[λλον as DΦ; the particle is absent in other codd. and Et. Gen.   747 κρωξ[η(ι): see above on Π₃₉

3230. HESIOD, *Erga*, 293–301, 763–4, 78 (or 789), 1–13

13 1B.125/F(c)   6·7 × 23·5 cm.   First century

Π₅₀. A tall strip of papyrus containing on the front excerpts from *Erga* in no obviously accountable order. The hand is a quickly written, upright, business one of medium size, in which letters are often linked to each other, and is probably to be assigned to the first part of the first century A.D. Cf. II **291** (P. Lond. 800), a document of A.D. 25/6, and P. Lond. 276B (Pal. Soc. II 182) of A.D. 15. XIX **2221**, a commentary on

Nicander, is of the same type. The back has been used (↓) for a private letter (l. 10] ̣αδελ-
φονεπιϲτολη [ ) also to be assigned to the early first century after Christ. A slight space
separates each excerpt from the last, except that *Op.* 763–4 are followed without interval
by a line from another passage.

Top of column

→	?	] ̣ο ̣ξ̣[
	293	]μενπα̣[
		]μενοϲ[
	295	]ϲδαυκαικειν[
		]κεμηταυτοϲνο ̣ε[
		]φιβαλληταιοδα̣[
		]γημετερηϲμ[
		]ευπερϲηδιονγε[
	300	]ηι ·φιλεηιδεϲε̣[
		]βιοτου ·δετεη[
	763	] ̣. ̣[ ]ι ̣[̣.] ̣αμπαναπ[
		] ̣μιξωϲιθε ̣. ̣ν ̣.[
	78 or 789	]αθαιμυλιου ̣ϲτελ[
	1	]πιεριηθεναοιδῆιϲικλειο ̣[
		]δίενεπετεϲφετερον[
		]αβροτοιανδρεϲομ[
		]ρητοιτεδιὸϲμεγ[
	5	]γαρβρ[̣.]αειρεαδεβ[
		]δαριζηλονμινυθε̣[
		]θυγ̣ειϲκολιονκαι[
		]βρεμετηϲο ̣ϲυπερ[
		]ωναϊωντεδικηιδ[
	10	]ωδεκεπερϲηετ[
		]ονεηνεριδω[
		]ενκενεπα̣[
		]η ·διαδαγ[

End of column

In the first line, the tip of a stroke rising to the right is closely followed by two curling up inwards
(I think an open-topped *o*), and these, again closely, by a stroke rising a little higher and looped over
to the left, resembling the top of the ξ in 764. But the letters οξ do not appear in the first half of the
verse anywhere in *Erga*　　　　294 is omitted by many quoting authors, but present in all manuscripts, including four other papyri　　　295 καικειν[οϲ: P. Berol. 21107, codd., and all quotations
give κἀκεῖνοϲ. Aristarchus commended καὶ κει- in such cases in Homer (sch. *Il.* 3. 402, *al.*), and Schaefer
conjectured it here　　　296 μήτ' αὐτὸϲ as Π₁₁Π₃₃ D, Laur. 32. 2, and quotations, against μήθ' αὐτῷ

of Proclus (?) and most codd.   764 The spacing indicates that λαοί not πολλοί stood before φημίξωσι, and therefore πολλοί not λαοί at the end of 763. Π thus agreed with Π₅, codd. and some quotations against Demosthenes, Aeschines, Aristotle, Favorinus, and Proclus   φημίξωσι is given by C, Et. Gen. A, the manuscripts of Aristides and Favorinus, and some of those of Demosthenes, Aeschines, and Proclus; other sources give -ξουσι or -ζουσι or -ζωσι   2 δί, i.e. Δί': some codd. and some quotations have δή   10 As iota is correctly written in long diphthongs elsewhere (300, 1, 9), the scribe may have understood Πέρση as vocative

3231. HESIOD, *Erga*, 225–45

57 171/B2   3·5 × 13 cm.   Second/third century

Π₅₂. A well-made upright capital of the mixed style of the later second century (or just possibly early third century) A.D. υ and τ both reach well below the line. The back is blank.

Upper margin	242	]·ηλαϲε·[
→	225	]δημοιϲιδιδουϲ[
		]αινωϲιδικαιων[
		]ανθευϲινε·[
		]··τροφοϲ·ουδεπ[
		]αιρεταˍˍυˍ[
	230	]ανδραϲιλ[
		]μηλοταεργαν[
		]πολυγβιˍˍ[·]·[
		]ανουϲ·μεϲ[
		]οῖϲκαταβεˍ[
	235	]οικοτατ[
		]μπερεϲ·ου[
		]ρειζειδω[
		]κηκαιϲχε[
		]εκμαιρετ[
	240	]ˍϲκακουαν[
	241	]αμηχαναˍ[
	243	]θιννθου[
		]·υθου[
	245	]μπ[

·   ·   ·

The verse in the upper margin appears to be 242 (omitted below) in the form in which it is quoted by Plut. *Mor.* 1040 c (from Chrysippus). ἐπήγαγε codd.   225 Π agrees with codd. in διδοῦσιν (διδῶντες Φ); Paley conjectured the subjunctive. See on the next line   226 -νωσι Π, Vat. gr. 904 (first hand) and 1825, Paley: -νουσι the rest   δικαιων is a new variant, for -ον of codd.   241 μηχανά[αται as Π₉, codd., and one of Aeschines' quotations: the other has μητιάαται   242 See above 244–5 are present; see on Π₄₃ above (p. 50)

3232. HESIOD, *Aspis*, 325–30

P.Oxy. A 8A/8 = C. 841   6·3 × 4·5 cm.   First century

Π_{51}. On the front (→) parts of four lines of an agricultural register in a regular round cursive of the first century A.D. On the back (↓) parts of 6 lines in a clear quickly made linear cursive also probably of the first century A.D.

$$\cdot\quad\cdot\quad\cdot$$

```
325    α[        ]ν[]δ[.].φ[]η[
       και[.]φεας θαρcυνου[
       χάιρετελυγκῆ.[
       νυν δη ζευc κρα[
       κύκνοντεξεναρ[
330    άλλο[....]ιτιέποcε[
```

$$\cdot\quad\cdot\quad\cdot$$

325 α[γχιμολο]ν, not -οc as J. The *ecthesis* marking a new paragraph is remarkable

3233. ISOCRATES, περὶ τῆc ἀντιδόcεωc 66–80

13 1B.132/A(1–2)a–b   Fr. B 6·8 × 19·9 cm.   First/second century

Four fragments from a handsome papyrus roll; the backs are blank. Fragments A, B, and C are from §§ 74–80 of Isocrates xv, περὶ τῆc ἀντιδόcεωc. Fragment D comes from Isocrates viii, περὶ τῆc εἰρήνηc, § 28. Either the roll originally contained several speeches, or we have part of two different rolls; or, more probably, fragment D belongs to the excerpt viii §§ 25–56 introduced at xv § 66, see below.

The scribe wrote a practised, upright, bilinear book-hand, similar to but less elegant than P. Lit. Lond. 132 (C. H. Roberts, *Greek Literary Hands*, pl. 13b). I should assign it to the late first or earlier second century. The only marks of punctuation are one elision (6) and one trema on iota (52; not written on hypsilon 16, 21, 24, 25). Iota adscript is omitted (10, 39), and there are two itacisms (48, 49). Some obvious errors have been corrected in the text (38, 49) or above the line (34, 39, cf. 13 n.), perhaps by the first hand; a correction of word-order (27) looks like a second hand.

In general, apart from errors of omission, **3233** coincides with the text of the Urbinas (Γ); note 12, where it supports a right reading of Γ^1 against all other manuscripts; and 41–2, where it ignores the unique reading of another papyrus, I 27 (Pack[2] 1281). But if fr. D is correctly placed in § 66, we may conclude that the scribe copied out the excerpt from Isocrates viii complete; and if so, **3233** shares the practice of the other manuscripts as against Γ, which gives only the opening and closing words (here as elsewhere, see Isocrates, ed. E. Drerup, 1906, pp. xciv f.). **3233** itself has two unique readings, one of them wrong (51), the other irrecoverable (15 n.).

Collated with the text of G. Mathieu (Budé, 1950).

Fr. D

. . . . .

επιθυμει]ν τ[ου cυμφεροντος   § 66 (= De Pace § 28)
και το]υ πλεο[ν εχειν των αλ-
λων ουκ] ειδενα[ι δε τας πρα-
ξεις τας ε]πι τ[αυτα

. . . . .

Fr. A

. . . . .

5   τερον ειρ]ημε[νων αλλως   § 74
τε και νυ]ν οτ᾽ου [μονον
μικροις] μερεςιν αλλ[ολοις ειδεςιν προ-
ειλομην] χρηςθαι προ[ς υμας
ταυτα] μεν ουν οπ[ως αν
10 υμιν cυ]μπιπτη π[οιηcομεν

. . . . .

Fr. B

. . . . .

χ[ρωμαι τοις λογοις δουναι   § 75
δ[ικην υμιν αλλ ει μη τοι-
ουτος οι[οις ουδεις αλλος της
μ[ε]γιcτης [τυχειν τιμωριας
15 ει τ[ιν]ες ου[ν υμων
υπελαβον [τοτε λιαν αλαζονι-
κον εινα[ι] και μ[εγα το ρηθεν
ουκ αν δικαιω[ς ετι την γνω-
μην ταυτην [εχοιεν οιμαι
20 γα[ρ] αποδεδω[κεναι την
υποςχεςιν κ[αι τοιουτους ειναι τους λογο[υς τους ανα-
γνωςθεντα[ς οιους περ εξ
αρχης υπεθε[μην] βου[λο-   § 76
25 μαι δ υμιν δια βρα[χ]εων [α-

πολογηϲαϲθα[ι] περι[ε]κ̣αϲ-
            β
του και ποιηϲαι ετι μαλ[λ]ο̣ν̣
καταφανεϲ ωϲ αλη[θ]η κ̣[α]ι̣ το̣-
τε προ̣ειπον και νυν λε̣[γ]ω̣

30   περι αυτων κ̣[αι] π̣[ρω]τον
μεν ποιοϲ γε̣νοιτ αν λ̣[ογοϲ
οϲιωτε[ροϲ η δικαι]οτε̣[ροϲ του
τουϲ π̣[ρογονουϲ εγ]κ̣[ω]μ̣[ια-
ζοντ[[α]]‘ο’[ϲ] αξιω[ϲ τηϲ α]ρ̣ετη[ϲ

35   τηϲ εκεινων [και των ερ-
γων των πεπ[ραγμενων αυτοιϲ
επειτα τιϲ αν π̣[ολιτικωτε-   § 77
ρο[[.]]ϲ και μαλλο[ν πρεπων
τη πολει ‘του’ τη[ν] ηγεμ̣[ονιαν α-

40   π̣ο̣φα̣[ι]νοντ̣[ο]ϲ [εκ] τ̣[ε των αλλων ευεργεϲιων [και των
κινδυνων ημετ̣[εραν ουϲαν

Fr. C

.   .   .   .   .

ϲυμφ̣]ερο̣ν̣[τ̣]ω̣ϲ [χρη δε τουϲ   § 79–80
νουν] εχον[τα]ϲ π̣[ερι αμ-

45   φοτερ]α̣ μεν ταυτ̣[α ϲπουδα-
ζειν α]υτοιν δε το[υτοιν το
με̣]ιζ̣[ο]ν και το πλ̣[ειονοϲ
α̣]ξιον προτειμαν [επειτα
κ[[ε]]‘α’κεινο [γ]εινωϲκε[ιν οτι

50   νομουϲ μεν θεινα̣ι [μυριοι
και των Ελληνων [και των
βαρβαρων ϊκ̣[ανοι γεγοναϲιν

].̣.[

.   .   .   .   .

Fr. A 7–8 The text restored in 7 is about 10 letters too long for the normal line-length. Since no shorter variant is likely, something must have been omitted.

    Fr. B Line-length : 18–24 letters.

12 δίκην υμιν: so *Γ*¹; δίκην ὑμῖν τὴν μεγίστην *Γ*²*Δ*mg.*Θ*; δίκην τὴν μεγίστην ὑμῖν *ΔE*. The space here is too short for τὴν μεγίστην.

13 τοι]ουτος: τοιούτοις codd., rightly. It is no longer possible to tell whether the omitted iota was added above the line, since the papyrus is torn away.

15 This line is unusually short (14 letters). It seems that the papyrus had something longer than the unanimous version of the manuscripts.

16 ὑπέλαβον με *Γ*²*Δ*²*E*, ὑπέλαβον cett. The line is long (23 letters) without με, though the argument from space is not rigorous enough to exclude the possibility that it was written.

[The Press reader, noting the reversal of μᾶλλον ἔτι in 27, offers the guess that the copyist also reversed the word order of ὑπέλαβον τότε, so that τότε fell in 15. If so, lines 15 and 16 would each have contained 18–19 letters and have fallen within the normal limits, see above. Note, however, that the person who corrected 27 did not indicate any change of word order above ὑπέλαβον.]

27 ἔτι μᾶλλον corrected to μᾶλλον ἔτι (so manuscripts). For *β α* (the second now lost in lacuna) used to reverse the word-order, cf. I **16** i 26, P. Amh. I 25. 25.

31 ποῖος: so *Γ*¹ cett.; ποῖός τις *Γ*² E.

32 ἢ δικαιότερος om. *Γ*¹, ins. *Γ*² mg.

33 εγ]κ[ω]μ[ια]ζοντος: so *Γ* cett.; -ζεσθαι E.

38 ρο[[.]]ς: the deleted letter may have been hypsilon.

41 f. και των] κινδυνων: so codd. και των αλλων κ. I **27**, which the space here does not allow.

Fr. C. 51 των ελληνων: τῶν ἄλλων Ἑλλήνων codd. Probably a simple slip; for the contrast οἱ ἄλλοι Ἕλληνες / ἡ πόλις (Athens), cf. e.g. viii §§ 14, 136, xv § 85.

52 ἴκ[ανοι: the first trace looks prima facie like the left-hand half of tau. I take it to be iota, joined at the top by the first half of a trema written as two dashes.

3234. THUCYDIDES I 73. 4–74. 3

37 3B.87/K(14)a   Fr. 1 6·3 × 9·6 cm.   First/second century
                  Fr. 2 1·1 × 3·9 cm.

Two fragments, the first from the beginning of a column with a top margin of 1·5 cm. The fragments are too small to determine if they come from a copy of a whole book or from a collection of speeches as in XIII **1621**. Approximately 28 lines are missing between them and no fibre matches have been found. This could be due to an intervening join of two sheets. It is also possible that fr. 2 belonged to the same column as fr. 1 (the column would have been at least 49 lines long) or that it was lower in its column than fr. 1 in its column (the column could then be no more than 30 lines). The back is blank.

The writing is a practised, plain, semi-documentary hand of a type found in both the late first and early second centuries. Although similar letter forms can be found earlier, e.g. XXVII **2471** of about A.D. 50, and later, e.g. P. Merton II 71 of A.D. 160–3, most letter forms and the style can best be compared with P. Lond. III 1177 of A.D. 113. Characteristic letters are the square β, ε with a high cross stroke which frequently closes the upper half and makes the letter extremely like θ, κ and τ broader and more flamboyant than the other letters, ϲ very frequently an almost closed curve and very similar to the larger form of ο. Punctuation is both by spaces (lines 3, 5, 10) and a combination of high stop and space (lines 6, 7). What difference there was between these two types, if any, is not clear.

In so far as one can judge the text in a section so small and free from divergences, it is, as expected, eclectic. Most of its differences from Hude's large edition (Leipzig, 1898–1902), with which a complete collation of the papyrus is given in the notes, are in the matter of ν-ἐφελκυστικόν, which the papyrus avoids and Hude favours. In the only two cases (lines 2 and 11) where it might be possible to speak of differing traditions, the papyrus presents the better reading, although in one case this is found in CEGMf and in the other in CG.

Fr. 1   →   οπ]ερ ϵϲχϵ μη κατα πολειϲ α[υ-
τον επιπλεοντα την πελοπ[ον-
νηϲον πορθειν αδυνατων [αν
οντων προϲ ναυϲ πολλαϲ αλλ[η-
5   λοιϲ επιβοηθϵιν τεκμηριον[
δϵ μεγιϲτον αυτοϲ εποιηϲε· ν[ι-
κηθειϲ γα[ρ τ]αιϲ ναυϲι· ωϲ ουκϵ[τι
αυτωι ομ[οι]αϲ ουϲηϲ τηϲ δυναμ[ε-
ωϲ κατα ταχ]οϲ τωι πλεονι το[υ
10   ϲτρατου ανεχ]ωρηϲε τοιουτου μ[εν-
τοι τουτου ξ]υμβαντοϲ και ϲαφ[ωϲ
δηλωθεντο]ϲ οτι εν ταιϲ ναυ[ϲι
των ελληνω]ν τα πραγ[ματα εγε-
νετο τρια τα ωφελιμ]ωτ[ατα εϲ

.   .   .
c. 28 lines lost

Fr. 2   .   .   .   .

].[.].[
τω το λ]οιπο[ν νεμεϲθαι επειδη ε-
45   δειϲα]τε υ[περ υμων και ου
χ ημων] το π[λεον εβοηθη-
ϲατε ο]τε γου[ν ημεν ετι ϲωοι ου
παρε]γενε[ϲθε ημειϲ δε απο τε
τηϲ ο]υκ ο[υϲηϲ
.   .   .   .

1 α[low horizontal trace   2 π[left upright and part of cross stroke   4 λ[small high and low traces   5 ν[very small high trace   6 δϵ traces of a low horizontal and oblique sloping down to right, then scattered traces   7 κηθϵιϲ low oblique sloping down to right (κ), cross stroke (η), traces of low curve, higher horizontal and scattered (θ), ϵ faint but visible under microscope   8 αυτωι right downward sloping oblique (α), traces of ντ, traces then curve of ω, then vertical (ι)   12 ναυ[traces of tops of letters   14]ωτ[traces of curve then long high horizontal   43].[.].[bottom of rounded letter, then, after a gap, a small trace of a foot   45 ν[high trace of curve   46 π[high horizontal   49]υκο[:]ν looks as if it may have been corrected

2 τὴν CEGM, τήν τε ABF, τε del. f.

2–3 πελοπ[ον]|νηϲον: so ABEFM, Πελοπόνηϲον CG; possibly only one ν or else ō in the papyrus.

3 [αν] omitted by C; spacing indicates that it was in the papyrus in this form or as ā.

6 ἐποίηϲε ABEFGc, ἐποίηϲεν CM Hude.

7 ναυϲι· ναυϲίν manuscripts. The high stop is very small, but even under a microscope no connection with ι is visible.

10 ἀνεχώρηϲε ACEFGM ἀνεχώρηϲεν B Hude.

11 τούτου ξυμβάντοϲ CG ξυμβάντοϲ τούτου ABEFMG₁.

43–9 How the restored lines in this fragment should be divided cannot be determined.

44 τὸ om. AB.

III. SUB-LITERARY TEXTS

3235-6. RHETORICAL DECLAMATIONS

Third century

The fragments collected under these numbers are of μελέται written in the *persona* of Demosthenes. (The technical term for the exercise would be Δημοσθένην ἀγωνίζεςθαι, cf. Philostratus, *Vitae Sophist.* 575.) Both **3235** and **3236** are written across the fibres in a severe style to be assigned probably to the third century; but two hands may be distinguished. **3235** is more widely spaced, not only between letters but between lines, and it displays a greater contrast between thick and thin strokes of the pen; and the columns are apparently shorter than those of **3236**. What is more, there are constant differences in some of the letter formations. Beta in **3235** lacks the horizontal bar at the base that it has in **3236**; xi has its top and bottom bars connected in **3235**, whereas in **3236** the centre is distinct; sigma and epsilon are invariably tall and narrow in **3235**, but often smaller and more rounded in **3236**, and in the case of epsilon the mid-stroke which is generally kept short in **3236** is regularly extended in **3235**; the stem of upsilon is a continuation of the right-hand side of the cup in **3235**, of the left-hand side in **3236**. Such differences take on special significance when they occur in such a standard type of script; and the inference that two manuscripts are represented is to some extent borne out by the writing on the front: in either case a register of amounts of land, but the fragments of **3236** have the declamation written the same way up as the document on the front, those of **3235** the other way up.

The alterations made in the texts, at any rate in **3236**, give the impression of textual revision rather than correction of scribal error, so that the pieces are probably autographs of contemporary compositions. As Demosthenic μελέται they are not particularly impressive, though the Attic is on the whole good and the writers knew their author well, at least the Philippic orations and the *De Corona*. They plagiarize somewhat clumsily.

Demosthenes figures quite large in the meletic repertoire as represented on papyrus, as is only to be expected: VI **858**, an attack on him which utilizes the *De Corona*; BKT 7. 4–13, a speech based on the *in Leptinem* and put into Leptines' mouth; XV **1799**, a vindication of Demosthenes' anti-Macedonian policy; cf. III **444**, which mentions Philip and the Macedonians, and II **216**, directed against Philip but in Asianic style. But these are the first certain papyrus examples of declamations actually in his person.

3235

28 4B.61/G(15)a

Fr. 1, 14·1 × 13·5 cm.
Fr. 2, 8·2 × 13·8 cm.
Fr. 3, 7·8 × 14·5 cm.

3235 is an Olynthiac, given a firm dramatic date of 349–348 B.C. by the historical situation set out in fr. 2. Though the speaker is not positively identified as Demosthenes, the political stance is clearly his, and that the speech is in his *persona* is not open to doubt. The *problemata* of μελέται are generally fictional but historically based: the argument of **3235** does not emerge.

Fr. 1

Col. i

↓

πανταεϲτιϙϋμετερα
τουτου[..]..ϙοψϙ]]‘ε[]χομεν′τουϲ
ορουϲτοδεϙυνϙυδετα
εντοϲπυλωνεαυτοιϲ
5   ]φυλαξαμ.ϙϋποβο
...]αιοϲδετιϲ.αινοθϙϲ
..].λ.ϙδεδουλϙϲε.⟩
]ειτϙ.λη..ϲειπειϙ
..]..ποιειτ..τϙϙϙη.ε
10   ].ϙωϙκτη..τϙϙ[[.]]
.αιουδεμεριζεταιαλ
]απαντ.ϙαπλωϲη
.αϲαποϲ.ερειϙβουλε
.αιειδε.ουτο[[υ]]ιϲαχθεϲ
15   ..]τοιϲλο..ιϲκαιμηδειϲ
..]τιϙϋμιϙϙτωνελλη
c. 6].[...]μενων

·   ·   ·   ·   ·

πάντα ἐϲτὶν ὑμέτερα,
τούτου[ϲ] ‘ἔχομεν’ τοὺϲ
ὅρουϲ· τὸ δὲ νῦν οὐδὲ τὰ
ἐντὸϲ Πυλῶν ἑαυτοῖϲ
5   ἐ]φυλάξαμεν, ὑποβο-
λιμ]αῖοϲ δέ τιϲ καὶ νόθοϲ,
μᾶ]λλον δὲ δοῦλοϲ, εἰ
δ]εῖ τὸ ἀληθὲϲ εἰπεῖν,
ἀν]τιποιεῖται τῶν ἡμε-
10   τ]έρων κτημάτων
καὶ οὐδὲ μερίζεται, ἀλ-
λὰ πάντων ἁπλῶϲ ἡ-
μᾶϲ ἀποϲτερεῖν βούλε-
ται. εἰ δὲ τούτοιϲ ἄχθεϲ-
15   θε] τοῖϲ λόγοιϲ καὶ μηδείϲ
ἐϲ]τιν ὑμῖν τῶν Ἑλλη-

Col. ii

```
.[c. 5]εγωτ.[
.....].εινπ[
....].ντευθ[
.....]αθην[
..φ[...]ππος[
οις.[..]cεκει[
ορκε.[.]υγγεν[
μεισειγαρτο[
γεν..πολεμ[
ε.cτηνελλα[
π.[..].[..]ρ[.]cκα[
εκειθενϋμ[
λεμων[[πολ[
χετα[
ανδρε[
ρικ[.]ππ[
τ.[
α[
```

.   .   .   .   .

Col. ii 5   .., κι suggested, perhaps νι

Fr. 2

Col. i	Col. ii	
]τω(ν)	cπ[.]νδουςποι...[	
]ν	ολυνθιους·ουτως	οὕτως
]ετ	ϋ.ωναμελουντῶ	ὑμῶν ἀμελούντω(ν)
	πὺδνααπωλετοου	Πύδνα ἀπώλετο, οὕ-
	τωςαμφιπ[.]λιςου	τως Ἀμφίπ[ο]λις, οὕ-
	τωποδ᾿τ᾿ιδαια[[ν]]ου	τω Πο᾿τ᾿ίδαια, οὕ-
	τωκινδυνευει.[	τω κινδυνεύει κ[αὶ
	νυνολυνθοςτα[	νῦν Ὄλυνθος· τὰ[ς
	γαρϋμετεραςα.[	γὰρ ὑμετέρας α.[
	.]..αςφιλιπποςπ[	.]..ας Φίλιππος π[
	..]μβανωναποα[	λα]μβάνων ἀπὸ Ἀ[μ-
	..]πολε....ρις[	φι]πόλεως ἄχρις [᾿Ο-
	.υνθουπροηλθε[	λύνθου προῆλθε[ν,

αλλακαινγγανα . . [ἀλλὰ καὶ νῦν ανα . . [

15   τε ⲉτο̣λυνθι̣ουϲφ . [τε ἐπ’ Ὀλυνθίους Φί-

λιπποϲαγα[.]ωτο̣ν̣[λιππος

πολε . ον . ⲉ . ο[

Col. i 1 τῶ   ii 9 . [, a high and a low trace (the latter thick), nearly joining; direction not clear, but suggesting an inward-curving upright   10] . ., the first trace high and thick, suggesting an upright joining another stroke of indeterminate direction; the second trace an upright or possibly the right-hand side of a curve   π[, or γ   14 . . [, surface rubbed: clear only, immediately after α, a low thick trace apparently slightly oblique   16 τ, or γ   γ[, or μ, λ, less good   17 . ., represented by two uprights ο̣, or ω   . (alterum), π, μ, ν

Fr. 3

Col. i	Col. ii
]αϲ και ⟩	κη[
] . [.]ϲ̣μερη	μ[
]ε̣ι και πο[.]	τε̣[
]ετε λα`μ′βα	εκ . [
5]παραχω ⟩	επι̣ . . . π[
]χηϲ Μακε	παντων̣[
]ε Φιλιππω	χειαειδ̣[
]αϲ αφιϲτα	μεϲηϲτ . [
]των Αθη	πολειϲει . . [
10]λυτ⟦ε⟧`αι′ϋμω(ν)	δημου̣ϲα̣ . [
] . Φιλιππος	μειϲω . . [
]γουμε ⟩	ρω̣γαπα[
]ανεται⟩	κτημα[
]ϋμετερου ·	ϲτι̣ν τα[.]θ[
15]τα̣ . αιτα	χ ϋμετερα[
]βουλεται ·	. . [.]λλαϲ ουχ[
]ϋμειϲ ο̣ι	. . .]ντατα̣[
] . α̣ειμε .	. .]ν̣κα̣[
]α̣ϲ̣[	.

In upper margin above col. i and intercolumnium, in informal hand:] . .ι̣κ[. .]`· Perhaps Δημο-cθ]ε̣ρικ[ός (sc. λόγος, or -κή, sc. μελέτη, or -κόν?); in which case this fragment will in fact be the beginning of the *declamatio*.

Col. i 1, 5, 12, 13: filler signs a zigzag shape   11] ., speck at line level   15 . ., ϲ poss.
17 ι̣, or ρ

	Fr. 4	Fr. 5	Fr. 6	Fr. 7
	. . . . .	. . . . .	. . . . .	. . . . .
	π.[	]..τ.[	]π[	]λυ[
	απ[	]τετ.[	].μ[	. . . . .
	πυδ[	]ϲιη[		
	.ιδ.[	]ϲυ[γ]γε[		
5	φιλτ[	]μη`[[δ]]´δ[		
	ανδρ[	]ιωνα.`.´[		
	κ̣ενη[	]βαϲπ[		
	μαχο[	].[		
	ευ[			
10	γαδ.[			
	πο̣ν̣θ[			
	⸗αλλα[			
	ϲι..[			
	μα̣[			
15	δ[			
	. . . . .			

Fr. 4　1　.[, low trace, perhaps υ　　　2　π[, or γ

Fr. i Col. i '. . . are all yours, these are the boundaries we have. But as it is, we failed to guard for ourselves even our territory this side of Thermopylae; some supposititious bastard, or slave rather, if the truth must be told, is laying claim to our possessions, and does not even go shares, but wants simply to rob us of everything. If these words annoy you and there is no one . . .'

1–3 Presumably 'Demosthenes' has been outlining the extent of the Athenian empire.

2 Perhaps ⟦ϲυνοψω⟧, but the papyrus is too mutilated to allow it to be confirmed. The tau of the following τουϲ is contiguous with the omega, so that its top stroke comes partly across it. Instead of ἔχομεν, ε[ἴ]χομεν (or ἔ[ϲ]χομεν) could be read, but ἐϲτιν favours the present tense. The change of person is unwelcome: perhaps emend to ἡμέτερα.

3 τὸ δὲ νῦν, used in preference to the regular νῦν δέ, displays acquaintance with adverbial τὸ νῦν.

3–5 Athens had in fact taken urgent action to prevent Philip passing through Thermopylae in 352 after his capture of Pagasae. Unless the composer is guilty of a bad anachronism, this phrase must be accounted to rhetorical licence. If the allusion is to Athenian failure to support the Phocians in their attempt to hold the pass in the summer of 346, it is a little late in the day to be warning of the danger to Olynthus (fr. 2). The crucial significance of the pass is clearly brought out at *De Cor.* 32, where Demosthenes affirms that Philip's purpose in restraining the false embassy from returning to Athens at once after the administration of the oath had been to prevent the Athenians sailing to Thermopylae and closing the pass, ἀλλ' ἅμ' ἀκούοιτε ταῦτ' ἀπαγγελλόντων ἡμῶν κἀκεῖνος (sc. Philip) ἐντὸς εἴη Πυλῶν καὶ μηδὲν ἔχοιθ' ὑμεῖς ποιῆσαι. (Cf. the opening sentence of Libanius' invective against Aeschines, or. XVII: Οὐκ ἦν, ὡς ἔοικεν, ἀρκοῦν Αἰσχίνη τούτῳ Πύλας ἀνοῖξαι Φιλίππῳ κτλ.) It may be that our author derived both the fundamental idea and the specific phrase ἐντὸς Πυλῶν from this passage.

4 ἑαυτοῖϲ for ἡμῖν αὐτοῖϲ could possibly be defended as Demosthenic, but the idiom belonged also to the κοινή.

5–8 Ineptly adapted from *Phil.* 3. 30–1: εἰ δέ γε δοῦλος ἢ ὑποβολιμαῖος τὰ μὴ προσήκοντ' ἀπώλλυε καὶ ἐλυμαίνετο, Ἡράκλεις ὅσῳ μᾶλλον δεινὸν καὶ ὀργῆς ἄξιον πάντες ἂν ἔφησαν εἶναι. Demosthenes' point is that Athenian losses are all the more intolerable as being suffered at the hands of a man who is not even a true-born Hellene (γνήσιος τῆς Ἑλλάδος), but our author seizes on the words δοῦλος and ὑποβολιμαῖος and transfers them into a context of literal fact.

10–11 What remains at the end of 10 is prima facie the mid-stroke of epsilon characteristically prolonged at the line end, with a trace of the extremity of its upper curve above. If so, there is a minimal trace before the epsilon which the limited amount of space requires to be iota, and thus ἵεται ('he rushes onward'?) all but enforces itself. However, this is scarcely tolerable Greek (and certainly not Demosthenic), and it seems preferable to regard the traces as an excised letter.

11 οὐδὲ μερίζεται: οὐδένι ἐρίζεται could equally well be read, but would be inferior in sense and language alike.

Col. ii 1 .[The traces are further to the left than would be expected for the first letter of the line. Unless the alignment was at a considerable slope, a marginal mark of some kind.

3 ἐντεῦθ[εν.
5 Φ[ίλι]ππος.
6–7 πολι]ορκεῖ or ἐπι]ορκεῖ, then [c]υγγεν[.
10 εἰς τὴν Ἑλλά[δα.
12–13 πο]λέμων.
14–15 Not necessarily ὦ ἄνδρες Ἀθηναῖοι.
16 Probably πε]ρικ[ό]πτ[-.

Fr. 2 Col. ii '. . bring the Olynthians into alliance(?). It was thus by your negligence that Pydna was lost, thus Amphipolis, thus Potidaea, thus even now stands Olynthus in danger. For Philip, anticipating your negligence on each occasion (?), has advanced from Amphipolis as far as Olynthus. Now at last rouse yourselves to action (?). Against the Olynthians Philip . . .'

This passage shows plainly that the declamation is an Olynthiac, with a dramatic date of 349–348 B.C. But the precise nature of the ὑπόθεσις remains unclear.

1–2 The Athenians are presumably being berated for failing to make alliance with Olynthus.

1 The Demosthenic compounds are ὑπο-, ἐκ-, and ἄσπονδος; perhaps ἐνσπόνδους here for all that. At the end probably either ποιεῖσθαι or ποιεῖν.

3 The Athenians' ἀμέλεια is a recurrent target for criticism throughout the Philippic orations. I note particularly *Ol.* 1. 10–11 (τὸ μὲν γὰρ πόλλ' ἀπολωλεκέναι κατὰ τὸν πόλεμον τῆς ἡμετέρας ἀμελείας ἄν τις θείη δικαίως), *Phil.* 1. 5 f. (φύσει δ' ὑπάρχει . . . τοῖς ἐθέλουσι πονεῖν καὶ κινδυνεύειν τὰ τῶν ἀμελούντων. καὶ γάρ τοι ταύτῃ χρησάμενος (sc. Philip) τῇ γνώμῃ πάντα κατέστραπται καὶ ἔχει—cf. *Phil.* 4. 47, 49), *Phil.* 1. 11 (οὐδὲ γὰρ οὗτος (sc. Philip) παρὰ τὴν αὑτοῦ ῥώμην τοσοῦτον ἐπηύξηται, ὅσον παρὰ τὴν ἡμετέραν ἀμέλειαν), *Phil.* 3. 5.

4–6 Perhaps the composer was unaware that Amphipolis was taken before Pydna. Demosthenes gives the towns in the order of their capture (*Ol.* 1. 12, cf. 8–9 and 5).

9–10 The word spanning these lines is presumably a noun governed by προ-, περι-, or προσλαμβάνειν: ἀμ[ελ]είας π[ρο|λα]μβάνων? Demosthenes does not use ἀμέλεια in the plural, but Plato and Aristotle do, and it is appropriate here: 'your negligence on each occasion'.

12 ἄχρις ['Ο]λύνθου. ἄχρις, it is generally agreed, is not Attic. That is not to say that the composer did not find ἄχρις in *his* Demosthenes.

14 ff. are difficult. The stops(?) in 15 and 17 are in a more watery ink, and should perhaps be ignored. Respecting the first stop, in 14–15 we could supply an imperative, e.g. ἀναςτ[ῆ]|τε, but then the subsequent asyndeton seems uncomfortable. Alternatively something like ἂν ἀργῆτε, 'if you do nothing', continuing 'Philip will attack the Olynthians', e.g. τὸν πόλεμον ἐπο[ίσει in 16–17 (this line of approach is due to Mr. Parsons); but then the opening ἀλλὰ καὶ νῦν seems inappropriate, and the whole thing very feeble. Remaining quite intractable is αγα[.]ω in 16, for which I have nothing plausible to suggest.

Fr. 3 Col. ii 14–15 οὐ]χ.
16 [ἄ]λλας or [Ἑ]λλάς.

Fr. 4 3, 4 Πύδ[να, Πο]|τίδα[ια: cf. 2 ii 4–6.

3236

29 4B.56/X(1–3)a

Fr. 1, 13 × 16·3 cm.
Fr. 2, 9·2 × 16·5 cm.

Two fragments, each with remains of two columns. The speech, patently in the person of Demosthenes, is directed against Aeschines. It looks a competent enough piece of work, though hardly distinguished. Fr. 1 combines an attack on Aeschines with an implicit exhortation to the Athenians to uphold their tradition of honour and self-sacrifice; reference to the exploits of Miltiades and Themistocles serves both ends. Fr. 2, in an apparent allusion to the 'wooden wall' Salamis oracle, seems to develop the metaphor of the fleet as a wall.

Fr. 1

Col. i

↓
```
 .ατρωονγαρε.τιν
τουτοαιςχινητωδε
δημωςωζειντηνελ
λαδακαιπολεωςπα
```
5
```
ςη.προκινδυνευειν
·τα·⟦δι⟧´αυτων⟦δα`ε´⟧εισφερον
τας`και´δαπα.ωμενους
εαν`δε´δεηκα[.]αυτ⟦ου⟧`η´ςα
φηρημενουςτηςπα
```
10
```
τριδοςουχιτωνεπιθρα
κηςχρ`κτ´ηματωναιςχι
νηαμφιπολεωςκαι
ειτιτοιουτονεςτιν
εντοιςθρακιοιςςειροις
```
15
```
καιβαραθρ.ιςωςελεγες
παλαιαλλατουπειρε
αιωςτηςακροπολεως
τηςελευςεινος·τουτ[.]
τοπατριον⌢τροπαιον⌢τωναθη
```
20
```
ν⟦αι⟧ων´τηςελλαδος`
εικοτωςεςτρατηγει
γαρουκαιςχινηςεχθες
```

πατρῷον γάρ ἐστιν
τοῦτο, Αἰσχίνη, τῷδε
⟨τῷ⟩ δήμῳ, σῴζειν τὴν Ἑλ-
λάδα καὶ πόλεως πά-
σης προκινδυνεύειν,
τὰ αὐτῶν εἰσφέρον-
τας καὶ δαπανωμένους,
ἐὰν {δὲ} δέῃ κα[ὶ] αὐτῆς ἀ-
φῃρημένους τῆς πα-
τρίδος, οὐχὶ τῶν ἐπὶ Θρά-
κης κτημάτων, Αἰσχί-
νη, Ἀμφιπόλεως καὶ
εἴ τι τοιοῦτόν ἐστιν
ἐν τοῖς Θρᾳκίοις ςιροῖς
καὶ βαράθροις, ὡς ἔλεγες
πάλαι, ἀλλὰ τοῦ Πειραι-
έως, τῆς ἀκροπόλεως,
τῆς Ἐλευςεῖνος. τοῦτ[ο]
τὸ πάτριον τῶν Ἀθη-
νῶν,
εἰκότως· ἐστρατήγει
γὰρ οὐκ Αἰσχίνης, ἐχθὲς

Col. ii

κα.π[..]ωηναποτ[	καὶ π[ρ]ώην ἀπὸ τ[
λουμεταβαϲεπι[	λου μεταβὰϲ ἐπὶ [τὸ
βημακαιμηδε[	βῆμα καὶ
ρημαδυναμ[	
5 τααθηναιων[	
ματ[.]ουδεδ..[	
αποτηϲιλια.[	
πηδηϲαϲτ[	
ϲιαϲαλλαμ[	ϲίαιϲ, ἀλλὰ Μ[ιλτιάδηϲ,
10 αλλαθεμιϲτ[	ἀλλὰ Θεμιϲτ[οκλῆϲ·
ομοιοιγεουγαρ[	ὅμοιοί γε, οὐ γάρ, [Αἰϲχί-
νηδημαγωγοιμ[	νη; δημαγωγοί. Μ[ιλ-
τιαδηϲ[.]ενουδετ[	τιάδηϲ [μ]ὲν οὐδὲ τ[οὺϲ
ϲυμμαχουϲαν[	ϲυμμάχουϲ ἀν[α-
15 μενωνμονουϲ[	μένων μόνουϲ [τοὺϲ
αθηναιουϲαντετ[	Ἀθηναίουϲ ἀντέτ[ατ-
τεπροϲπαϲαντη[	τε πρὸϲ πᾶϲαν τὴ[ν
ϲτρατ[[ε]]ιαντηνβ[	ϲτρατιὰν τὴν β[α-
ϲιλικηνϲυδετα[	ϲιλικήν, ϲὺ δὲ τὰ[ϲ οὐ-
20 δεμαχαϲεκλειπ[	δὲ μάχαϲ ἐκλείπ[ειν
αξιοιϲταϲτωνϲυ[	ἀξιοῖϲ τὰϲ τῶν ϲυ[μ-
μαχωνθεμιϲτοκ[	μάχων. Θεμιϲτοκ[λῆϲ
μεναυταϲϋπερτη[	μὲν αὖ τὰϲ ὑπὲρ τῆ[ϲ

6 ..[, minimal traces   7 .[, low trace, apparently oblique

Fr. 2

Col. i		Col. ii	

<table>
<tr><td></td><td></td><td>τριηρεις.χη[</td><td>τριήρεις ἔχη[τ</td></tr>
<tr><td>.   .   .   .   .</td><td></td><td>αλλοητειχος[</td><td>ἄλλο ἢ τεῖχος [</td></tr>
<tr><td>]των[</td><td></td><td>κτητονκαι[</td><td>κτητον καὶ [</td></tr>
<tr><td>].ντα</td><td></td><td>ϲαιδυναμεν[</td><td>ϲαι δυναμεν[</td></tr>
<tr><td>]θαλατ[</td><td>5</td><td>ταυτασενεβα[</td><td>ταύτας ἐνέβα[ινον</td></tr>
<tr><td>]να</td><td></td><td>ϋμωνοιπρογ[</td><td>ὑμῶν οἱ πρόγ[ονοι</td></tr>
<tr><td>5   ]ημεις</td><td></td><td>τατουϲκινδυ[</td><td></td></tr>
<tr><td>]τρο</td><td></td><td>..ϲαθηναιων[</td><td></td></tr>
<tr><td>].με</td><td></td><td>.τεραϲπολεις[</td><td></td></tr>
<tr><td>]ααμει</td><td>10</td><td>τειχοϲυμεινα[</td><td>τεῖχος ὑμεῖν α[</td></tr>
<tr><td>]μιτο</td><td></td><td>λεϲτεροναπολ[</td><td>λέϲτερον Ἀπολ[λ-</td></tr>
<tr><td>10   ]καιπαν</td><td></td><td>πυθιεμαρτυρ[</td><td>Πύθιε, μαρτύρ[</td></tr>
<tr><td>].εκων‘[[..]]’</td><td></td><td>ουτοϲοτειχιϲμ[</td><td>οὗτος ὁ τειχιϲμ[ὸϲ</td></tr>
<tr><td>].ϲαϲ</td><td></td><td>τουπυθιουκαια[</td><td>τοῦ Πυθίου καὶ ἀ[νά-</td></tr>
<tr><td>]ενθα</td><td>15</td><td>λωτοϲεϲτινκα[</td><td>λωτός ἐϲτιν κα[</td></tr>
<tr><td>]προ</td><td></td><td>τωθαρρουϲινϋ[</td><td>τω θαρροῦϲιν υ[</td></tr>
<tr><td>15   ]υποα</td><td></td><td>εξεϲτικαταφ[</td><td>ἔξεϲτι καταφ[</td></tr>
<tr><td>].εδε</td><td></td><td>.αι[[ϋ]]ποτετουδ[</td><td></td></tr>
<tr><td>]γονοι</td><td></td><td>ταγηνεπιμελ[</td><td></td></tr>
<tr><td>]οιχει</td><td>20</td><td>καιπροϲεπιϲκ[</td><td></td></tr>
<tr><td>].[..].[.].τ.</td><td></td><td>ζετεαναλαμ[</td><td></td></tr>
<tr><td>20   ].[..]εκαι</td><td></td><td>νετε‘τα...επινουν’[[ταειπονο[</td><td></td></tr>
<tr><td></td><td></td><td>..ειδεμηκατ[</td><td></td></tr>
</table>

Col. ii 8 .., 9 ., scattered traces on misplaced fibres; perhaps only one letter before ϲ in 8   9 .[, speck at letter-top level   18 ., high horizontal: τ, ξ, ϲ, possible, not ν   τ, corrected from (rather than to) ο or ρ?

Fr. 1 'For it is a tradition of this people, Aeschines, to keep Greece safe and to bear the brunt of danger for every city, by contributing and spending out of their own pockets, even, should it be necessary, if deprived of their country itself—not of their possessions in Thrace, Aeschines, Amphipolis and whatever of that sort lies in the Thracian barns and pits, as you used to say, but of the Piraeus, of the acropolis, of Eleusis. This is the tradition of Athens—and rightly so: for the commander of the forces was not Aeschines, who only yesterday or the day before came up on to the speaker's platform from the tholos(?) . . . : no, he was Miltiades, he was Themistocles—leaders on a par with you, Aeschines, were they not? Miltiades, without even waiting for the allies, proceeded to draw up the Athenians unsupported against the entire Persian army; while you think fit to desert our allies' battles when they are not even battles(?). Themistocles . . .'

Col. i 2 τῷδε ⟨τῷ⟩. The slip is surprising in view of the familiarity with Attic otherwise shown.

5 προκινδυνεύειν: the word of the Marathon oath, *de Cor.* 208. Ptolemy of Naucratis was given the nickname 'Marathon' ἐπειδὴ ἐν ταῖς Ἀττικαῖς τῶν ὑποθέσεων τῶν Μαραθῶνι προκινδυνευσάντων θαμὰ ἐμνημόνευεν (Philostratus, *Vit. Soph.* 595).

6 ·τα· '⟦δι⟧'. Apparently two stages of correction. First δι was substituted for τα, the latter being cancelled by a dot on either side; then δι was crossed through, thereby conferring a *stet* on τα.

8 {δέ}. Though δέ represents the emended version, I do not see that it can stand without the further (unmade) alteration of ἀφηρημένους to ἀφαιρουμένους.

10–18 Clearly dependent on *De Chers.* 44–5 (almost = *Phil.* 4. 15–16), which runs: οὐ γὰρ οὕτω γ᾽ εὐήθης οὐδείς ὃς ὑπολαμβάνει τὸν Φίλιππον τῶν μὲν ἐν Θρᾴκῃ κακῶν (τί γὰρ ἂν ἄλλο τις εἴποι Δρογγίλον καὶ Καβύλην καὶ Μάςτειραν καὶ ἃ νῦν ἐξαιρεῖ [καὶ κατασκευάζεται];) τούτων μὲν ἐπιθυμεῖν καὶ ὑπὲρ τοῦ ταῦτα λαβεῖν καὶ πόνους καὶ χειμῶνας καὶ τοὺς ἐσχάτους κινδύνους ὑπομένειν, τῶν δ᾽ Ἀθηναίων λιμένων καὶ νεωρίων καὶ τριήρων καὶ τῶν ἔργων τῶν ἀργυρείων καὶ τοσούτων προσόδων οὐκ ἐπιθυμεῖν, ἀλλὰ ταῦτα μὲν ὑμᾶς ἐάσειν ἔχειν, ὑπὲρ δὲ τῶν μελινῶν καὶ τῶν ὀλυρῶν τῶν ἐν τοῖς Θρᾳκίοις cιροῖς ἐν τῷ βαράθρῳ χειμάζειν. ὡς ἔλεγες is apparently a fiction of the composer.

16–17 Πειρεαιως: either a misspelling of Πειραιέως or an unsuccessful shot at the Attic form (Πειραιῶς).

19–20 The oblique strokes marking off τρόπαιον and τῆς Ἑλλάδος may possibly be intended to indicate not deletion but an alternative version (τρόπαιον for πάτριον, τῆς Ἑλλάδος for τῶν Ἀθηνῶν).

21 εἰκότως: evidently taught as a characteristically Demosthenic idiom; cf. ὅμοιοί γε, οὐ γάρ ii. 11.

21 f. ἐστρατήγει γὰρ οὐκ Αἰσχίνης. The switch to the third person, and the reversion to direct address at ii 11, may be deliberately affected. Theon of Alexandria recommends such variation as being ἐπιτερπέστερον (74 f. Spengel ii).

22–Col. ii 3 The jibe, along with some of the phraseology, is apparently taken from *De Cor.* 130: ... ὀψὲ γάρ ποτε—ὀψὲ λέγω; χθὲς (contemporary texts may have had εχθες) μὲν οὖν καὶ πρώην ἅμ᾽ Ἀθηναῖος καὶ ῥήτωρ γέγονε. (This extract is quoted at a later date by the rhetorician Tiberius, π. Δημοσθένους cχημάτων § 9, as an example of ἐπιδιόρθωσις—the self-correction ὀψὲ λέγω; etc.—but our author does not avail himself of this figure.) ἀπὸ τ[±4]λου presents many possibilities, of which I mention only τῆς πηλοῦ, τοῦ ὄχλου, and τῆς θόλου. If the last, the disparaging point will be in clumsy modification of two passages of a similar quasi-biographical nature in the *De Fals. Leg.*, each directed against Aeschines: 314 ... ὁ τέως προσκυνῶν τὴν θόλον, 249 ... καὶ τὸ τελευταῖον ὑφ᾽ ὑμῶν γραμματεὺς χειροτονηθέντες δύ᾽ ἔτη διετράφησαν ἐν τῇ θόλῳ, πρεσβεύων δ᾽ ἀπέσταλτο νῦν οὗτος ἐκ ταύτης.

3–9 I cannot give a plausible restoration of these lines. The nearest I can get to a coherent sense is μηδὲ [ἐν εἰπεῖν]|ρῆμα δυνάμ[ενος πρὸς]| τὰ Ἀθηναίων [πράγ]|ματ[α] οὐ δεδεχ[μένον] ἀπὸ τῆς Ἰλιάδος, 'unable to utter a single word on Athenian affairs not taken from the Iliad'. This is open to objection not only on account of its bad Greek, especially in the matter of negatives, but also because it makes lines 3 and 4 too long. ἀπὸ τῆς Ἰλιάδος, however, is hard to avoid: the reference seems to be a dig at Aeschines' quotations in his speech against Timarchus.

8–9 πηδήσας calls to mind ἀνεπήδησεν ἐπὶ τὸ βῆμα at *In Ctes.* 173, where Aeschines reviews Demosthenes' life in much the same way as Demosthenes in turn reviews his at *De Cor.* 129–31. Rea suggests ἐπι]|πηδήσας τ[αῖς ἐκκλη]|cίαις.

9–10 ἀλλὰ Μ[ιλτιάδης,] ἀλλὰ Θεμιστ[οκλῆς I take as picking up ἐστρατήγει γὰρ οὐκ Αἰσχίνης at i 21 f., but ἄλλα ... ἄλλα is also a possibility.

11–12 ὅμοιοί γε, οὐ γάρ, Αἰσχίνη; δημαγωγοί: a Demosthenic idiom: *In Tim.* 106 ὅμοιός γ᾽ οὐ γάρ; ὦ ἄνδρες Ἀθηναῖοι, Cόλων νομοθέτης καὶ Τιμοκράτης, ibid. 181 (= *In Androt.* 73) ὅμοιόν γε, οὐ γάρ; τοῦτο τοῖς προτέροις ἐπιγράμμασιν, *De Cor.* 136, cf. 318. I take it that coί is to be 'understood' and that δημαγωγοί has a neutral not a 'bad' connotation, but it may be that the composer did not properly understand the use of the idiom and intended δημαγωγοί to imply a distinction between Aeschines as a rabble-rouser and such statesmen as Miltiades and Themistocles.

12 ff. Marathon and Salamis held pride of place in the tradition of Athens as the saviour of Greece, and were no doubt a stock theme in Attic declamations. The appeal to Athens' glorious past is couched in these terms in the third century B.C. μελέτη P. Hib. I 15. 106: ὡς ἀνάξιόν ἐστιν, ὦ ἄνδρες Ἀθηναῖοι, τῶν ἐμ Μαραθῶνι καὶ Cαλαμῖνι κινδύνων διατελεῖν ὑμᾶς τὸ cύνολον ἀπογιγνώσκοντας τὴν ἡγεμονίαν κτλ. How much of a commonplace this sort of thing became may be judged by Ptolemy of Naucratis' nickname Marathon.

Direct comparison is too common a technique of disparagement to be significant in itself, but a particular influence here may well be the comparison that Aeschines draws between Demosthenes and statesmen of past days at *In Ctes.* 181 ff. Common points of detail are that the question at issue is their generalship, and that the list of past statesmen is headed by Themistocles and Miltiades (but in that order in Aeschines): πότερον ὑμῖν ἀμείνων ἀνὴρ δοκεῖ Θεμιστοκλῆς ὁ στρατηγήσας ὅτ' ἐν τῇ περὶ Cαλαμῖνα ναυμαχίᾳ τὸν Πέρcην ἐνικᾶτε, ἢ Δημοcθένης, ὁ νυνὶ τὴν τάξιν λιπών; Μιλτιάδης δέ, ὁ τὴν ἐν Μαραθῶνι μάχην νικήcας, ἢ οὗτος; Our author seems to have taken the opportunity of turning the comparison back on Aeschines himself—an opportunity that the Ur-Demosthenes rejected (*De Cor.* 314 ff.).

14 ἀν[α leaves the line somewhat short but is hardly to be doubted. A filler sign may have been used.

18 βαcιλικήν is no doubt another conscious Atticism. Demosthenes habitually refers to the king of Persia as βαcιλεύc, and uses the adjective at *Pro Lib. Rhod.* 5.

19–20 The restoration τὰ[c οὐ]|δὲ μάχαc avoids a repetition of the slip at i 2 (i.e. τά[c]|δε ⟨τὰc⟩ μάχαc). Though it gives a greater rhetorical point than would τὰ[c τῇ]δε μάχαc, it is linguistically very bold.

24 Continue on the lines of: Θεμιστοκλῆc μὲν αὖ τὰc ὑπὲρ τῆ[c ἁπάντων τῶν ῾Ελλήνων ἐλευθερίαc cυνειλεγμέναc τριήρειc . . ., cὺ δὲ . . .

Fr. 2 The ultimate source of this fragment appears to be the famous Salamis oracle, the second of the Delphic oracles given to the Athenian envoys when Attica was threatened by Xerxes: Hdt. 7. 141. Whatever disputes as to its meaning there were at the time, the interpretation that established itself was that the wooden wall stood for the ships. In rhetorical literature, the line τεῖχος Τριτογενεῖ ξύλινον δίδοι εὐρύοπα Ζεύc is cited by Theon as an example of a trope (*Progymn.* 81 Sp. ii), and Philostratus quotes it in the introduction to the *Vitae Sophistarum* (481). Libanius alludes to the oracle in connection with the victory at Salamis: *or.* XV 40 τὴν δὲ (sc. ναυμαχίαν) ᾗ προσόμοιον οὐδέν, δι' ἣν ἡ Cαλαμὶc ὑπὸ τοῦ Πυθίου θεοῦ θεία προσείρητο, cf. XV 37 ναυμαχίαι μετὰ χρησμῶν κατορθούμεναι. The oracle, and especially the τεῖχοc ξύλινον, held an important place in βίοι of Themistocles: cf. Plut. *Them.* 10, Corn. Nep. *Them.* 2. 6–8, Polyaen. *Strat.* I 30. 2. Unless this passage is to be interpreted simply by reference to the naval reforms successfully carried through by Demosthenes, the allusion here may be taken as implying that a similar course of action to that enjoined by the oracle is being recommended, i.e. that the hypothesis consists of a motion that the Athenians abandon the city and resort to the fleet. Cf. Philost. *Vit. Soph.* 543, on a declamation by Polemo: (Δημοσθένης) ξυμβουλεύων ἐπὶ τῶν τριήρων φεύγειν ἐπιόντος μὲν Φιλίππου, νόμον δὲ Αἰcχίνου κεκυρωκότος ἀποθνήcκειν τὸν πολέμου μνημονεύcαντα. (For a *problema* under the original circumstances cf. Apsines 332 Sp. i: ὁ Θεμιστοκλῆc πείcαc ἐκλείπειν τὴν πόλιν γράφει αὐτοὺc καὶ ἐμπρῆcαι τὸ ἄcτυ, cf. also Syrian. II 203 SR (non-fictitious), which quotes the τεῖχοc line.) If this is so, the occasion envisaged will be one when the city was in imminent danger from Philip: the spring of 338 is evidently suitable. (The fictional basis, if not the death-penalty liability of Polemo's theme, could be that after Philip's capture of Elatea Thebes had rejected Athens' overtures and accepted alliance with Philip.)

Col. i 17 πρό]γονοι.

Col. ii 1–6 e.g. τριήρειc ἔχη[τ' οὐδὲν] ἄλλο ἢ τεῖχόc [τι οὐχὶ] κτητὸν καὶ [ὑμᾶc cῷ]cαι δυνάμεν[ον· εἰc γὰρ] ταύταc ἐνέβα[ινον] ὑμῶν οἱ πρόγ[ονοι . . ., 'that in the triremes what you have is a wall, uncapturable(?) and able to save you, for it was these triremes that your forefathers used to board . . .'.

1 Or ἔχη[τε τί. The tradition behind the metaphor makes it less Isocratean than it would otherwise have been.

2–3 οὐχὶ] κτητόν, 'not gettable', i.e. 'uncapturable'? Not Demosthenic; nor are the alternatives ἄ]κτητον, δύc]κτητον.

5–6 Cf. *De Cor.* 204, εἰc τὰc τριήρειc ἐμβάντεc.

6–9 I cannot restore. In 8 Dr. Rea suggests, instead of the obvious Ἀθηναίων, Ἀθῆναι ὤν[ηcαν: ἑτέραc πόλειc may follow in 9, but a coherent sense remains difficult to achieve. με]τὰ τοὺc κινδύ[νουc εὐ]θὺc Ἀθῆναι ὤν[ηcαν] ἑτέραc πόλειc is surely not tolerable, either in itself or in the context.

9–11 e.g. τ[ί γὰρ] τεῖχος ὑμεῖν ἀ[cφα]λέcτερον Ἀπόλ[λωνοc; 'For what safer wall have you' (or, with ἀ[ν ἀcφα]λέcτερον, 'could you have') 'than Apollo?', i.e. than Apollo's, the wall mentioned by the oracle.

I suppose this is preferable to punctuating after ἀϲφαλέϲτερον and continuing Ἄπολ[λον] Πύθιε, which would invert the normal order of Πύθιοϲ Ἀπόλλων.

11–12 ὦ] Πύθιε, μαρτύρ[ει μοι, or μαρτύρ[ομαί ϲε. For the apostrophe of Apollo cf. E. G. Turner, *Eos* xlviii (1956), fasc. 2 (*Symbolae R. Taubenschlag dedicatae II*), 143–6, on P. Hamb. 132.

13–14 οὗτος ὁ τειχιϲμ[ὸϲ ὁ] τοῦ Πυθίου καὶ ἀ[νά]λωτόϲ ἐϲτιν, 'this the Pythian's wall is actually uncapturable', rather than τειχιϲμ[ὸϲ] τοῦ Πυθίου, 'this wall is the Pythian's and uncapturable'?

15 ff. e.g. κα[ὶ οὕ]τω θαρροῦϲιν ὑ[μεῖν] ἔξεϲτι . . . Then neither καταφ[ραγῆ]ναι nor καταφ[ράϲϲεϲ]θαι suits the traces at the beginning of 18, but an object would be expected with an active verb such as καταφ[ρονῆ]ϲαι ('your enemies') or καταφ[υλά]ξαι ('yourselves').

What follows is also difficult. The starting point for restoration seems to be 19–21, presumably ἐπιμελ[εῖϲθε] καὶ προϲεπιϲκ[ευά]ζετε. ἐπιϲκευάζειν is especially used of refitting ships; the προϲ- compound is rare and late. What precedes? τῶν κα]τὰ γῆν suggests itself (despite its inappropriateness to προϲεπιϲκευάζετε), but 18 remains a puzzle. In 18, two letters have been tampered with. υ was simply crossed out. τ was altered and has a double dot above it: perhaps an attempt was first made to convert it to ο, then the unsatisfactory result cancelled by the dots and a new start made. This will give us ποτε ουδ[. Perhaps take ποτε with what precedes, and go on with something like οὐδ[ὲν τῶν κα]τὰ γῆν ἐπιμελ[εῖϲθε] καὶ προϲεπιϲκ[ευά]ζετε, though we should want this to be imperative, despite οὐδέν not μηδέν: 'take no thought for affairs on land and refit (the ships) anew.' Some of the declamations of ps.-Libanius are very lax in the matter of negatives (and cf. on Fr. 1 Col. ii 3–9). But I cannot claim to be happy about this.

21–2 Perhaps ἀναλαμ[βά]νετε ταῦτα ἐπὶ νοῦν, 'recall these things to mind', is the amended version.

23 Probably a warning, εἰ δὲ μή.

3237. GLOSSARY TO HOMER, *Iliad* i. 302–23

27 3B.44/K(1–2)a   Fr. 1, 9×25·5 cm.   Early third century

One column, a few traces of a previous column, and one unplaced scrap remain of this third-century word list. The reverse is mostly blank with traces of ink in one corner. The hand is a medium-sized sloping style with the angular letter forms characteristic of the third century (cf. Roberts, *GLH* 19a–19c). The only lectional signs are a trema (line 27) and a marginal mark (line 7) probably used to alert the reader that ερωηϲει has been glossed twice. A second hand, smaller and rather faded, has annotated line 13 and added καλλιπαρηον at the foot of the column.

The text is a familiar type, generally thought to be a product of the schoolroom and known to be related to the *Scholia Minora*. For a discussion of such texts see A. Calderini, *Aegyptus* 2 (1921) 303 ff. and A. Henrichs, 'Scholia Minora zu Homer I', *ZPE* 7 (1971) 97–119.

Lemmata and glosses coincide in the main with P. Strassburg inv. Gr. 33 (Pack[2] 1163) re-edited by A. Henrichs (op. cit. 142–5), cited here as P. Strass. with col. and line number. Other abbreviations used in the commentary are those listed in XXIV **2405** introd.

Fr. 1

Col. i   Col. ii

→

		Col. ii (a)	Col. ii (b)
		. . . . .	
		]...[	].[
(302)		πε]ιρη[ca]ι	πειραθητ[ι
(302)		γ]νωω[cι]	γνωcι‖οιδε [ουτοι]
(303)		αι]ψα[	τ]αχεωc
(303)	5	[κελαινον]	μελαν
(303)		[ερωηcει]	υποχ[ω]ρηc[ει]
→		[....]περιχυθη[cε]τα[ι]	
(304)		τω	ουτοι
(304)		αντιβιοιcι	εξ εναντι[αc]
(304)	10	μ]αχεccαμενω	μαχεcθεντε[c]
(305)		α[νc]τητην	ανεcτηcα[ν]
(305)		λυcαν	διελυcαν
(306)		ειcαc	ιcαc (m²) τοιχου[c]
(307)		οιc	τοιc εαυτου
(308)	15	προερυccε	προειλκ[υcεν]
(309)		εκρεινεν	διεχωρη[cεν]
(311)		ειcεν	εκαθιcεν
(310)		βηcεν	ενεβιβαcεν
(311)		πολυμητιc	πολυβ[ο]υλ[οc]
(312)	20	υγρα κελευθα	την θαλαccα[ν]
(313)		απολυμαινεcθα[ι]	α[ποκαθαι-
			ρεcθα[ι]
(313)		ανωγεν	παρεκελευετο
(314)		λυματα	καθαρματα
(315)		ερδον	επετελουν
(315)	25	τεληεccαc	τελειαc
(316)		ατρυγετοιο	ακαρπου
(317)		ϊκεν	παρεγενετο
(318)		πενοντο	ενηρ[γο]υν
(321)		οτρηρω	δραcτικοι
(321)	30	θεραποντεc	υπουργοι
(322)		ερχεcθον	παραγενεcθε
(323)		ελοντε	λαβομενοι
(323)		αγεμεν	αγειν

Col. i:

    .   .   .   .   .

]c

]

]

]αc

5   ].c

]

(279)   cκηπτουχοc cκηπτρο]φοροc

   .   .   .   .   .

15 l. προερυccεν   18 l. βηcε   30 l. θεραποντε

(323) (m²) καλλι[παρ]ηον καλας [παρ]ειας εχουςαν

35   καλην

Fr. 2 (unplaced)

```
    .           .        .
          ].[
          ]cεc[
          ]τρε.[
          ]οδ.[
    .        .      .      .      .
```

1].[trace of rounded letter   3 At end, trace of upright   4]οδ.[indefinite traces.

Col. i 4 D Pa ἐξ ἐναντίας.
7 So D Pa P. Strass. VII 19.
Col. ii 2 So D Pa. P. Strass. VIII 7 πείραςον.
3 οἶδε, separated from γνῶςι by two oblique strokes, appears to have been added later. οὗτοι
supplied from D Pa.
4 So D Pa P. Strass. VIII 10.
5 So Ap D Pa P. Strass. VIII 9.
6–7 The lemma is glossed twice; placed in the left margin against the second gloss there is a sign,
a slightly arched horizontal with a downward and backward tick at the right-hand end.
ὑποχωρήςει so Hsch. περιχυθήςεται cf. D περιρρήςεται.
8 So D Pa.
9 D Pa ἐναντίοις.
11 So D Pa.
12 So Pa. D ἔλυcαν.
13 D Pa P. Strass. VIII 13 ἰcοτοίχουc.
14 So Pa.
15 So Pa. Ap D P. Strass. VIII 18 καθείλκυcεν.
17 So Ap D Pa P. Strass. VIII 16.
18 So D Pa P. Strass. VIII. 17.
19 So Ap D Pa P. Strass. VIII 19.
20 So Ap. D Pa τὴν διὰ θαλάccηc ὁδόν.
21 So D Pa P. Strass. VIII 22–3.
22 D Pa ἐκέλευcεν.
23 So Eust. p. 169, 1. 1.
24 So D P. Strass. VIII 27.
25 So Ap D Pa P. Strass. VIII 28.
26 So D Pa.
27 So D.
28 So D Pa P. Strass. IX 1.
29 So Pa.
30 Homer has the dual θεράποντε. P. Strass. IX 6 has θεραπόντας. However, both this text (line
29) and P. Strass. IX 2 enter the dual form of the modifying adjective ὀτρηρώ, probably uncorrupted
because of its metrical position.
32 So Pa.
33 So D.
34–5 M² has added καλλιπάρηον, apparently overlooked at line 310. The restoration following
D on *Il.* i 143 and P. Strass. VIII 20 fits the traces that remain, but is far from secure.

G

3238. GLOSSARY TO HOMER, *Iliad* i–ii

31 4B.1/M(1–2)a   Fr. 1, 30·7 × 16·8 cm.   Early third century

One considerable fragment and several smaller pieces of a darkish, brittle papyrus-roll remain, which contain a Homeric glossary written on the back of an account. The largest fragment holds four columns of a word list covering *Il.* i 405?–538. Although the side and lower margins are broken off, the upper margin for columns 3 and 4 is preserved. A smaller fragment (2·6 × 8·0 cm.) contains the beginnings of words from *Il.* ii 385–93. The hand is the same throughout, a small, sloping 'Severe Style', comparable with VI **852** (Eur. *Hypsipyle*), though smaller, and with P. Ryl. III **529** (medical treatise), characteristically used for space-saving copies of bulky texts. The scribe usually writes iota adscript on verbs (e.g. lines 114 and 119) but not consistently on nouns. There are a number of errors, most of which are uncorrected.

The glosses are more extensive than usual (cf. XXIV **2405**, gloss 1) but do not contain material other than that found in the *Scholia Minora*. This glossary coincides in part with P. Ant. II 70 (Pack² 1167), P. Mil. Vogl. III 120 (Pack² 1168), and P. Colon. inv. 2281 (edited by A. Henrichs, *ZPE* 7 (1971) 229–52). All coincidence with these texts is indicated in the notes. Other abbreviations are as given for **3237**.

Fr. 1   Col. i

            ·   ·   ·   ·

(?)	]..[	].υιω Δι[
(418)	]..[	]τωι διο
(418)	μεγαροις[ι	].
(419)	τερπικεραυν[ωι]	τωι τερπο-
5	μεν[ωι τοι]ς κεραυνοιϲ	
	εϲτι Δ[ιος ε]πιθετον	
(420)	αγαννιφον	αγανιφετωδη
	χειμερινον	
(421)	ωκυποροις	ταχειαις
10 (422)	μη[νιε]	οργιζου
(422)	παμπαν	παντελωϲ
(423)	αμυμονας	αγαθουϲ
(424)	δ[αι]τα	ευωχιαν
(424)	[ε]πονται	ακολουθηϲουϲιν
15 (426)	[χ]αλκοβατεϲ	ιϲχυρωϲ βεβηκοϲ

7 l. αγαν νιφετωδη   9 l. ωκυποροιϲι

(426) δω   δωμα ο[ι]κημα

(427) γουνασο[μαι]   γονυπετησω

(429) ευζωνοιο   καλοζωνου

(430) απηυρων   αφειλαντο

20   (432) [π]ολυβενθ[ε]ος βαθειαις

(434) [ι]στοδοκη   τη δεχομενη

         τον ιστον επικλιθεντα

(433) [ιστια]   αρμενα

(434) [πελα]σαν   προσεγγισαι εποι-

25   ησαν

(435) [καρπα]λιμως   ταχεως

(435) [ερετμ]οις   [κ]ωπαις

(434) [προτονοις ο] προτονος εστι

       [το σχοινιο]ν απο της του

30   [ιστου κεφ]αλης ε[[κ]]῾ξ΄ημ-

       [μενον προ]ς την πρωραν

(434) [υφεντες   ε]πιχαλασαντες

       [. . . . .] . . [.] . . . . .

(436) [ευνας τας α]γκυρας δια το ε-

35   [. . . . .]ασθαι αυταις

       [την ναυν]

       [. . . . .] . α [] πο[   ]

     .   .   .   .   .   .

Col. ii

     .   .   .   .

(461) διπτυχα   . [   ]

(461) ωμοθετης[αν   . . . .]

40   εστιν[. . . . . μ ε-]

     . ρους [[ο]]῾ω΄μ[. . . . .]

     επικα . [. . . . .]

     εν τω πυρι[. . . . .]

(462) σχιζης   σ[   ]

45   (462) αιθοπα   μ[ελανα   ]

20 l. βαθειας   41 .ρους, dot of ink, not letter

(463)   λειβε   ϵπ[ϵcπϵνδ]ϵ

(463)   πϵμπωβολα τ[ριαιν]οϵιδϵιc

       οβϵλιcκοι [ϵκ μ]ιαc

       αρχηc πϵν[τϵ ο]βϵλους

50   ϵχοντϵc

(464)   ϵπαcαντο   ϵγ[ϵυc]αντ[ο]

(465)   μιcτυλλαν   δι[ϵκο]πτον

(465)   οβϵλοιc   οβϵλιcκοιc

(466)   πϵριφραδϵωc   ϵμπϵ[ι]ρωc

55   (466)   ϵρυcαντο   ϵιλκυcαν

(468)   δαινυντο   ϵυωχ[ο]υντ[ο]

(468)   ϵδϵυϵτο   ϵνδϵηc ην

(468)   δαιτοc ϵϵιcηc τηc ϵιc ιcον

       ϵκα`c′τ[[η]]`ω′ μϵμϵριcμϵν[ηc]

60   μϵριδοc

(469)   ϵξ ϵρον ϵνϵντο [ϵ]ξϵπλ[η-]

       ρωcαν την ϵπιθυμ[ιαν]

       οπϵρ ϵcτιν ϵπληρω-

       cαν

65   (470)   ϵπϵcτϵψαντο   πληρϵιc ϵποι-

       ηcαν του οι[[κ]]`ν′ου τους κρατη-

(471)   ραc νωμηcαν διϵδ[ω]καν

(471)   δϵπαϵccιν   ποτηριοι[c]

(472)   πανημϵριοι   δι ολης ημϵραc

70   (472)   μολπη   ωδη[ ]

(473)   καλον αϵιδοντϵc[ ]κ[αλωc]

       αιδοντϵc [   ]

(473)   [παιηονα]   πα[ιαν]

       [ωδηc] ϵιδ[οc]

      .   .   .   .

Col. iii

75   (480)   [πϵταcc]αν   ηπλωcαν

(481)   [πρ]ηcϵ[ν]   ϵφυηcϵν

52 l. μιcτυλλον   **58** l. δαιτοc ϵιcηc   **59** l. ϵκαcτω   **61** l. ϵξ ϵρον ϵντο   **76** l. ϵφυcηcϵν

(482) [στ]ειρ[η   η ϲ]τε`ι´ρα εϲτι το εξεχον
          . . . . .του κατα την πρω-
          ραν της τροπ[ε]ωϲ ξυλον
80   δια το ϲτερεον ειναι
(482) ιαχε   εφωνει
(483) εθεεν   ετρεχε
(483) διαπρηϲϲουϲα   διαπερωϲα
(485) ηπειροιο   τ(ηϲ) γη[ϲ]
85 (486) υψου   ειϲ υψοϲ
(486) ψαμαθο`ι´ϲ   ψαμαθοϲ καλει-
          ται η παραθαλαϲϲιοϲ αμ-
          μοϲ
(486) τανυϲϲαν   παρετειναν
90 (487) εϲ[κι]δναντο   [ε]ϲκεδαννυντο
(490) [κυδ]ιαν[ε]ιρα[ν] εν ὁ η οι ανδρεϲ
          [ευ]δοξ[ου]νται
(491) φθινυθε[ϲκε]   φθινει
(492) αυθι τοτε ε̣ν εκεινω τω τοπω
95   η ειϲ εκ[εινον το]ν τ̣ο̣πον
(492) ποθε[εϲ]κε   [εποθ]ει
(492) αϋτ[ην]   [τ]ην μαχην
(495) εφετμεων   εντολων
(497) ηεριη   ορθρινη
100 (498) ευρυοπα ητοι μεγαλο-
          φθαλμον η μεγαλο-
          φωνον δια ταϲ βρο̣ντ(αϲ)
(501) [ϲ]καιηι   αριϲτεραι
(501) [α]νθερεωνοϲ   [υπο το γε-]
105   [νε]ιον τοπου δι[α το ε-]
          [κει] πρωτον α[νθειν ταϲ]
          [τρ]ιχαϲ
(505) [ωκυ]μορωτατο̣[ϲ   ]
(507) [απου]ραϲ   α[   ]
110 (508) [μητιε]τα   [   ]
          .   .   .   .

77 l. ϲτειρα   86 l. ψαμαθοιϲ   91 l. εν η οι ανδρεϲ   102 βρο̣ν ^τ

Col. iv

(518)	[ε]χθοδοπη[c]αι	εις εχθ[ραν]	
(518)	[ελ]θειν		
(518)	εφηcει[c]	αναπειcεις	
(519)	ερεθηι[c]ιν	ερεθιζηι	
115 (519)	ονειδειοις	ονειδιcτικοι[c]	
(520)	αυτως	ματαιως	
(521)	νεικει	κακολογει	
(522)	αποστιχε	αποτρεχε	
(522)	νοηcηι	ιδηῑ	
120 (525)	εμεθεν	εμου	
(526)	τεκμωρ	τελος η τε[κμη-	
	ριον		
(526)	παλιναγρεπτον	παλιλλη-	
	πτον		
125 (526)	απατηλον	απατητικον	
(527)	ατελευτητον	ατελεcτον	
(528)	κυανε[η]cιν	μελαιναις	
(529)	αμβροсιαι	θειαι	
(529)	χαιται	κομαι	
130 (529)	επερρωςαντο	επεcιcθηcαν	
(532)	αλτο ηλατο	α`ι΄γληεντος	
	λαμπρου		
(533)	εον	το εαυτου	
(534)	εδεων	καθεδρων	
135 (534)	cφου	του [[εạ]]cαυτου	
(534)	ετλη	[υ]πεμ[ει]νε	
(537)	cυμφρα[cc]ατο	[cυν]εβουλευcατο	
(538)	αργυροπεζα	.[...]....η	

Fr. 2

]ωcπ..καικ[	].πεζα[
140]νος....ε..[	]...τηϛ[
].ει.[	]ε..[
]..[	

.   .   .   .   .   .

123 l. παλιναγρετον   130 l. επεcειcθηcαν   131 l. αιγληεντος

Fr. 3

Iliad ii 385–93

Col. i   Col. ii

. . . .

].		κρ[ινωμεθα	(385)
↓	]και	πα[υcωλη	(386)
	]..	ηβ[αιον	(386)
	]μεν	τελ[αμων	(388)
	].	5	αc[πιδοc	(389)
	].		αμ[φιβροτηc	(389)

Gap of 4 lines

].	11	.[	
		κα[μειται	(389)
		ευξ[οον	(390)
		τιτα[ινων	(390)
	15	.[	
].		μιμ[ναζειν	(392)
].		αρκ[ιον	(393)

. . . .

Col. i Traces of the glosses are too broken to permit restoration.

Fr. 4 (unplaced)

] τ.[
]κα.[

Fr. 1   Col. i

Lines 1 and 38 already stand a line or more higher than 75 and 111, which are shown by the margin to be the first of their columns. It is therefore unlikely that many lines, if any, stood above 1 and 38.

1 The letters that remain suggest Κρονίωνι glossed Κρόνου υἱῷ, Διί. Κρονίωνι occurs at 397 and 405; since nothing in the intervening lines seems remotely to suggest this gloss, it is probably only out of order.

2 So D Pa. τωι διο seems to have been added to the right of another entry (cf. line 67).

3 D Pa gloss οἴκοιc: here οἴκοι]c would fit space and trace.

4–5 Sim. D Pa. The supplements in 5–6 are dubious in that both lacunas give space for 8–10 letters. A longer supplement could be constructed for 6, but I do not see how to expand 5, given the parallels. Perhaps the papyrus surface was damaged before writing.

7–8 D τὸν λίαν νιφόμενον κατὰ τὰ ὑπὸ τοῖc νέφεcι μέρη.

9 D ταχέωc πλεούcαιc; Pa ταχυπλόοιc.

10 So D Pa.

11 So D Pa.

12 So Ap D Pa.

13 So D Pa.

14 End of the lemma is -ονται, dubiously restored to ἕπονται, the reading preferred by Aristarchus to ἕποντο, because (1) -ονται is clear (2) the space will permit only 2–3 letters before this and (3) a form of ἀκολουθέω is the usual gloss for ἕποντο. D ἠκολούθησαν; Pa ἠκολούθουν.

15 So D.

16 Ap D δῶμα; Pa οἴκημα.

17 So D.

18 D καλῶς καὶ εὐστόλου; Pa εὐστολίστου. καλοζωνου is unattested but not an unlikely formation (καλλι- in Homer). Cf. LSJ for other καλο- compounds.

19 ἀφείλαντο: for the assimilation of strong aorists to the sigmatic forms cf. J. H. Moulton, *Grammar of the Greek New Testament* ii 214 ff.

20 Cf. D Pa.

21–2 Cf. Schol. A τὸ κατὰ τὴν πρύμναν ἐξέχον ξύλον καθ' οὗ κλίνεται ὁ ἱστός.

23 So D Pa.

24–5 D πελασθῆναι ἐποίησαν.

26 So D Pa.

27 So Pa.

28–31 Cf. Schol. BT τὰ ἀπὸ πρύμνης εἰς πρῶραν διήκοντα σχοίνια.

32 Traces before χαλασαντες fit]πι. Perhaps a compound ἐπιχαλάσαντες? D Pa χαλάσαντες. Cf. lines 46 and 96.

33 Too damaged to restore securely.

34–6 A variant of D παρὰ τὸ εὐνάζειν τὴν ναῦν . . . καὶ ποιεῖν ἵστασθαι? Spacing seems to demand that ε- (line 34) and]ασθαι (line 35) be part of the same word and the large space after the break in line 36 would seem to indicate that the gloss is complete. It is possible to restore, e.g. ε/ξαψ]ασθαι or ε/φιστ]ασθαι, but neither is appropriate with αὐταῖς, which should require a passive verb. τὴν ναυν is the likeliest supplement for line 36.

37 Perhaps πρυμνης]ία [α]πο[γεια | σχοινία (so D Pa).

Col. ii 38 Only an ink dot remains of the gloss. Ap δύο; D διπλώσαντες; Pa διπλοῦν.

39–43 From the remaining letters, the gloss appears to be a variant of Hsch: τὸ ἀφ' ἑκάστου μέρους τοῦ ἐσφαγμένου ἱερείου ἀφαιρεῖν ἔτι ὠμοῦ ὄντος, καὶ ἐπιτιθέναι ἐπὶ τὴν θυσίαν.

44 Only traces of sigma remain. D ἐπὶ σχιδῶν; Pa σχίδαξιν.

45 μέλανα restored with D Pa.

46 While the traces do not exclude σπένδε (so Ap), the space requires a longer word. ἐπέσπενδε restored with D Pa.

47–50 Sim. Ap πέντε ὀβελίσκοι τριαινοειδεῖς ἐκ μιᾶς ἀρχῆς.

51 The traces fit ἐγεύσαντο. So D Pa P. Ant. II 70. 2.

52 So Ap. D Pa διέκοψαν.

53 So D P. Ant. II 70. 5.

54 D Pa πάνυ ἐμπείρως. P. Ant. II 70. 8 ἐμπείρως.

55 So D Pa.

56 So Pa.

57 So D Pa.

58–60 Sim. Hsch τῆς ἐξ ἴσου μεριζομένης εὐωχίας.

61–4 ενεντο by dittography. Pa ἐπλήρωσαν τὴν ἐπιθυμίαν.

65–6 Sim. Ap πλήρεις ἐποίησαν.

67 So D.

68 So D Pa.

69 So Ap D Pa.

70 So Pa.

71–2 So D Pa.

73–4 παιήονα? Nothing of the lemma remains; the gloss begins with pi and beneath it]ϝιδ[. The reconstruction is suggested by D παιάν, ᾠδῆς εἶδος.

Col. iii 75 So D.

76 So Ap D Pa.

77–80 Cf. Schol. on *Odyssey* ii 428 (στείρη): τῇ τρόπιδι διὰ τὸ στερεὸν εἶναι καὶ διὰ τὸ στεροῦσθαι ἐν αὐτῇ τὴν ναῦν. Also D: τῇ τρόπιδι τῆς νεώς, ἐπεὶ στερεωτέρα τῶν σανίδων ὑπάρχει· ἐπὶ γὰρ τῷ ξύλῳ τούτῳ ὥσπερ ἐπὶ θεμελίῳ τινὶ ἐποικοδομεῖται τὰ ἄλλα ξύλα τῆς νεώς. At the beginning of line 78 there are traces of 5 letters (possibly ξυλου) then a clear του. The rest of the gloss (κατὰ . . . εἶναι) is coherent without this, but it does not appear to be a later addition. τρόπεως restored in line 79, because it fits the traces and the more common genitive τρόπιδος does not. The sense as well as the parallels indicate that the word is appropriate.

81 D μεγάλως ἤχει.

82 So Ap D Pa.

83 So D Pa P. Ant. II 70. 19.

84 So Pa P. Ant. II 70. 21.

85 D Pa P. Ant. II 70. 22 ἐφ' ὕψους.

86–8 Cf. Ap ἡ παραθαλάσσιος ἄμμος.

89 Pa ἐνέτειναν.

90 So D.

91–2 D ἐνδόξους ἄνδρας ἔχουσαν. The scribe placed a dot above omicron to indicate that it was written in error.

93 D Pa διέφθειρεν. Apparently]φθινει, not ε]φθινεν.

94–5 Ap ἐν τούτῳ τῷ τόπῳ; cf. D Pa αὐτόθι.

96 D ἐπέποθει; Pa ἔποθει. Only the -ει remains, but space available favours the shorter word.

97 So Ap Pa.

98 So Ap D Pa.

99 So D Pa.

100–2 Sim. D: ἤτοι μεγαλόφθαλμον, παρὰ τοὺς ὦπας, ἢ μεγαλόφωνον, παρὰ τὴν ὄπα, ὅ ἐστι τὴν φωνήν. διὰ τὰς βροντ(άς) read by M. E. Weinstein.

103 So Ap D Pa.

104–7 Sim. Ap ὑπὸ τὸ γένειον τόπου ἀφ' οὗ ἄρχεται ἀνθεῖν. D τοῦ ὑπὸ τὸ γένειον τόπου. παρὰ τὴν ἐξάνθησιν τῶν τριχῶν.

108 D ταχυθανάτου; Pa ταχυθανατώτατος.

109 Ap ἀφορίσας; D ἀφελόμενος; Pa ἀφελών.

Col. iv 111–12 ἐλθεῖν? Traces fit this better than the other possibilities, e.g. D ἐχθρὸν καταστῆναι.

113 Cf. D Pa.

114 D ἐρεθίζει.

115 So D Pa.

116 So D Pa.

117 So D.

118 Cf. D.

119 D Pa θεάσηται. The iota adscript of the gloss has a horizontal line placed over it. I have been unable to find any parallel or to suggest a plausible explanation for its being so marked. Possibly the line was intended as a *trema*, though I can produce no closer example of misuse than αινειαϊ (dative), P. Bodm. I *Il.* 5. 450.

120 So D Pa P. Mil. Vogl. III 120. 1.

121–2 So D. Ap P. Colon. inv. 2281 iii 17 τέλος only.

123–4 So Ap. Cf. D Pa.

125 So D Pa.

126 So Pa P. Colon. inv. 2281 iii 20.

127 So D Pa P. Colon. inv. 2281 iii 22.

128 So D P. Colon. inv. 2281 iii 23.

129 Ap αἱ κεχυμέναι κόμαι; D P. Colon. inv. 2281 iii 24 τρίχες.

130 So D Pa.
131 So Hsch; D καθήλατο.
132 So D Pa P. Colon. inv. 2281 iv 3.
133 D πρὸς τὸ ἴδιον.
134 So D Pa P. Colon. inv. 2281 iv 4.
135 D Pa ἰδίου.
136 So D.
137 So D Pa.
138–42 ἀργυρόπεζα has occasioned a lengthy gloss, too little of which remains for certain restoration. See the material collected in *ZPE* 7 (1971) 243. Line 139 might be]ωσπερ και κ[. Line 140 -νος suggests a restoration like P. Colon. inv. 2281 iv. 8–11 (*ZPE* l.c.) οἱ μὲν ἀπὸ τῆς πέζης τοῦ χιτῶνος. Fragment 2 seems to belong to this gloss because of the clearly readable].πεζα[. Lines 141–2 may be part of new entries, but too little remains to be certain.

3239. ALPHABETIC 'GLOSSARY'

33 4B.79/D(1–3)   13·8 × 13·1 cm.   Later second century

This puzzling fragment, originally complete in three columns, comprises an alphabetical list of words with what, for lack of a better term, must be called definitions. The small number of lemmata, fifty-three, including line 27, combined with the arrangement, as well as the contents themselves present problems which thus far have failed of solution. **3239** is probably not a glossary to a particular poem, unless that poem were alphabetically arranged or exceedingly repetitive, because the arrangement would have been inconvenient and also because that explanation does not take into account the peculiar 'place-holding' nu in line 27. Nor does it seem based on an acrostic principle, as there is often more than one entry for each letter. It is far too short for a lexicon. Nor does it appear to have been a school exercise, both on the basis of the writing (see below) and also because of the lack of corrections in a second, i.e. teacher's, hand, although the sometimes rather fanciful definitions might possibly be the work of an unprepared scholar.

Alphabetical lists of words do occur in school exercises in syllabification, cf. Pack² 2676 = O. Tait II 2193 or in lists of particular kinds of words, e.g. words in -ους, cf. Pack² 2718 = J. G. Milne *JHS* XXVIII (1908) p. 124 iv. Pack² 2654 = P. Tebt. II 278 has an alphabetical list of occupations followed by an acrostic story, both of which may have been used as a way of teaching the alphabet. In both Pack² 2718 and 2654 there is only one entry per letter of the alphabet. Alphabetical glossaries are also found in Pack² 2119–28. The definitions given in them are usually more common words synonymous with the lemmata, possibly with an explanation of the derivation and sometimes with examples of usage from various authors. Obviously the relation between **3239** and any of these is tenuous, first because of the shortness of the list, second and more important because of the strangeness of the 'definitions' given, for example mouse defined as 'vainglorious' (26), bathing attendant as 'rotten fate' (34). All the surviving lemmata, so far as can be seen, are substantives. Beyond that there seems to be no connection between them. The index to *PMG* yields no connection with magical texts, which goes against the assumption that **3239** interprets religious or oracular symbols; nor is there any relation with the *Hieroglyphica* of Horapollo. Some entries might be taken as 'kennings' or riddles: Tryph. π. τρ. 4 (Spengel, *Rh. Gr.* iii 195) κατὰ δὲ γλῶτταν (sc. γίνεται αἴνιγμα), ὅταν τὴν μὲν θάλατταν εὐρυγάστορα λέγῃ, τὴν δὲ Ἀθηναίαν μαρμαρῶπιν, τὸν δὲ μῦν δολιχοῦρον (with the last cf. **3239** 26). But I have found no real parallels in the list of W. Schultz, *Rätsel aus dem hellenischen Kulturkreise* ii (1912) 135–46; and some items are clearly unsuitable.

From the papyrus itself one must conclude that the main motivation of the author was, somehow, alphabetical, cf. the nu in line 27; and it seems very likely that the lemmata were written, in each column at least, before the definitions, cf. in col. i the mistaken placing and erasure of what appears to have been αρουρα after line 6, in col. ii the spacing of the blank second half of line 27 and possibly the mistake caused by the two-line entry at lines 31 and 32.

The papyrus is written on the backs of two documents, *A* having col. i and most of col. ii, *B* having the rest. *A* and *B* are pasted together upside down relative to each other and the edge of *A* overlaps the first three letters of *B*. Neither is dated, although the writing is of the first century. *B* appears to be an account involving grain, *A* is very scrappy and indistinct. There is a washed-out heading at the top of *B* and the spacing suggests that its full height is preserved. The consequence of this is that at several places in **3229** large vertical fibres and the pasting have interfered with the writing.

The left-hand half of col. i, and the right-hand two-thirds of col. iii, have been torn away. But the full original height seems to be preserved.

The clumsy upright hand begins with some attempt at literary style, but becomes smaller and more cursive as the text proceeds. Beta (open-topped) and eta (y-shaped) almost always have the cursive form. It is of the class in which hypomnemata are written and should perhaps be assigned to the later second century.

Col. i

↓

]πικρονκακον

]αιειοινος

].ιλαραγεωργια

]..φιλ[ε]ιπατροκλον

5   ] κυνηγικονηγημα

]κυλιας ανθος

]τονος

]αρουρ α

]πολεμονποιει

10   ]λεσχη

]ηδονηθεων

]χαρμ αμεθης

]πεταμενοσθεος

]παραγων

15   ]ρϋιοσαναξ

]μημερια

]εβεια

].ηπιστις

]

20   ].

Col. i 3]. high and low ink, as if from vertical   4].. high traces in paler ink, ος possible
6 Below are traces of washed out letters, αρουρα?   7]τ possibly pi but not gamma   11 θ
very smudged, after ω traces probably because the scribe was thwarted by the large fibre and had to
begin the nu again   16 for μη λα, αλ, or χη can be read, the first two if written rather small
18]. three small traces on two fibres consistent with an oblique sloping down to right followed immediately by an upright alpha or mu?   20]. high trace of curve opening to right

Col. i

```
        ] πικρὸν κακόν
        ] αἰεὶ οἶνος
        ]. ἱλαρὰ γεωργία
        ].. φιλεῖ Πάτροκλον
  5     ] κυνηγικὸν ἤγημα
        ]κυλίας ἄνθος
        ]τονος
        ] ἄρουρα
        ] πόλεμον ποιεῖ
 10     ] λέςχη
        ] ἡδονὴ θεῶν
        ] χάρμα μέθης
     δ ] πετάμενος θεός
        ] παράγων
 15     ] ὁ υἱὸς ἄναξ
         ]μημερια
         ]εβεια
        ].η πίςτις
        ]
 20      ].
```

Col. ii

	ιϲιϲ	ημεγαλη[.]λπιϲ
	κυων	ιταμο ϲπει.ατ...
	κα[λ]αθοϲ	ειϲερια
	λυχνοϲ	τοδεξιονφεγγ`ο´
25	μολιβοϲ	μεγα βαροϲ
	μυϲ	περπ εροϲ
	ν	
	ξυϲτρα	ελαδι ουϲπανιϲ
	οι[..].ε.ι	ηδονη[.]ειν
30	οι[κο]δομοϲ	παραβολ[..]
	οϲαραπιϲ	αλεξανδρειαν
		κοϲμει
	οιν[ο]ϲ	οξοϲ
	παραχυτηϲ	ϲαπρατυχη
35	ρητωρ	ερ[[κ]]γομωροϲ
	ραβδ οϲ	οδηγ οϲαγαθη
	ρωμ η	ξειν ηπ ολιϲ
	ϲιμιν[.]ϲ	ϲεμι δαλιϲ
	ϲυναγοροϲ	περπε ρονϲτομα
40	ϲιμι .ιϲ	οκαλοϲαηρ
	ϲτεφανοϲ	εκαϲτ ω
	τυχη	ονανθεληπλουϲι`ο´
	υδρο []..οϲ	δευρε ϲω πο.ει
	υδρο []φοροϲ	διψω
45	υπηρ ετηϲ	αντι κυριοϲ

Col. ii 22 *ι.* nu or rho   After τ an upright (blotted at middle height, corrected?)   26 *υϲ* corrected from η ?   27 The gap between 26 and 28 is only slightly larger than between 25 and 26 or 28 and 29   40 *.ιϲ* two tiny traces a mid-height on edge   43 *ϲω* fibre interferes with *ω* which is not very clear and may be another letter   *πο.ει*: either *πορει* or *ποιει* (there are no traces of the upper loop of rho, but the lower loop is like rho in *ϲαπρα* line 34)

Col. ii

	Ἶϲιϲ	ἡ μεγάλη [ἐ]λπίϲ
	κύων	ἰταμὸϲ πειρατίϲ
	κά[λ]αθοϲ	εἰϲ ἔρια
	λύχνοϲ	τὸ δεξιὸν φέγγο(ϲ)
25	μόλιβοϲ	μέγα βάροϲ
	μῦϲ	πέρπεροϲ
	ν	
	ξύϲτρα	ἐλαδίου ϲπάνιϲ
	οι [..].ε .ι	ἡδονη[.]ειν
30	οἰ[κο]δόμοϲ	παραβολ[..]
	ὁ Ϲαρᾶπιϲ	Ἀλεξανδρείαν
		κοϲμεῖ
	οἶνοϲ	ὄξοϲ
	παραχύτηϲ	ϲαπρὰ τύχη
35	ῥήτωρ	ἐργόμωροϲ
	ῥάβδοϲ	ὁδηγὸϲ ἀγαθή
	Ῥώμη	ξείνη πόλιϲ
	ϲιμιν[ι]ϲ	ϲεμίδαλιϲ
	ϲυνάγοροϲ	πέρπερον ϲτόμα
40	ϲιμι.ιϲ	ὁ καλὸϲ ἀήρ
	ϲτέφανοϲ	ἑκάϲτῳ
	τύχη	ὃν ἂν θέλῃ πλούϲιο(ν)
	ὑδρο[]..οϲ	δευρεϲῳ ποιεῖ
	ὑδροφόροϲ	διψῶ
45	ὑπηρέτηϲ	ἀντικύριοϲ

Col. iii

υϲ [ῦϲ ⌊

φ...ϲ[

φορμ[

χα..[

50   χαρω[

χαρω[

χιμ.[

ψι[

ωροϲ[

———

Col. iii 52 χ is very faint, possibly another letter between it and ι   53 ψ very faint, possibly space for a small letter between it and ι   54 ω corrected from o?

Col. i In 5 the 'definition' is certainly complete, for blank papyrus precedes; so probably in 11 and 12. Starting from this alignment, and allowing for limited irregularities of margin as in col. ii, we may assume that 1–4 also are complete, and that 6–10 may (but need not) lack one or two letters at the beginning.

1 ἀνάγκη]?

2 If αἰεί is right, it must be adjectival; the obvious lemma is then ἀμβροϲία (as the wine of the gods, already in Sappho 141 L–P). But if the line began unusually far to the left, we could try κ]αίει, etc.

3 Perhaps ἡ ἱλαρά, unless the first trace is stray ink.

4 Ἀχιλλεύϲ]. Before φιλεῖ perhaps]ὃϲ.

5 κυνηγικόν has a clear meaning, though the word is rare (τόποι P. Grenf. II 71 i 15; χώρα? Evagr. *HE* 3. 32). ἥγημα is quoted in the sense 'that which guides' from Inscr. Perg. p. 246. 27, in the sense 'thought, purpose' from LXX *Ez.* 17. 3 (hence in Photius, etc., see Stephanus s.v.). If the meaning here is 'that which leads in hunting', Ἄρτεμιϲ would be a suitable lemma.

6 An extremely puzzling definition. A spelling error must be assumed. Two possible readings are κοιλίαϲ ἄνθοϲ poetic and unexampled, but perhaps suitable for αἰδοῖα, or ϲ]κυλείαϲ ἄνθοϲ with ἀϲπίϲ.

7 If τόνοϲ, perhaps ἁρμονία]?

9 Ἄρηϲ?

10 λέϲχη is the only possible reading. Perhaps the lemma was βουλευτήριον.

11 Γανυμήδηϲ]?

12 Διόνυϲοϲ]?

13 Ἔρωϲ].

15 Strangely expressed definition. Ζεύϲ fits the alphabetic scheme.

16 θερ]μημερία would fit the traces, but occurs usually in the plural, cf. LSJ s.v. Possibly the lemma is ἥλιοϲ *vel sim.*

17 -ϲ]έβεια.

18 The traces might allow ἡ κ]αλὴ πίϲτιϲ. Cf. 21.

21 This title does not occur in the magical papyri or the Isiac aretologies. The closest is PMG XXIV a 1 μεγάλη Ἴϲιϲ ἡ κυρία.

22 For the connection of κύων with ἰταμόϲ cf. Aeschylus fr. 282N. I print πειρατίϲ as a misspelling of πειρατήϲ; but it is possible that the scribe corrected τιϲ to τηϲ. πειρᾷ τιϲ might also be read, but suits ἰταμόϲ less well.

24 δεξιόν: well-omened? favourable to lovers or travellers?

26 The connection is less clear than usual here: possibly a reference to the Batrachomyomachia (there are no braggart mice in Aesop). πέρπεροc and its compounds are well attested in the literary Greek of the Hellenistic and Roman epochs, see *LSJ* and especially Lampe, *PGL* s.v.

29 οι[..].ε.ι: the lacuna may hold one or two letters; then traces of a descender followed by a high trace; then the beginning of epsilon. After epsilon: alpha, lambda or possibly gamma. Dr. Rea suggests οἰ[νό]μελι ἡδονὴ [π]εῖν: this is very attractive, though]μ is not the most obvious reading of the traces.

30 παραβολ[: the space allows παραβολ[ή, -[ον, -[οc. I see no obvious sense. It is tempting to write παραβολ[ή, and refer to the image of the man who built his house on a rock, NT Matt. 7. 24. But we might not expect an allusion to a Christian parable so early.

31 ὁ Cαρᾶπιc: no other entry has the article. Possibly he intended 'Οcαρᾶπιc as a by-form of 'Οcέραπιc and 'Οcορᾶπιc.

34 cαπρὰ τύχη: cf. PMG XIII 635 τὴν cαπρὰν εἱμαρμένην. In a literal sense, some parachytae had a degraded lot in life, see Cumont, *L'Égypte des Astrologues*, 141 f. But notice also that cαπρὰ τύχη is an anagram of παραχύτηc.

35 ἐρ[[κ]]γόμωροc: the scribe apparently wrote ερκο and corrected it to εργο; there is also stray ink round the rho, but not enough to prove that it was corrected. The word intended must be ἐργόμωκοc, which is glossed *adulator, ambitiosus, ancillarius, ancillula, assentator, fuco, stlatarius* (Goetz, *CGL* vii 527, with derivatives; cf. Hsch. E 5668 ἐργομωκῶν ἐμπαίζων).

36 The walking-stick of the blind or old? (For ῥάβδοc as the equivalent of βακτήριον, see NT Matt. 10. 10, etc.)

37 Cf. ξένων πόλιc of Alexandria in the *Oracle of the Potter*, *ZPE* 2 (1968) 206, line 30.

38 S. Stephens suggests cίμιν[ι]c = *seminis*. But the connection is obscure, and the case (genitive or mistaken plural) is strange.

39 cυνάγοροc: the Doric form is the only one which fits the traces.

40 M. W. Haslam has suggested Cίμιλιc ὁ καλὸc ἀ⟨ν⟩ήρ (Ser. Sulpicius Similis, Prefect of Egypt 107–12). If this were correct, it would provide a lower limit for dating the text.

41 ἑκάcτῳ is an exceptionally odd definition. There might be doubts about the reading: sigma could be omicron; the descender of tau is very thick (corrected); omega is widely separated from tau (but the scribe may have left a space to avoid thick fibres, as at the same point in 36–9 though not in 40). It is just possible that a narrow letter originally stood before epsilon, if the single point of ink is significant. But I have found no other satisfactory reconstruction; ἐραcτῶ(ν) can be excluded, since kappa is virtually certain.

42–3 ποιεῖ is written slightly higher than the preceding words. I assume therefore that it carries over from 42.

43 ὑδρο[].οc: before οc, what looks at first sight like the loop and part of the descender of rho. But if so, the descender ends short with an uncharacteristic curl to the right. Other possibilities are no more attractive: theta (malformed), beta (but elsewhere the scribe uses an open-topped form). Perhaps the letter has been corrected. The word as written was one letter shorter than ὑδροφόροc in 44; and the 'definition' was apparently δεῦρ' ἔcω.

45 ἀντικύριοc is new, but cf. ἀντιβαcιλεύc, etc. Better so than Ἀντικύριοc or ἀντὶ ⟨τοῦ⟩ κύριοc (which would produce a 'definition' much more explicit than any of the others).

47 Perhaps φ..ιc[; φύcιc not suggested.

48 φόρμιγξ, φορμόc, etc.

49 χα..[: the first traces looks very like nu or pi. No attested word or name begins χαπ. Even for χαν- the possibilities are few: χάννα? Χαναάν (cf. on 30)?

50 Χάρων?

52 χίμα[ιρα (cf. 46)? But perhaps χι.μ.[should be read.

54 Ὦροc (cf. 21, 31)? ὡροc[κόποc?

H

IV. OFFICIAL DOCUMENTS

3240. Official Correspondence

34 4B.78/D(10–12)b   16·1 × 13·2 cm.   c. 88/9

A warped fragment of the bottom of a column containing copies of two or three letters, the last one of which at least is official. It is not clear if this fragment belongs to a roll or is a single sheet of copies of letters pertaining to one dispute, see 2 n. Parts of the left and bottom margins, 3·6 and 2·0 cm. respectively, survive, but the full width of the left margin is not preserved. The back is blank.

The subject of the lower portion of the column is a boundary dispute of some duration, the history of which goes back at least as far as the term of Flavius Heracleides, predecessor of Junius Hestiaeus as strategus, and conceivably continued for forty years after this letter, see 14–16 n. Junius Hestiaeus is a new strategus and the period available for Flavius Heracleides is narrowed by this papyrus. The prefects C. Septimius Vegetus and M. Mettius Rufus gave instructions in the case.

$$\cdot \quad\quad \cdot \quad\quad \cdot \quad\quad \cdot \quad\quad \cdot \quad\quad \cdot$$

→   c. 17   ]ει..[c. 18

             c. 16   ] Φλαουίω[ι   c. 15

             c. 16   ]ηγηϲαϲ.[..].[c. 12

.[c. 14   ].εγενο.[.]..ωεν[c. 7

5   ...[c. 13   ]ητου διὰ ἀφοριϲμοῦ κατὰ τ̣[ὰϲ

ἀϲφ[αλείαϲ.   (ἔτουϲ) . Α]ὐτοκράτοροϲ Καίϲαροϲ Δομιτιαν[οῦ

Cεβαϲτοῦ Γερ[μανικοῦ, Φαμ]ενὼθ ιγ‾.   (vac.)

ἄλληϲ. Μέττιοϲ Ῥοῦφοϲ Ἰουνίωι Ἑϲτιαίωι ϲτρ(ατηγῷ) Ὀξυρ(υγχίτου) χ(αίρειν).

Διονύϲιοϲ Διονυϲίου διὰ ἀναφο(ρίου) μοι ἐνέτυχε λέγων

10   γε]γραφέναι Οὐέγετον τὸν κράτιϲτον Φλαουίωι Ἡρ[α-

κλείδ]ηι τῶι πρὸ ϲοῦ ϲτρατηγή[ϲα]ντι περὶ ἀρουρῶν αὐ-

τοῦ τῶν] ἡρπαϲμένων ὑπὸ τ̣[ῶν] γιτόνων ἵν' αὐτῶι κα-

τὰ τὰ]ϲ ἀϲφαλείαϲ ἀφορι̣[ϲθῶ]ϲιν, ἄχρι δὲ τούτου μηδὲν

πεποι]ῆϲθαι. βούλομαι [οὖν ϲ]έ, εἰ μηδὲν περὶ τοῦ πρά-

15   γματοϲ ἐπο]ι̣ήθη{ι}, [[.]] γεν[όμενον] ἐπὶ τοὺϲ τόπουϲ ἑκάϲτ(ῳ)

τὸ ἴδιον ἔδα]φοϲ ἀπο̣[καταϲτ]ῆϲαι. ἔρρωϲο. (ἔτουϲ) η″

Αὐτοκράτορο]ϲ Καίϲαροϲ [Δομιτιανο]ῦ Cεβαϲτοῦ Γερμανικοῦ

         c. 20   ].[c. 10   ]   (vac.)

     8 ϲτρ^L οξυρ‾ χ^L   9 αναφ°   12 l. γειτόνων   15 εκαϲ^τ

5 ff. '. . . through a determination of boundaries according to the title deeds. Year *n* of Imperator Caesar Domitianus Augustus Germanicus, Phamenoth 13(?).

'(Copy) of another. Mettius Rufus to Junius Hestiaeus strategus of the Oxyrhynchite nome, greetings. Dionysius son of Dionysius applied to me in a petition stating that Vegetus, *vir egregius*, wrote to Flavius Heracleides who was strategus before you concerning the arouras of his which were stolen by the neighbours in order that the boundaries might be determined for him according to the title deeds, but nothing has been done yet. I desire you, if nothing has been done about the matter, to go to the locality and restore to each his own land. Farewell. Year 8 of Imperator Caesar Domitianus Augustus Germanicus . . .'

2 Φλαουίω[ι. Restore perhaps Ἡρακλείδηι again, cf. 10–11. Possibly this is the first line of the letter of Vegetus mentioned in 10. There is just room for Cεπτίμιος Οὐέγετος at the beginning of the line, but not for ἄλλης or ἀντί(γραφον). Alternatively there is room for ἄλλης. Μέττιος Ῥοῦφος. In either case the letter would be extremely short. The traces of l. 1 are extremely small and faint, but could possibly be read as]ϲεβα[, i.e. as part of the titulature closing a preceding letter.

6 For ἀϲφάλειαι meaning title deeds see R. Taubenschlag, *Law*², 275.

8 The earliest definite date for Mettius Rufus is 3 August A.D. 89, though he may have taken office in the spring of A.D. 89, see *BASP* 4 (1967) 89 and *ZPE* 17 (1975) 277. The date in 7, if it really were Phamenoth 13 = 9 March A.D. 89, would not exclude the possibility that Mettius Rufus was the writer of the letter.

Junius Hestiaeus is a previously unknown strategus in office sometime in A.D. 88/9, see 16–17.

10 The earliest known date for Vegetus, prefect of Egypt, is 8 February A.D. 85, the latest 26 February A.D. 88, see *BASP* 4 (1967) 89 and *ZPE* 17 (1975) 277.

Flavius Heracleides is known from PSI XII 1235. 2 as strategus some time between A.D. 80 and 90, but not in 83. This document indicates that he must have been in office after 83 some time in the prefecture of Vegetus and before the date of this letter.

12 For encroachment by neighbours cf. BGU II 616, P. Petaus 24.

13 ἀφορι[ϲθῶ]ϲιν. Cf. P. Flor. III 319. 9.

14–16 For the restorations cf. BGU II 616. 5 ff. ἀξιῶ ἐ[π]ιτα[γ]ῆναι [τῷ τ]ῆ[ϲ] κώμης κωμογρ(αμματεῖ) γενέϲθα[ι] ἐπὶ τού[ϲ] τόπους ϲὺν τῷ ὁριοδικ(τῇ) καὶ ἀναμετρῆϲαι [τ]ὴν πᾶϲα⟨ν⟩ γῆν καὶ ἑκάϲτῳ τὸ ἴδιο[ν] ἀπ[ο]καταϲτήϲῃ (l. -ϲτῆϲαι). This is a request possibly similar to one Dionysius may have written to Vegetus. In it, in P. Petaus 24, and in P. Flor. 319 of *c.* A.D. 133–7, which may possibly be connected with our document as the petitioner is 'son of Dionysius', the writers assume that the village scribe is in charge of the examination. There is no sign of him in our document.

3241. Notifications to Tax-farmers

5 1B.59/H(i)   14 × 14 cm.   11 February A.D. 163

Two adjacent documents from a τόμος ϲυγκολλήϲιμος, both addressed to a pair of contractors for the ἐγκύκλιον, the tax on transfers of property. The first is a statement of payment of the charges due on the manumission of a female slave, the second, written by the same man on the same day, appears to concern the same transaction and refers to a public registration at Alexandria.

In manumissions three payments are to be distinguished: the ransom price, or λύτρα, paid to the slave's owner; the tax due upon the transaction, the ἐγκύκλιον; and a separate charge of 10 dr. (The suggestion made at XXXVIII 2843, that the 10 dr. are the tax itself, is to be rejected.) The first of the present documents records the payment of the last two of these, and the 10 dr. charge now has a name, the πρ]ο- πρατικόν. The purpose served by this first letter, virtually complete, is something of a puzzle. It is not an acknowledgement of payment by the recipients, but a statement of payment by the payer, and since it incorporates acknowledgement of a receipt (9–10 ὧν [καὶ c]ύμβολον ἔcχον), it was clearly not intended to serve as a receipt itself (by being countersigned by the taxmen). A precise parallel for the form of the letter is found in I **61**, a statement made by an Oxyrhynchite ex-strategus of the Arsinoite nome to public bankers at Oxyrhynchus of the payment of a fine he had incurred by his failure to produce official papers when required. That letter, however, does not provide an immediate solution to the problem. (The revised readings of E. G. Turner in *JEA* 38 (1952) 88 n. 6, do not affect the basic form. Expand to cύμβολ(ον) in 19.) In **3241** a possible explanation is that the money had been paid directly into the state bank, instead of passing through the hands of the tax farmers (cf. I **96**, where a tax official pays the ἐγκύκλιον on the sale of a slave into the bank; cf. P. Fay. 64, P. Osl. III 116). It would be a reasonable, perhaps obligatory, course of action to notify the circumvented taxmen, the nominal payees. A comparable explanation is available for **61**, if the fine had been paid into a bank in the Hermopolite, where the man was currently strategus.

The matter might be more intelligible if the second of the present letters had survived intact. As it is, the significance of the publication through the *katalogeion* at Alexandria is not at all clear. It may refer to the δημοcίωcιc of the manumission at Alexandria. If the current view of the identity of the senders of I **48**, **49** and II **349** is correct (see **XXXVIII 2856** 2 n.), it was the duty of the ἐγκύκλιον farmers, at any rate at the end of the first century, to notify the local agoranomus of the details of the manumission and authorize him to proceed with the registration. There would be no need for this to be done if the deed had already been entered at Alexandria. (Cf. IX **1200**, where a request is made to the archidicastes to inform the Oxyrhynchite record office of the registration of a deed of sale through the *katalogeion*.) In view of the identity of the addressees, it seems less likely that the registration in question is that of a deed certifying the legal title to the slave, and hence with the man's right to dispose of her (cf. I **73**, where an agreement registered through the *katalogeion* is mentioned in connection with a registration of a slave before agoranomi).

Above the first column are some scribblings in two different hands, apparently unrelated to the main text. The most legible of them read :]οκαιοκαιμουι( ) | περιτωνcυν | cυμτ...ωιγου[[περι]]....των.

On the back, not transcribed here, is what appears to be a prose encomium on the *aulos*.

Col. i

→   Θεα....] Cαραπίωνος ἀπὸ Ὀξυρύγχων [πόλ(εως)
       δι]ὰ Cαραπίωνος Ἀπολλωνίου φροντι[cτοῦ
       Αὐρ]ηλίῳ Ἀντιόχῳ καὶ Ἡρακλείδῃ ἐνκυ[κλι-
       ών]αις χαίρειν. Διέγραψα ὑμεῖν ὑπὲρ Πρ[
5   ..]ης δούλης ἐλευθερωθείςης ὑπ' ἐμοῦ τὸ

τῆ] c ἐλευθερώcεωc αὐτῆc ἐνκυκλιακὸν

..].. υc ὂν ἐν δραχ(μαῖc) πεντήκοντα δύο, (γίνονται) (δραχμαὶ) νβ,

καὶ πρ]οπρατικοῦ δραχ(μὰc) δέκα, (γίνονται) (δραχμαὶ) ι, γείνονται

ἐπὶ] τὸ αὐτὸ δραχ(μαὶ) ἑξήκοντα δύο, (γίνονται) (δραχμαὶ) ξβ, ὧν

10 καὶ c]ύμβολον ἔcχον. Cαραπίων Ἀπολλω-

νίου ὁ] προγεγραμμένος φροντιcτὴς αὐτὸc

τὸ γράμ]μα ἔγραψα. Ἔτουc τρίτου Αὐτοκράτοροc

Καίcαροc] Μάρκου Αὐρηλίου Ἀντωνείνου Cεβαcτοῦ

καὶ Αὐτο]κράτοροc Καίcαροc Λουκίου Αὐρηλίου

15 Οὐήρ]ου Cεβαcτοῦ, Μεχεὶρ ῑζ.

Col. ii

Θεα.... Cαραπ[ίωνοc ἀπὸ Ὀξυρύγχων πόλ(εωc)

διὰ Cαραπίων[οc Ἀπολλωνίου φροντιcτοῦ

Αὐρηλίω Ἀντ[ιόχω καὶ Ἡρακλείδῃ ἐν-

κυκλιώναιc χ[αίρειν.

20 .[..].. περιη[

δούληc Πρειμ[

λιοπηc δημ[οcιω-

διὰ τοῦ ἐν Ἀλεξαν[δρείᾳ καταλογείου.

Cαραπίων Ἀπολλ[ωνίου ὁ προγεγραμμέ-

25 νοc φροντιcτὴc [αὐτὸc τὸ ὑπόμνημα

ἐπιδέδωκα. Ἔτουc [τρίτου Αὐτοκράτοροc

Καίcαροc Μάρκου Αὐρη[λίου Ἀντωνείνου

Cεβαcτοῦ καὶ Αὐτοκ[ράτοροc Καίcαροc

Λουκίου Αὐρηλίο[υ Οὐήρου Cεβαcτοῦ,

30 Μεχεὶρ ῑζ.

Col. i 'Thea- son of Sarapion of Oxyrhynchus, through Sarapion son of Apollonius, manager, to Aurelius Antiochus and Heraclides, contractors for the transfer tax, greeting. I have paid you, on behalf of the slave . . . freed by me, the transfer tax for her manumission, the sum being fifty-two drachmas of coined silver, 52 dr., and for warranty fee ten drachmas, 10 dr., that is in sum total sixty-two drachmas, 62 dr., for which I have had a receipt. I, Sarapion son of Apollonius the abovementioned manager, have personally written the statement. Year 3 of Imperator Caesar Marcus Aurelius Antoninus Augustus and Imperator Caesar Lucius Aurelius Verus Augustus, Mecheir 16.'

1 Θεαγένης is far and away the commonest name in Θεα-, but the traces do not commend it. Θεάνωρ is an attested name that is perhaps acceptable, but too little remains to be certain.

3 Αὐρηλίῳ Ἀντιόχῳ: Aurelius occasionally appears as the nomen of romanized Greeks before the Antonine Constitution. I know of no earlier occurrence without a praenomen than this.

The heirs of an Aurelius Antiochus are mentioned in III **512**, a document of A.D. 173. The nomen at this date greatly increases the chances of identity.

3–4 ἐνκυ[κλι|ών]αις (guaranteed by 18–19 ἐν]κυκλιώναις), a new title, equivalent to τελῶναι ἐγκυκλίου (XVII **2111** 18, P. Vindob. Worp 1. 5). ἐγκυκλιακοί (XX **2281** 3, P. Mich. II 123 verso vii 16, BGU III 914. 5, P. Osl. III 118. 1) will probably have been officials.

4–5 I take it that the lines were spanned by the slave's name, whose manumission is apparently the subject of the second letter also, where the name is Πρειμ[. Attested female names in Πρει-/Πρι- are Πρεῖμα, Πριμιάνη, and Πριμέλλα. Πρ[ειμι|άν]ης and Πρ[ειμίλ|λ]ης are thus possibilities.

5–7 The rate of the manumission tax is unknown except in the case of Roman citizens, who were liable to the *vicesima libertatis*. The raising of the greco-egyptian tax, in so far as it related to an alienation of property, evidently devolved upon the ἐγκύκλιον farmers, as is suggested also by the phrase διὰ τοῦ ἐγκυκλίου καὶ ὧν ἄλλων καθήκει in some manumission documents (P. Strasb. 122. 11, SB III 6293. 6). The ἐγκύκλιον on sales was 10 per cent (A. C. Johnson, *Economic Survey*, 558 f., S. Wallace, *Taxation*, 228, 230, 448 n. 60, 449 n. 75), but the manumission tax was not necessarily the same (a 2 per cent rate, also raised by the farmers of the ἐγκυκλίον, was levied on mortgages, II **243**). However, 52 dr. are paid on the sale of a slave at I **96** (A.D. 180) and again at P. Hamb. 79 (second century), so that though slave prices varied considerably, it seems quite possible that the manumission tax was also a 10 per cent rate.

Since it is the purchaser, and in the case of mortgages the mortgagee, who pays the ἐγκύκλιον in the Roman period, the presumption would be that the manumission tax was payable by the manumitted slave (as it is at P. Hib. I 29. 7, Ptolemaic), out of his or her peculium. But payment by the owner on the slave's behalf may have been regular practice. (At P. Tebt. II 407. 25 (A.D. 199?) a man who declares to his wife that he wishes to free some slaves standing in her name has himself paid the taxes due: διαγράψας πάντ]ᾳ τᾳ ὑ[π]ὲρ αὐτῶν τέλη τῆς ἐλευθερώσεως.) Similarly the ransom price itself, the λύτρα, was paid not by the slave but by a third party. The slave's legal incapacity will account for both the payments in question being made, at least nominally, by someone other than the beneficiary of the transaction.

6–7 ἐνκυκλιακὸν |[..]..νς ὂν ἐν δραχ(μαῖς). For ἐγκυκλιακός in description of the tax (rather than of the collector) cf. P. Mich. II 123 verso vii 19 δαπάνη(ς) ἐνκυκλιακο(ῦ). The problem is, what to supply in 7? The upsilon and sigma are good readings, not open to much doubt; they are preceded by lettertops difficult to interpret, perhaps most satisfactorily taken as]λο. So τέ]λους? But why the genitive? Hardly ὑπὲρ τέ]λους, even if there were room. τέ]λο{υ}ς, however desirable, arouses the misgivings to which the jettisoning of available evidence among deficient is properly liable. But I find no answer that saves the phenomena. τέλ(ος)] δέκατον (or any other fraction) cannot be read; nor does it seem to help if the following ον is taken not as ὂν but as the termination of our *verbum petitum* (it would be admissible in itself: for omission of the participle in this phrase, cf. I **56** 8).

8 The standing charge of 10 dr. occurs in various other documents relating to manumissions, viz. I **48, 49, 50**, XXXVIII **2843**, P. Lugd. Bat. XIII 24, cf. IV **722**. Usually without a name, it is here called the [πρ]οπρατικόν. So far as I know the only other occurrence of this word is at P. Col. inv. 480 (P. Col. I = W. L. Westermann, *Upon Slavery in Ptolemaic Egypt*; *c.* 198–197 B.C.) 14, where it is synonymous with προπωλητικόν (ibid. 9–10), which itself is found elsewhere only in the Revenue Laws of Ptolemy Philadelphus (SB *Beiheft* I) 55. 15. [προπρατικόν is unaccountably missing from all the standard lexica.] It is apparently not a brokerage fee but a charge for warranty against eviction: see, on προπωλητής and related words, J. Partsch, *Griechische Bürgschaftsrecht* i, 340–58, esp. 349 f. and 354 n. 3, cf. P. M. Meyer, *Jur. Pap.* 35. 1. 11 f., and F. Pringsheim, *Greek Law of Sale*, 429–44, esp. 441. In sales of the Roman period the warrantor is the vendor himself (Pringsheim 439 ff., Taubenschlag *Law*[2], 251 n. 4), but it now appears that in the case of manumissions it was the state that undertook the liability for any eviction of the freedman from his freedom. This interpretation is suitable for the Columbia papyrus, where the προπρατικόν/προπωλητικόν is payable τῇ πόλει, i.e. to Alexandria. The same explanation has been given of the charges paid as βεβαιωτικόν or ὑπὲρ βεβαιώσεως (P. M. Meyer, *Festschrift Otto Hirschfeld gewidmet*, 151). Pestman, *Marriage and Matrimonial Property in Ancient Egypt* 41, investigating property conveyances from bridegroom to bride, shows that πρόπρασις is equivalent to the demotic sḫ (n) db3 ḥd, the deed which declares that the purchase money has been paid in full and to the vendor's satisfaction and which precedes the vendor's relinquishing his title to the property (this

being effected by a further deed). If a comparable procedure is to be envisaged for manumissions, record of the payment of the προπρατικόν (the charge upon the πρόπρασις?) will presumably have served to give the freedman security from eviction once the transaction was completed.

The expansion προπ(ρατικοῦ) is now available for **50** 3 (A.D. 100), a banker's chit recording payment on a manumission.

20 ὑ[με]ῖν would satisfy the exiguous remains.

20–2 Perhaps 20 περὶ ἧ[ς —, 22 δημ[οσιώσεως τετελειωμένης, cf. IX **1200** 7.

22]λιοπης: the reading is secure (not, e.g., ἐνκύκ]λιον ἧς). A more precise identification than is given in the first letter? ἐπικεκλημένης Καλ]λιόπης? μητρὸς Καλ]λιόπης?

25–6 τὸ ὑπόμνημα] ἐπιδέδωκα: 'I have made the declaration', cf. I **73** 23–4.

3242. Declaration of Property

22 3B.15/G(4–7)(a)   15 × 16 cm.   A.D. 185–7

A general property return, complete except at the foot, blank on the back, addressed to both the strategus and the royal scribe by Dionysia, an Antinoite woman, acting through Sarapion son of Longinus of Oxyrhynchus. She registers, in response to a call issued by the prefect Pomponius Faustianus (185–7), the property that she owned at the village of Sko in the Oxyrhynchite nome.

In form it follows the usual pattern, see A. M. Harmon, *YCS* 4 (1934) 135 ff.; S. Avogadro, *Aegyptus* 15 (1935) 131 ff.; and Cl. Préaux, *CÉ* 75 (1963) 117 ff.; other parallel documents: P. Harris, 74 (A.D. 99); P. Merton I 13 (98–102); P. Mil. Vogl. III 191–2 (130–1); PSI (ed. Bartoletti, 1965) no. 9 (161–2); PSI XIII 1325 (176–80); BGU XI 2022 (202); 2023 (198–201); P. Strasb. 192 (207); SB VIII 9878 (259); P. Vindob. Boswinkel 3 (279).

The present document is the first return known to me in response to a general call issued by Pomponius Faustianus. A point of interest is that Dionysia reports that part of her property was registered in the public records by her ancestors in the periods after the third year of Vespasian (A.D. 70/1) and the first of Titus (A.D. 79). This means that the property was preserved in the same family for over a hundred years. This is perhaps the longest history of a property in the same family that has been reported in the papyri of the period (Harmon, op. cit. p. 141, considered thirty-five years the longest history of a family property he was able to trace).

→   Διοφάνει cτρ(ατηγῷ) καὶ Ἁρποκρατίωνι βασιλ(ικῷ) γρ(αμματεῖ)
        παρὰ Διονυcίας Cαραπιάδος τῆς καὶ Θαμουνίου Ἀντινοΐ-
        δος διὰ Cαραπίωνος Λογγείνου ἀπ' Ὀξυρύγχων πόλεως. ἀπο-
        γράφομαι κατὰ τὰ κελευσθέντα ὑπὸ Πομπωνίου Φαυστια-
5   νοῦ τοῦ λαμπροτάτου ἡγεμόν[ο]ς τὸ ὑπάρχον μοι περὶ
        κώμην Cκὼ τῆς ἄνω το(παρχίας) ἐκ τοῦ Ἀπολλωνίου κλήρου
        ἀμπέλου ἀρχαίας ἐν ᾗ φοίνεικ(ες) καὶ ἀγρόδ(ρυα) καὶ καλαμεί-

1 cτρ⳽, βασιλ γρ⳽   2–3 αντινοϊδος   6 το)   7 φοινεικ⳽, αγρο⳽ l. ἀκρόδ(ρυα)

ας (δίμοιρον) μέρος (ἀρουρῶν) δ (ἡμίσους) ις λβ οὐςῶν (τέταρτον) μέρος ἀπὸ ἐπιγρ(αφομένων)

ὅλων (ἀρουρῶν) ιη (τετάρτου) ῆ οὐςῶν ἐν ὀνόματι τῶν προγόνων μου

10 δηλωθεισῶν διὰ δημοσίων λόγων ἐν τοῖς ἀπὸ γ (ἔτους) Οὐες(πασιανοῦ) καὶ α (ἔτους) Τίτου χρόνοις, παραδείςου ὁμοίως ἐκ νότ(ου) τῆς α(ὐτῆς) ἀμ(πέλου) cὺν διαψείλ(ῳ) (δίμοιρον) μέρος (ἀρούρης) αῆ δηλωθέντος διὰ δη- μοςίων λόγων ἀνῆχθ(αι) ἐν τοῖς προκειμένοις χρόνοις, οἰκοπέδ(ων) καὶ διαψείλ(ου) καὶ κυκλευτηρίου καὶ (ἡμίσους) μέρους

15 ὑδρευμάτων (δίμοιρον) μέρος (ἀρούρης) (τέταρτον) ῆ [ὅ]περ ἐςτὶν τὸ ἐπιβάλ- λον ἐμοί τε καὶ κοινωνῷ μου [(τέταρτον)] μέρος τῆς διὰ δη- μοςίων λόγω[ν ἀ]ναγραφομένης ἐν οἰκο(πέδοις) (ἀρούρης) α (ἡμίσους). γείτ[ο- νες τῶν προκειμένων νότ(ου) κ[αὶ] ἀπηλ(ιώτου) ἐμοῦ καὶ κοινω- νοῦ μου, βορρᾶ ἄμπελος Cαραπ[ί]ωνος Ἀνδρονείκου,

20 λιβὸς ἄμπελος. καὶ ὁμοίως ἀ[πογ]ρ(άφομαι) τὸ ὑπάρχον μοι (δίμοιρον) μέρος περὶ τὴν α(ὐτὴν) Cκὼ ἐκ τ[οῦ] Ποςιδίππου κλή(ρου) παραδ(είςου) (ἀρουρῶν) ις̣ .[..]. ῆ. γείτον[ες] πάντοθεν ἐμοῦ καὶ [κ]οινω[νοῦ μου]. καὶ ὁμ[οίως ἀ]πογρ(άφομαι) περ[ὶ] Μ[ο- νίμου ..[.........].κ.[........]...[

25 ..[...]...[

. . . . . .

8 β), Ꝃ δ∟ις∧λβ, δ΄, l. (τετάρτου) μέρους, επιγρς   9 Ꝃ∟ιηδ΄ῆ   10 γςουες)   11 ας, νοτ, ᾱ
12 αμ), διαψειλβ),Ꝃ∟αῆ   13 ανηχθ   14 οικοπεδ, διαψειλ, ς΄   15 β), Ꝃ∟δῆ   17 οικο)
Ꝃ∟ας΄   18 νοτ, απηλ   20 α[πογ]ρς   21 β), ᾱ, κλη   22 παραδ Ꝃ∟   23 α]πογρς

'To Diophanes, strategus, and Harpocration, royal scribe, from Dionysia, daughter of Sarapias alias Thamounion, of Antinoopolis, by agency of Sarapion son of Longinus, from the city of the Oxyrhynchi. I register in accordance with the orders issued by Pomponius Faustianus, the most glorious prefect, the two-thirds share of an ancient vineyard, in which there are date palms and fruit trees, and of a reed bed, which I hold in the vicinity of the village of Sko in the upper toparchy from the *clerus* of Apollonius, amounting to $4 + \frac{1}{2} + \frac{1}{16} + \frac{1}{32}$ aruras, which are a fourth share from the full listed number of $18 + \frac{1}{4} + \frac{1}{8}$ aruras, which are in the name of my forebears and reported in the public records in the periods from the 3rd year of Vespasian and from the 1st year of Titus; likewise a two-thirds share of garden-land on the south side of the same vineyard including infertile ground, amounting to $1\frac{1}{8}$ aruras, reported in the public records to have resulted from agricultural improvements in the aforesaid period; a two-thirds share of building land and infertile land and a water-wheel and of a half share of water sources, amounting to $\frac{1}{4} + \frac{1}{8}$ aruras, which is the quarter share devolving upon me and my partner of the $1\frac{1}{2}$ aruras listed in the public records as building land. Boundaries of the aforesaid properties are:— on the south and east, property belonging to me and my partner; on the north, a vineyard belonging to Sarapion son of Andronicus; on the west, a vineyard. And likewise I register the two-thirds share of garden-land, amounting to $16 + ?$ aruras, which I hold in the vicinity of the same (village of) Sko from the *clerus* of Posidippus. Boundaries on all sides are:—property belonging to me and my partner. And likewise I register in the vicinity of Monimu . . . .'

1 It is perhaps improbable that this Diophanes was identical with a Diophanes who—ten years later—appears as strategus of the Oxyrhynchite nome, *c.* 197–200. There are other strategi in the interval, see H. Henne, *Liste des stratèges*, 31, and G. Mussies, P. Lugd. Bat. XIV, p. 26, no. 275. Another strategus, Isidorus, was in office on 25 May A.D. 186 (II **237** vi 32–6). It is not clear whether this Diophanes was his predecessor or his successor.

Harpocration is already known as royal scribe and deputy strategus in A.D. 186, see II **237** vi 36, vii 10, SB I 5693. 4, XXIV **2414** 22?

4 Pomponius Faustianus was prefect of Egypt at least from December/January A.D. 185/6 to September A.D. 187, see *BASP* 4 (1967) 102.

Here we have a general call for property registration later than the one issued by M. Sempronius Liberalis, see Omaggio all' XI Congresso Internazionale di Papirologia (PSI ed. Bartoletti) 9. 5 n.

10–11 ἀπὸ γ (ἔτους) Οὐεc(παcιανοῦ) καὶ α (ἔτους) Τίτου. It is not clear what the two dates signify. One possibility is that they are the dates of the two earliest general property returns in which the family of Dionysia laid claim to this land. They are not, however, among the known dates of the general returns listed in *YCS* 4 (1934) 184.

The long history of this family property is another indication of the stable and prosperous conditions of the second century. Other cases of family property with a history of two or more generations from the papyri of the second century are those of the families of Heron son of Hermanoubion, BGU III 959 (149), P. Berl. Leihg. 18 (163), of M. Valerius Turbo, BGU VII 1574, 1565 (169), 1662 (181–2), of Onesicrates son of Ptolemaeus, BGU III 919 (second century), of Sabina Apollonarion, PSI XIII 1325 (176–80).

22 (ἀρουρῶν) ιϛ . . [. .] . ῆ. Before ῆ = (ὀγδόου) the trace looks like the upright of d = (τετάρτου). If so, probably the whole figure ought to be read ιϛ ʃ′ d ῆ = 16 + ½ + ¼ + ⅛, even though the lacuna seems somewhat too wide. The oblique stroke after the (ἡμίcουc) sign may have been unusually long.

3243. REPORT TO A PREFECT OF EGYPT

14 1B.202/L(b)   Fr. 1, 32 × 20 cm.   A.D. 214/15

A reply to the prefect of Egypt, Septimius Heraclitus, from the strategus of the Themistes and Polemon districts of the Arsinoite nome, concerning corn supplies. It is written in an accomplished 'chancery' hand (which shows that proficiency in this impressive style was not confined to the prefect's office), stylistically looser than the otherwise very similar XIX **2227**, which is roughly contemporary. Alpha and omicron occasionally 'float' to the top of the line, as in P. Berol. 6925 (*tav.* 2 of the plates given by G. Cavallo in *Aeg.* 45 (1965) 215–49). The calligraphic intent is underlined by the presence of two rough breathings. The letter extended to a second column, which is mostly lost, so that the date clause is missing, but it is the balance in hand from the harvest of Caracalla's 22nd year (A.D. 213/14) that is in question, and the document is probably to be dated around the end of 214 (see further 2 n.). It may be that the prefect's demand for the information sought had been prompted by the impending imperial visitation: cf. PSI VI 683, a survey undertaken on the orders of the epistrategus on the occasion of Septimius Severus' visit to Egypt in 199. **3243** was presumably intended, when written, to be the copy actually sent to Alexandria, but it was probably rejected on account of the original omission of the imperial titles.

The papyrus reveals that the Mons Claudianus was still being quarried in this period. Hitherto the latest evidence of its exploitation has been Hadrianic.

On the back are three columns of private accounts (not transcribed) covering a period of just over a month. The most frequently recurring item is wine.

Fr. 1

Col. i   Col. ii

→   Αὐρηλίωι Ϲ[ε]πτιμίωι Ἡρακλείτωι τῶι λαμπρ[οτάτω]ι

        ἡγεμόνι (vac.) Καλπούρνιος Ἰϲίδωρος ὁ καὶ Ἁρπ[ο]κρατί-

        ων ϲτρατηγὸϲ Ἀρϲινοΐτου Θεμίϲτου καὶ Πολ[έ]μων[οϲ

        μερίδων   (vac.)   χαίρειν.

5   Λαβών ϲου γράμματα, δέϲποτα ἡγεμών, προϲτάϲϲοντα

        ἐμοί τε καὶ τῷ τῆϲ ἑτέραϲ μερίδοϲ ϲτρατηγῷ τὴν ἀπὸ

        καρπῶν τοῦ δευτέρου καὶ εἰκοϲτοῦ ἔτουϲ τοῦ κυρίου   δ[

        ἡμῶν αὐτοκράτοροϲ Ϲεουήρου᾽ Ἀντωνίνου Εὐτυχοῦϲ Εὐϲεβοῦϲ   ε[

                Ϲεβαϲτοῦ᾽ λοιπογραφουμένην

        εἰϲ ἣν ἡμέραν κομιζόμεθά ϲου τὰ γράμμ[α]τα ἐν

10   το]ῖϲ θηϲα[υροῖϲ ν]έμειν καὶ δ[ηλ]ῶϲαί ϲοι πᾶ[ν τὸ] ἀπο-

        κείμενον μ[έτ]ρον προϲθ[εῖϲι] πόϲον ἤ[δη] παρ-

        εδόθη εἴϲ τε τροφὰϲ κτηνῶ[ν] τῶν ἐν Θηβα[ίδ]ι ϲτρα-

        τευμάτων καὶ εἰϲ χρείαϲ τῶν ὑπηρετούντων   ].,[

        τοῖϲ Πορφυρειτικοῖϲ καὶ Κλαυδιανοῖϲ μετάλλοιϲ   του[

15   ἔτι τε κ[αὶ] εἰϲ τὰϲ ἐπὶ τ[όπ]ων γεινομέν[αϲ] ϲυνηθε[(ἔτουϲ) .[

2 ἰϲιδωροϲ   3 αρϲινοϊτου   9 ην̈ (sic)   13 ϋπηρετουντων

Fragments of col. ii?

Fr. 2   Fr. 3

  .   .   .   .

         ].[   ].[...].[

     ]ρουκαια..[   ]ν μέρο[ϲ] καὶ [

    ἑ]κατέρου τὴν π.[   ]θαι μέτρον τι ὠ[

     ]ν τῶν ἀπὸ του.[   ] δαπανήματα κ[

5   ]ειϲ τε ϲτρατιωτικ[5   ]ου μέροϲ επ[

    ].πωενδαπ.να[   ].οταξ[..]τα[

    ]αϲθη.[..].ϲκα.[   ]ιθ.[

    ἐπι]ϲτοληι[.   .   .   .

3 ὠ

Fr. 2 6]. πω ἐν δαπάνα[ιϲ? The first letter is probably alpha or epsilon (not rho, nor iota).
7 Θηβ[αίδ]οϲ looks likely.

Fr. 4

. . . . .

]ϲ εἰϲ τὰϲ πρ[

]πενευθει[

].ουγε[

. . . . .

'To Aurelius Septimius Heraclitus, most illustrious prefect, from Calpurnius Isidorus also called Harpocration, strategus of the Themistes and Polemon departments of the Arsinoite, greeting.

On receipt of your letter, my lord prefect, instructing me and the strategus of the other division to distribute(?) the ⟨grain?⟩ that is in balance in the granaries from the harvest of the 22nd year of our lord emperor Severus Antoninus Felix Pius Augustus up to the date we receive your letter and to report to you the total amount remaining, adding how much has already been given over for provisions for the animals of the troops in the Thebaid and for the requirements of the men serving in the Porphyrite and Claudian quarries, as well as for the customary local . . .'

Col. i 1 The earliest attested date for the prefecture of Septimius Heraclitus is 16 March, A.D. 215 (Stein, *Die Präfekten*, 115). The fact that the strategus here does not yet call himself Aurelius makes it likely that Heraclitus was in office at any rate a few months before then (see next note).

2 The strategus is new in this nome, i.e. not in G. Bastianini, *Gli strateghi dell' Arsinoites in epoca romana*, p. 57. In XXXVIII **2876** Calpurnius Isidorus also called Harpocration is strategus of the Memphite nome. The editors put forward reasons for dating that document 'early in the sole reign of Caracalla' (14–16 n.). They mention the document published under this number and also another, published in this volume as **3263**: in **3263**, written just after 29 August A.D. 215, our man is, as here, strategus in the Arsinoite, but he appears with the additional nomen Aurelius. Evidently he acquired the name in the course of his tenure of office in the Arsinoite, as a result of the Antonine Constitution. The Constitution had begun to affect nomenclature early in the 23rd year of Caracalla, A.D. 214/15 (*JEA* 48 (1962) 124–31), so that the absence of 'Aurelius' here establishes a rough *terminus ante quem*. But the reference to the λοιπογραφουμένη of the 22nd year suggests that the end of that year is passed (otherwise, moreover, one might expect specifically 'of the *current* (τοῦ ἐνεϲτῶτοϲ) 22nd year'), i.e. that the prefect's letter to which the present document is the response was written later than 29 August 214. A date in the last few months of 214 is therefore probable.

Isidorus' immediate predecessor in the Arsinoite nome may have been the well-known Sarapion also called Apollonianus (or Apollonius) who was strategus there in 210, but this cannot be regarded as certain, for Sarapion is last attested in that office on 31 July of that year (P. Flor. III 317; it is unsafe to infer from XVIII **2184** that he was still in office in 214).

5 δέϲποτα ἡγεμών is a deferential phrase, used elsewhere only in private petitions to the prefect. It may be that the strategus is asking for an extension of time or some other indulgence.

6 The prefect's letter will have been addressed simply ϲτρατηγοῖϲ Ἀρϲινοΐτου, cf. PSI VI 683. 5.

τῷ τῆϲ ἑτέραϲ μερίδοϲ ϲτρατηγῷ: the strategus of the Heraclides division at this time may or may not have been either Aurelius Aelius(?) Isidorus, in office some time between January and May 216, or Aurelius Hierax also called Ammonius, attested for May–June 213 (Mussies, P. Lugd. Bat. XIV p. 18; Henne, *Liste des stratèges*, p. 57; Bastianini, op. cit., pp. 47 f.).

6–8 τὴν . . . λοιπογραφουμένην: sc. ἀννῶναν? But its ellipse at so early a date would be surprising. Perhaps the noun has been inadvertently omitted: ὑπόϲταϲιν (P. Tebt. II 336. 7), κριθήν?

λοιπογραφεῖν, an accounting term, means to carry over, whether in arrears (debit) or in balance (credit): cf. P. Col. V 1 verso 1a introd., *Berl. Leihgabe* 1 recto iii 20 n. The item of reference will be the assessment of corn for dispatch to Alexandria and thence to Rome. ἡ λοιπογραφουμένη could theoretically be corn which should already have been sent but which (whether through administrative incompetence or deficiency of the harvest) had not been (cf. XXII **2341** 25), or the surplus remaining in hand after the amount due had been sent off. Which meaning it has here will depend on the verb governing it in 10; if ν]έμειν, either interpretation will give sense of a kind, see note below.

10 ν]έμειν: only slight traces of ϵ and μ remain, but the strong stylization of the hand makes for precision in identification. Of ϵ there remains only the top of the upper loop, but any reading other than ϵ would be forced. μ is represented by a trace on an isolated fibre level with the foot of the following ϵ, and lower and to the left of this by a rightward hook, characteristic of mu but found now and again also with kappa, and incompatible I would say with any other letter unless anomalously formed. If the letter were kappa one would expect other parts of it to be visible, perhaps the top of its vertical and the extremity of its lower leg. But mu is not entirely free from objection either, for elsewhere it is invariably ligatured to the following letter, in the case of epsilon to the top of the lower half (the top half being ligatured in turn to the next letter again); whereas here there is no stroke coming in to the middle of epsilon. θησα[υροῖϲ will have taken up most of the lacuna: it could contain one more letter, perhaps two, hardly more.

Unless some such error as γεμ⟨ίζ⟩ειν is postulated, ν]έμειν is practically unavoidable. If it is right, one must assume that the corn in question was assigned to the use of the military (cf. J. Lesquier, *L'Armée romaine*, 350–68), and that the strategi had had previous instructions specifying the amounts and the recipients (cf. e.g. P. Amh. II 107). Whatever the verb, ἐν τοῖϲ θηϲαυροῖϲ construes not with it but with λοιπογραφουμένην, cf. BGU III 976. 24, 977. 3.

ν]έμειν, however, makes it difficult to extract a reasonable sense. If the strategi are to disburse the balance (i.e. the corn left over after the quota for Alexandria had been filled and the military requisitions met), the second instruction, to inform the prefect of the amount left in store, is nonsensical, for there will of course be none. There are various ways of circumventing this (λοιπογραφουμένην might not mean in balance but in arrears, so that the amount of the civil annona in arrears is to be diverted to local needs; or τὸ ἀποκείμενον μέτρον includes some kind of grain that does not come under ἡ λοιπογραφουμένη, or grain from previous years), but it remains true that if the communication is connected with the impending imperial visit, as seems very likely, the orders one might expect would be, as Mr. Parsons suggests, *not* to make any further distribution but on the contrary to hold all remaining stocks in store until the government should know what resources are available. Working then from sense to text: ἔχειν (or ϲχεῖν, intrinsically preferable but palaeographically inferior) is a forced and scarcely tolerable reading, while ἕκειν (l. ἔχειν) would involve a phonetic error not uncommon but in this document unexpected and unparalleled. ἀρι]θμεῖν (virtually a technical term of book-keeping and stock-taking) has stronger claims to consideration, for θ, though not a wholly satisfactory reading, is perhaps an acceptable one; however, I am not sure that the lacuna can accommodate so much.

11 προϲθ[εῖϲι] πόϲον: otherwise προϲθ[εῖϲι]ν ὅϲον. The participle may have been in another case, but προϲθέντεϲ, the likeliest alternative, would be rather too long for the lacuna.

14 On the Mons Porphyrites and Mons Claudianus, see D. M. Meredith, 'Roman Remains in the Eastern Desert of Egypt' *JEA* 38 (1952) 94–111, and refs. ibid. 98 n. 4, 101 n. 3. For the military supervision of the quarries see Lesquier, op. cit. 239–43, and A. C. Johnson, *Economic Survey*, 241 f. The papyrus demonstrates that the Mons Claudianus was still being exploited under Caracalla. The general assumption, from which Meredith however demurs (pp. 109 f.), has been that it was permanently abandoned after Hadrian (C. Préaux, *CÉ* 51 (1951) 359).

3244. OATH OF OFFICE[1]

3 1B.81/C(1)b   8·0 × 20·7 cm.   3 December A.D. 228

This is a piece of a *tomos synkollesimos* containing two joined copies of the same document (cf. XXXVI **2764**). The right-hand piece, of which the text is here presented, is complete at the top and at both margins. Of the left-hand piece not much survives—merely enough to show that the texts are identical and to supply the date

[1] Described as P. Oxy. ined. 15 in A. K. Bowman, *The Town Councils of Roman Egypt* (American Studies in Papyrology XI, 1971), Appendix IV.

missing in line 32. In the same folder were seven other scraps, including a piece possibly from the same *tomos* of which the right-hand text preserves parts of sixteen lines of a similar document.

The text is an oath of office of the familiar type, see E. Seidl, *Der Eid*, 76–80, P. Leit. 12 and most recently XXXVI **2764** with citation of similar documents. In this case the office—that of supplying fish for the city—is probably not liturgical; more likely the man works as a *misthotes* under the supervision of the agoranomi or eutheniarchs. For a similar oath applied to a non-liturgic office see I **83** where an egg-seller undertakes to sell his produce only in the market.

Aurelius Sarapion son of Achilleus addresses Aurelius Theon also called Maximus, a (previously unattested) prytanis of the bule of Oxyrhynchus, swearing to fulfil the duty of supplying fish and and offering as his surety Aurelius Theon son of Theon. The back of the papyrus contains two dockets one of which probably describes the contents of the whole *tomos*; the other, which I have not been able to read fully, probably refers only to this text.

An additional point of interest is the occurrence on this papyrus of an example of the *damnatio memoriae* of Severus Alexander (see 11 n.).

→ (m. 1) Αὐρηλίῳ Θέωνι τῷ καὶ
     Μαξίμωι γυμν(ασιαρχ) ἐνάρχ(ῳ)
     πρυτάνει τῆς Ὀξ(υρυγχιτῶν) πόλ(εως) διέπο[ν-]
     τι καὶ τ[ὰ π]ολειτ(ικὰ) τῆς α(ὐτῆς) πόλ(εως)
 5 Αὐρήλι[ο]ϲ Ϲαραπίων Ἀχιλ-
     λ[έ]ωϲ μητρὸϲ Διεῦτοϲ
     ἀπ' Ὀξυ(ρυγχιτῶν) πόλεωϲ μεταβό-
     λοϲ τῆϲ αὐτῆϲ πόλεωϲ.
     Ὀμνύω τὴν Μάρκου
 10 Αὐρηλίου Ϲεουήρου
     [[Ἀλεξανδρου]] Καίϲαροϲ
     τοῦ κυρίου τύχην χο-
     ρηγήϲειν τῇ πόλει
     ἀνενδεῶϲ τ[ὸν]
 15 ἰχθὺν ἀπὸ ιϛ' τοῦ
     ὄντοϲ μηνὸϲ Χοιὰκ ἐφ'
     ὅϲον οἱ τοῦ Μονίμου

2 γυμνϛ εναρχ 3 οξϛ πολ 4 [π]ολειτ τηϲ α) πολ 7 οξυπολεωϲ 12 Filler at end of line (also in 13, 15); final letter extended in 7, 9, 10, 17, 18, 19, 23 15 ἰχθυν?

ἐποικίου ἁλεεῖς
ἐργάζονται εἰς τὸ ἐν
20   μηδενὶ μεμφθῆναι
ἢ ἔνοχος [ε]ἴην τῷ ὅρκῳ.
παρέσχο[ν] δὲ ἐμαυτοῦ
ἐγγυητὴν Αὐρήλ[ιο]ν
Θέωνα Θέωνος
25   μητ(ρὸς) Διογενίδος [τ]ῆς α(ὐτῆς) πόλ(εως)
παρόντα καὶ εὐδοκοῦν-
τα. (ἔτους) η′
Αὐτοκράτορος Καίσαρος
Μάρκου Αὐρηλίου
30   Ϲεουήρου ⟦Ἀλεξάνδρου⟧
Εὐσ[ε]βοῦς Εὐτυχοῦς
Ϲεβαστοῦ Χ[ο]ιὰκ [ζ′].
(m. 2)   Αὐρήλιος Ϲα[ραπίων]
Ἀ]χιλλ[έως ὤμοσα]
35   τὸν ὅρκ]ον ὡ[ς πρόκειται.]
        Traces of two more lines

.   .   .   .

Back ↓ (m. 3)   ἐγγυητὴς Αὐρήλιος
Θέων ε.δ.λ...
40   σουχειωμεν[.].

→ (m. 4)   χειρόγ(ραφα) ἐγγύ(ων)

25 μη^τ, πο^λ   α̣∴27 ∠ η′   39 smudged; attempted erasure?   41 χειρογ ͦ εγγυ

(1st hand) 'To Aurelius Theon also called Maximus (ex-?) gymnasiarch, prytanis-in-office of the city of the Oxyrhynchites, administrator of the city funds of the same city, Aurelius Sarapion son of Achilleus, whose mother is Dieus, from the city of the Oxyrhynchites, merchant of the same city. I swear by the fortune of Marcus Aurelius Severus (Alexander) Caesar the lord that I will faultlessly provide fish for the city from the sixteenth of the present month Choiak as long as the fishermen of the village of Monimou are working, in such a way as to incur no blame or may I be liable to the consequences of the oath. And I present as my surety Aurelius Theon son of Theon, whose mother is Diogenis, of the same city, who is present and consenting. Year 8 of Imperator Caesar Marcus Aurelius Severus (Alexander) Pius Felix Augustus, Choiak [7]. (2nd hand) I, Aurelius Sarapion son of Achilleus, have sworn the oath as stated above ... Back: (3rd hand) Surety Aurelius Theon ... (4th hand) Deeds of surety.'

1–4 Aurelius Theon alias Maximus was previously unattested as prytanis, see A. K. Bowman, *The Town Councils of Roman Egypt*, 131. For the title διέπων καὶ τὰ πολιτικά, ibid. 59.

7–8 For μεταβόλοι of fish see WO II 647, 1449, PSI VII 737, WO I p. 136.

11 The name Alexander is obliterated here and in line 30, and also in the corresponding lines of the other copy. This is evidently an example of the *damnatio memoriae* of Severus Alexander which is known from Egyptian inscriptions (SB V 8478, 8482 = Lepsius, *Denkmäler* xii, Taf. 92, nos. 333 and 344, SB III 7018) and from elsewhere (cf. *RE* ii (1896), 2527). I have not been able to parallel this on papyrus. In P. Ryl. II 297 (descr.) where the editors report the obliteration of Augustus I find nothing corresponding to their description of the erasure.

12–13 χορηγήϲειν. For the term χορηγία applied to a non-liturgic office see XXXI 2569 15–16. Cf. also P. Lond. III 974 (p. 115), containing a declaration of surety for a καρπώνηϲ who is to supply fruit in Hermopolis; the verb there used is ὑπηρετέω. The situation in P. Got. 3 is probably different— the man who was to provide fish for the visit of Caracalla in A.D. 215–16 was εἰϲδοθείϲ (line 6), which indicates that the post was a liturgy.

16–17 ἐφ' ὅϲον. The reading is not certain, but we must have a phrase which connects with the following words to describe the conditions of the service. At the end of 16 we have really only a ligature leading from epsilon and no trace of a vertical. Omicron and sigma at the beginning of 17 fit the traces comfortably; the word ends with a short vertical which suits the right-hand stroke of nu. The phrase makes reasonable sense and implies that the fishing was a seasonal activity. An alternative possibility is ἕ|ωϲ ἄν... ἐργάζονται (1. ἐργάζωνται), i.e. 'until the fishermen ... are working', implying that he is to replace them. But this suits the traces less well and the sense is more difficult because it makes the man directly responsible for getting the fish, whereas a μεταβόλοϲ is more naturally understood as a middleman between the fishermen and the market. Unfortunately the other copy does not preserve this section.

18 On fishing in Egypt see San Nicolò, *Vereinswesen* i 94–7, Besta, *Aegyptus* 2 (1921), 67–74. Recently published documents connected with fishing are P. Leit. 14, P. Wis. 6 (cf. *ZPE* 12 (1973), 262), 37.

30 [[Ἀλεξάνδρου]]: see 11 n.

32 The date is supplied from the other copy where zeta is clearly to be seen.

33 ff. For the form of the endorsements see e.g. VI 972, XXXVI 2764. The last letter surviving in 35 is more like omega than the beginning of καί, making it unlikely that καὶ ἐκτελέϲω κτλ. was included here. The endorsement by the surety will have read: Αὐρήλιοϲ Θέων Θέωνοϲ ὀμόϲαϲ τὸν ὅρκον ἐγγυῶμαι τὸν Ϲαραπίωνα ὡϲ πρόκειται (cf. XXXVI 2764 36–8), but the traces in the last two lines are too indeterminate to offer a reading.

39–40 This docket has escaped decipherment. Line 39 is somewhat smudged, but I do not think that ἐπιδέδωκα can be read. The second letter looks like nu, the fourth could be epsilon, but in the fifth there is no trace of the bottom stroke which delta would require. Line 40 is more frustrating because the first seven letters, at least, seem clear but make no sense in any plausible articulation. Ϲουχείῳ is the most plausible reading but there is no evidence for such a building in Oxyrhynchus, nor would its connection with the present document be easily explained. Ϲοῦχοϲ appears in XXXI 2598, but the editor reasonably suggests a connection with the Fayum. To read ϲοῦ χειρόγραφον *vel sim.* would be to force the orthography with no gain in understanding.

41 For this docket compare P. Lips. 52 verso.

3245. REPORT OF A PUBLIC PHYSICIAN[1]

7 1B.1/XI–XII(e)   11·6 × 19·3 cm.   A.D. 297

A piece of a *tomos synkollesimos* consisting of one fairly well preserved document, to which is attached, at the right-hand side, a small fragment of another document. The main piece is incomplete at the foot and lacks the ends of lines after line 7. Its back is blank, unlike that of the small fragment.

[1] Described as P. Oxy. ined. 18 in A. K. Bowman, *The Town Councils of Roman Egypt* (American Studies in Papyrology XI, 1971), Appendix IV.

The document contains a report submitted by a public physician and although the fragment on the right is too small to yield any significant information the occurrence of υπηρ[.]. [in line 24 (ὑπηρ[ε]τ[ου?) and the docket on the back suggest that the subject was the same. One significant point emerges in the fact that the report was submitted to a prytanis of Oxyrhynchus named Aurelius Aelurion alias Hesychius (here first attested as prytanis, see 3 n.). Such reports were usually addressed to the strategus in the third century, later to the logistes. The present text dates to a time of change in the municipal administration of Egypt. The position of strategus was clearly on the wane, but the institution of the logistes did not occur until several years later.

Documents of this type are reasonably common in the second, third, and fourth centuries A.D. They are discussed in detail by K. Sudhoff, *Ärtzliches aus griechischen Papyrusurkunden* (1909), 240 ff. and in P. Osl. III, pp. 100–3 (to the examples there cited add XII **1556** and PSI V 455). Apart from the address the present text does not differ significantly from the other examples. Aurelius Thonius, the public physician, reports that, as a result of instructions from the prytanis engendered by a petition from two Oxyrhynchites, he has examined the person in question and adds the details of the physical damage observed.

Col. i

→ (m. 1) ἐπὶ ὑπάτων τῶν κυρίων ἡμῶν Αὐτοκράτορος Μαξιμιανοῦ
    Σ[ε]βαστοῦ τὸ ε′ καὶ Μαξιμιανοῦ ἐπιφανεστάτου Καίσαρος τὸ β′.
    Αὐρηλίῳ Αἰλουρίωνι τῷ καὶ Ἡσυχίῳ γενομένῳ ὑπομ(νηματογράφῳ)
    β[ουλευ]τῇ τῆς λαμ(προτάτης) πόλεως τῶν Ἀλεξ(ανδρέων) γυμ(νασιαρχ)
                βουλ(ευτῇ) ἐνάρχῳ
5   πρυτάνι τῆς λαμ(πρᾶς) καὶ λαμ(προτάτης) Ὀξυρυγχιτῶν πόλεως
    παρὰ Αὐρηλίου Θωνίου ἀπὸ τῆς αὐτῆς πόλεως
    δημοσίου ἰατροῦ. ἐπετράπην ὑπὸ σοῦ διὰ Αὐρηλ(ίου)
    Εἰρηναί[ο]υ ὑπηρέτου τῆς τάξεως ἐκ βιβλι[δίων ἐπι-]
    δ]οθέντων σοι ὑπὸ Αὐρηλίων Διδύμου καὶ Πτολε[μα]ί[ου]
10   Διονυσίου τοῦ καὶ Ἀρτεμιδώρου ἀμφοτέρω[ν ἀπὸ]
    τ]ῆς λαμ(πρᾶς) καὶ λαμ(προτάτης) Ὀξ(υρυγχιτῶν) πόλεως ὥστε ἐφιδεῖν τ[ὸν ἐνγεγραμ-]
    μένον τοῖς βιβλιδίο[ις] αὐτῶν Παταρε[ῦτα]
    καὶ ἣν ἐὰν καταλάβω διάθεσιν ἐνγράφως π[ροσφωνεῖν.]
    ὅθεν ἐφῖδον τοῦτο[ν] ἐν τῇ αὐτῇ πόλει ἐπὶ παρ[όντος]
15   τοῦ αὐτοῦ ὑπηρέτου ἔχοντα ἐπὶ τοῦ πήχους [τῆς δεξιᾶς]

3 υπομ𝄖   4 λαμ𝄖, αλεξ′ γυμ𝄖 βουλ   5 l. πρυτάνει, λαμ𝄖 και λαμ𝄖   7 ὑπο, αυρηλ
11 λαμ𝄖 και λαμ𝄖 οξ̄   14 l. ἐφεῖδον (cf. Mayser-Schmoll, I i pp. 175–6)   15 ὑπηρετου

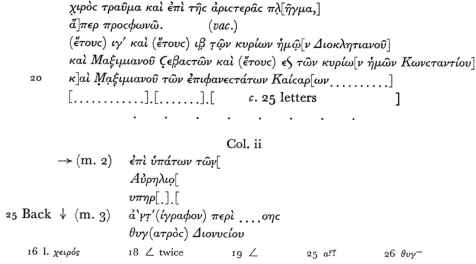

χιρὸς τραῦμα καὶ ἐπὶ τῆς ἀριϲτερᾶϲ πλ[ῆγμα,]
ἅ]περ προϲφωνῶ.   (*vac.*)
(ἔτους) ιγ΄ καὶ (ἔτους) ιβ τῶν κυρίων ἡμῶ[ν Διοκλητιανοῦ]
καὶ Μαξιμιανοῦ Ϲεβαϲτῶν καὶ (ἔτους) ες τῶν κυρίω[ν ἡμῶν Κωνϲταντίου]
20   κ]αὶ Μαξιμιανοῦ τῶν ἐπιφανεϲτάτων Καίϲαρ[ων.........]
[............].[.......].[*c.* 25 letters   ]
·   ·   ·   ·   ·   ·   ·   ·   ·

Col. ii

→ (m. 2)   ἐπὶ ὑπάτων τῶγ[
          Αὐρηλιο[
          υπηρ[.].[
25 Back ↓ (m. 3)   ἀ`γτ΄(ίγραφον) περὶ ....οηϲ
          θυγ(ατρὸϲ) Διονυϲίου

16 l. χειρόϲ   18 ∠ twice   19 ∠   25 αργτ   26 θυγ⁻

(1st hand) 'In the consulship of our lords Imperator Maximianus Augustus for the fifth time and Maximianus the most illustrious Caesar for the second time. To Aurelius Aelurion also called Hesychius, formerly hypomnematographus, councillor of the most glorious city of the Alexandrians, (ex-?) gymnasiarch, councillor, prytanis-in-office of the glorious and most glorious city of the Oxyrhynchites from Aurelius Thonius from the same city, public physician. I was instructed by you through Aurelius Irenaeus, assistant of your office, in consequence of a petition presented to you by the Aurelii Didymus and Ptolemaeus, sons of Dionysius also called Artemidorus, both from the glorious and most glorious city of the Oxyrhynchites, to examine the Patareus mentioned in their petition and to make a written report on the condition in which I found him. Accordingly I examined this man in the same city in the presence of the same assistant, having on the forearm of his right hand a wound and on his left hand a blow. Which I accordingly report. Year 13 and year 12 of our lords Diocletian and Maximian Augusti and year 5 of our lords Constantius and Maximianus the most illustrious Caesars . . . (3rd hand) Copy concerning . . . . oe daughter of Dionysius.'

2 The letters after alpha of Ϲ[ε]βαϲτοῦ are virtually obliterated, but the numeral ε is clear.

3 Aelurion is known from PSI V 461. 9–10 (A.D. 290) where the name Ἡ[ϲυχίῳ may now be restored; he is here first attested as prytanis, see introd. and *The Town Councils of Roman Egypt*, 133.

12 The name at the end of the line is difficult to read. Παταρεῦϲ seems to fit best the surviving traces (it occurs in P. Mil. Vogl. II 110). Or is it the ethnic Παταρέ[α, 'the man from Patara'? Πατεββῆ[ν is also a possible reading.

16 πλ[ῆγμα. Lambda looks to be the best reading for the second letter. πληγή is far more common than πλῆγμα but the meaning of the latter is closer to what is required here; πληγή means the act of striking rather than the results of the act (cf. τύμματα πληγῶν, PSI V 455. 16–17). The remains do not suit πε[λίωμα, nor is it plausible to emend the text to π⟨ε⟩λ[ίωμα.

20 The month and day are lost at the end of the line.

21 A subscription by the physician will have followed here, as for example in VI **896** 37 ff.: ἐπιδέδωκα προϲφωνῶν ὡϲ πρόκειται. An oath is unusual in this type of document (P. Osl. III, p. 102).

25 ἀ`γτ΄(ίγραφον). The last two letters are written very cursively above the line and the first letter of περί has been corrected. The usual term for a document of this kind is προϲφώνηϲιϲ, but the initial letter certainly looks like alpha. As for the name, the last three letters seem secure but the beginning is very cramped and indistinct. In the absence of other suitable names Ἀρϲι´νόηϲ must be regarded as a possibility.

I

3246. Fragment of a Petition[1]

31 4B.11/B(1–2)a   20·5 × 7·7 cm.   A.D. 297/8(?)

A fragment of a petition of which virtually only the address survives. The only clue as to its content is the occurrence of the word χῶμα in 10. Several features of the papyrus suggest that this fragment was originally part of a large document. The first two preserved lines, which contain the date, are in a different hand from the rest. A trace of ink above the iota of Διοκλητ[ιανοῦ looks like the foot of a descender in a previous line. Lines 4 ff. are indented and we should therefore assume that the first three lines constitute the end of a document written above and that at line 4 a new document commences. The back of the papyrus is blank.

What is left of the document—an address to the strategus from five people including two women—contains a couple of points of interest. This strategus has only been attested once, in IX **1204** 2 where his name was read as Ζηνογένει. In line 4 of the present text we have Ζηναγένι and Dr. R. A. Coles, who has seen IX **1204**, kindly informs me that Ζηναγένει should be read there. The male petitioners carry a normal sequence of municipal titles, but the father of one of the women has the curious title ὑπομν(ηματο-γράφου) ἀπὸ cτεφάνου, a qualification which is, so far as I know, unparalleled. It is therefore difficult to elucidate its meaning, though it is obviously connected with the crown of office. Perhaps it means that the man had filled the office but not worn the crown, or vice versa (cf. SB V 7996. 97).

· · · · · · · ·

→   [*c.* 20 letters   ].[

(m. 1)   (ἔτους) ιδ καὶ ιγϛ´ τῶν κυρίων ἡμῶν Διοκλητ[ιανοῦ καὶ Μαξιμιανοῦ Cεβαcτῶν καὶ ϛϛ Κωνcταντίου καὶ

      Μαξιμιανοῦ τῶν ἐπιφανεcτάτων Κα[ιcάρων

(m. 2)   Αὐρηλίῳ Ζηναγένι cτρατηγῷ ᾿Οξυρυγχίτου[(vac.)

5   παρὰ Αὐρηλίων ῾Ωρίωνος τοῦ καὶ Cαραπίωνος γενομένου ὑπ[ομν]ημα(τογρά-
      φου) πρυταν(εύcαντος)

      καὶ Cεύθου τοῦ καὶ ῾Ωρίωνος ἀμφοτέρων γυμναcιάρχων καὶ Θωνίου το[ῦ]
      καὶ Θεογένους

      ἐξηγητοῦ καὶ Κλαυδίας ῾Ηλιοδώρας θυγατρὸς Κανωπίωνος γεν[ο]μένου ὑπο-
      μν(ηματογράφου) ἀπὸ

2 ⌐   4 l. Ζηναγένει, οξυρυγ᾿χιτου   5 υπ[ομν]ημαϛ´ πρυτανϛ´   7 υπομνϛ´

[1] Described as P. Oxy. ined. 11 in A. K. Bowman, *The Town Councils of Roman Egypt* (American Studies in Papyrology XI, 1971), Appendix IV. When that note was written **3247** (inv. no. the same) was thought to be another piece of the same document but subsequent examination shows this to be wrong, though the hands are quite similar.

ϲτεφάνου καὶ Τεχωϲοῦτοϲ τῆϲ καὶ Εὐδαιμονίδοϲ θυγατρὸϲ Διδύμ[ου] τοῦ καὶ
Εὐδαίμονοϲ γυμν(αϲιαρχ) βουλευτοῦ, τῶν πάντων τῆϲ λαμπρᾶϲ καὶ λαμ(προτά-
τηϲ) Ὀξυρυγχ[ι]τῶν πόλεωϲ,

10 καὶ [τῶν κ]οινωνῶν. ἔϲτιν τ[ο]ίνυν, ἄριϲτε τῶν [ϲτ]ρατ[ηγῶ]ν, χῶμα ἐν οἷϲ κε-

. . . .

9 γυμνϛ, λαμϛ

(1st hand) 'Year 14 and 13 of our lords Diocletian and Maximian Augusti and 6 of Constantius
and Maximian the most illustrious Caesars [month and day]. (2nd hand) To Aurelius Zenagenes,
strategus of the Oxyrhynchite from the Aurelii Horion also called Sarapion, formerly hypomnematographus and prytanis and Seuthes also called Horion, both gymnasiarchs, and Thonius also called
Theogenes, exegetes, and Claudia Heliodora daughter of Canopion formerly crowned (?) hypomnematographus and Techosous daughter of Didymus also called Eudaemon (ex- ?)
gymnasiarch, councillor, all of the glorious and most glorious city of the Oxyrhynchites, and their
partners. Best of the strategi, there is a dyke [on our land . . .]'

2 It is difficult to be sure that this constitutes another date for the office of Zenagenes (IX **1204**
is dated to A.D. 299) for two reasons: first, the reading of the date is not beyond doubt, though years
14 and 13 seem most likely; even if correct, it is not certain that this would necessarily refer to Zenagenes
since the indentation of the lines following suggests that this dating clause may well be the end of a document. In texts of this kind it is common to find documents ranging over more than one year so the
date of the petition to Zenagenes could be different. All that being said, however, the evidence of **3247** 17
(same inv. no.) makes it probable that Zenagenes was in fact strategus in 298. There is a Zenagenes
also in XVIII **2187** 30 (A.D. 304), but he has no title.

3 If this date clause is the end of a previous document the month and day will have concluded
this line.

5 The presidency of Aurelius Horion also called Sarapion was not previously attested.

7–8 ἀπὸ ϲτεφάνου: see introduction.

10 For the form of address cf. P. Cair. Isid. 64. 4. The plural relative which follows χῶμα presumably refers forward to something in the lost portion. The sense seems likely to be something like:
ἐν οἷϲ κε[κτήμεθα ἐδάφεϲι . . . .

3247. FRAGMENT OF A PETITION[1]

31 4B.11/B(1–2)a   11·2 × 21·1 cm.   16 August, A.D. 298

On this papyrus are preserved the left-hand sides of 23 lines of a petition, written
in a hand very similar to the second hand of **3246**. To judge from what is missing of the
date clause in line 22 the surviving portion represents little better than a third of the
original piece. The back of the papyrus is blank.

Since so much is missing it is impossible to reconstruct the sense of the petition
with any plausibility but the remains, which include three occurrences of the word
ἀπαιτεῖν (10, 12, 13), suggest that the subject may have been the exaction of taxes.
Perhaps the petitioner is complaining of having been subjected to exactions beyond
the legal requirements. The addressee of the petition is probably the same as in **3246,**
the strategus Zenagenes.

[1] See footnote to **3246.**

→   Αὐρηλ]ίῳ Ζην[αγένει

     .....] Ἀρτεμίδωρος [

     ....τ]ῆς πριουάτης τοῦ κυρίου μου [

     τάξει ἀποκατασταθῆναι ὡς τὰ περὶ τοτ.[

5   πρότερον Ἀκοντίου περὶ κώμην Μερμ[έρθα

     κατὰ τὴν ἐμὴν ἀπουσίαν ὄντος περ[

     ων Πασίωνος καὶ Ἀμμώνιος ἀμφότερο[ι

     εἴκοσι ἀλλὰ καὶ ὑπὲρ ὧν ἡ σύμβιος Κλαυδί[α

     φορτία ἀρουρῶν τριῶν ἐκτεθίσης .[

10   σαρων ὁ τῶν ἀπαιτηθέντων ὑπὸ .[

     τακοσίας εἴκοσι. τὸ μὲν οὖν ἑκάστου κεραμ[ίου

     παιτῆσθαι ξέστας οἴνου χιλίου⟨ς⟩ ἑξακος[ίους

     τούτους εἰς τὴν νῦν ἀπαιτουμένην.[

     χιμαῖα γράμματα λάβωμαι κα[τε]πείγεσθαι [

15   .[.].[..].α...[..].τα.χας.[ἵ]να μηδέν σοι [

     στρατιώτην κατακελ[ε]ύσειν τοῦ ...[

     τα. (ἔτους) ιδ″ καὶ ιγ″ καὶ ϛ″ .[

     μο....οις οἴνου κεραμι[

     καὶ τούτων τὰ ναῦλα τῆς Θηβαΐδ[ος

20   κεράμια ἑκατὸν καὶ τούτων τ.[

     νος ὀφ(ικιάλιος?) ἐπάρχου οἴνου κεραμ[ι—

     Διοκλητιανοῦ καὶ Μαξιμιανοῦ Ϲ[εβαστῶν

     Καισάρων, Μεσορὴ κγ‾.

---

9 l. ἐκτεθείσης   19 θηβαϊδ[

1 Although there is only a very narrow bit of papyrus above this line there are no traces of ink and it seems probable that this was the first line of the document. The name of the strategus Zenagenes should certainly be restored here (cf. **3246**). If he was in office in 298 (line 17) we may now extend his tenure of the post (cf. IX **1204**, A.D. 299). The great width of the document will easily have accommodated the names of the addressee and the petitioner.

3 This must be a reference to the *magister rei privatae*, and, as such, will be the earliest occurrence of this office. The earliest known holder of the post was Pomponius Domnus who was in office in Thoth of 298 (P. Beatty Panop. 1. 120). Since the date of the present text is only a month earlier than that (cf. 17 n.) it is not unreasonable to suppose that his name will have occurred here. By A.D. 299 Pomponius Domnus appears to have become *rationalis* (IX **1204** 12). The form of the reference will be something like: τῇ τοῦ διασημοτάτου μαγίστρου τ]ῆς πριουάτης τοῦ κυρίου μου[name .....] τάξει.

5 Ἀκοντίου. The name is not in *NB* or Foraboschi, *Onomasticon Papyrologicum Alterum*.

14 I am indebted to Dr. Rea for the suggestion that this should be restored as ἀποχιμαῖα (cf. ἀπόχιμος in P. Cair. Preis. 13; 13; 14. 13). *Addendum lexicis*, if correct.

16 There is no obvious explanation for the fact that this and the following lines are indented about 2 cm. But since it is clear that this line does not begin a sentence it can hardly be the start of a new document. καταϲκελ[ε]ύϲειν could be interpreted as κατὰ κελ[ε]υϲειν (l. κέλευϲιν), in which case it might be followed by τοῦ διᾳ[ϲημοτάτου, i.e. 'according to the order of the most perfect . . .'. Either the name or the title of a high-ranking equestrian official would be suitable to complete the phrase.

17 The date is A.D. 297–8. Line 22 will also have contained a year date, preceding the month and day in line 23. When a papyrus contains more than one document the year dates need not necessarily be the same, but since there is no indication that this is the case here (see 16 n.) it seems probable that the date in 22 will have been the same as that in 17.

19 ναῦλα: see O. M. Pearl, *TAPA* 83 (1952) 74–9.

22–3 See 17 n.

3248. FRAGMENT OF AN OFFICIAL DIARY[1]

22 3B.14/C(4–7)b   7·0 × 9·5 cm.   Third century

This small scrap of papyrus contains the beginnings of lines of what must have been an interesting document. Unfortunately only part of the text, at the left-hand margin, has survived intact. The text consists of entries, arranged by date, referring to events of a public nature. Calendars containing lists of public festivals are known in the papyri, the most extensive Egyptian examples being XXXI 2553 and P. Osl. III 77. The present text, however, differs from these in two significant respects. First, it records events which apparently have no religious significance, e.g. a meeting of the town council (line 10); second, the entries are arranged under consecutive days at the end of Thoth and the beginning of Phaophi with no omissions, a special notation being used to mark blank days (lines 8–9). This is not paralleled in the religious calendars.

It seems most likely, in fact, that this is a fragment of an 'Amtstagebuch', of which the best known example is W. *Chr.* 41, recording the activities of a strategus. Other examples are PSI XIV 1444 and XLII 3072–4. The present text, however, does not seem to be concerned with the strategus. Perhaps the best clue to its nature comes in line 12 where ὁ ἐξηγ[ητής is mentioned immediately after the date. Given the format of the document, this seems to support the idea that the official whose activities are recorded here was the exegetes, perhaps the president of the κοινόν of exegetae, or one of the κοινόν serving a term of duty on a rota. The entry in line 10 conforms with the theory that the town council met regularly on the last day of the month (cf. *The Town Councils of Roman Egypt*, 36).

The back of the papyrus contains the faded remains of three lines, mostly illegible, perhaps by two different hands, the first of which (↓]τοῖϲ ἄλλοιϲ ἱεροῖϲ[ ) is separated from the others by a space of about 5 cm.

[1] Described as P. Oxy. ined. 24 in A. K. Bowman, *The Town Councils of Roman Egypt* (American Studies in Papyrology XI, 1971), Appendix IV.

$$\cdot \quad \cdot \quad \cdot \quad \cdot \quad \cdot$$

→   ..μ[.]..[

     ἔν τε τῷ Cεβαϲτ[είῳ

     ϟϛ′   ἱερᾶϲ οὔϲηϲ [

     καὶ Καπιτω[

5   κζ′   θεωρία ἐξ.[

     τῷ θεάτρῳ [

     ἐπιτελεϲθει.[

     κη′   οὐδὲν ὑπ[...]..[

     κθ′   οὐδὲν ὑπ[

10   λ′   νομίμηϲ βουλῆϲ [

     (vac.) τῷ βουλευτηρί[ῳ

Φαῶφι   α′   ὁ ἐξηγ[ητήϲ

     β′   ἱερᾶϲ οὔϲηϲ.[

     οντοϲ εγ[

15   ].,.τη..[

$$\cdot \quad \cdot \quad \cdot \quad \cdot \quad \cdot$$

3 ϊεραϲ   8 ϋπ[9 ϋπ[13 ϊεραϲ

1 The traces of the first letter suggest pi, but the second does not favour, for example, πομ[π]ῆϲ, which would fit the context.

2 For the Cεβαϲτεῖον at Oxyrhynchus see e.g. XXXI 2553 12. This entry is paralleled in XLII 3072 5:].ἔθυϲεν ἔν τε τῷ Cεβαϲτείῳ[.

3 Cf. BGU II 362 iv 11.

4 A reference to the Capitoline games, first celebrated at Oxyrhynchus in the reign of Aurelian (BGU IV 1074. 10, P. Osl. III 85, cf. XLIII 3135)? In which case this text will date to the last quarter of the third century.

5 Perhaps ἐξη[γητοῦ should be restored here. For the duties of the exegetes see P. Jouguet, *La Vie municipale dans l'Égypte romaine*, 315–18. On θεωρία see P. Osl. III 77. 18 n.

6 Cf. XLII 3072 3:]ϲεν εἰϲ τὸ θέατρον κἀκεῖ τω[.

8–9 These entries presumably cover blank days. The phrase might be οὐδὲν ὑπάρχει or ὑπεμνηματίϲθη *vel sim.*

10 Cf. the *Lex Palmyrenorum* (Abbot and Johnson, *Municipal Administration in the Roman Empire*, no. 89. 6) which has the phrase νομίμου βουλῆϲ.

15 One is tempted to see a reference to the office of strategus here and the traces of the first few letters are consonant with a reading of ϲ]τρατη but the traces following cannot be made to fit gamma.

3249. NOMINATION TO A LITURGY

11 1B.145/C(b)   9·2 × 14·6 cm.   September–December, A.D. 326

This text was originally part of a *tomos synkollesimos*, but only a scrap of the document attached at the left has been preserved. This contains exiguous traces of the ends of three lines. The main text is complete at the top and the left margin, with only a few letters missing at the right-hand side. The lost portion will have contained the name of the nominee, the date, and endorsement by the official. The back of the papyrus is blank.

The nomination is cast in the form usual for this period (cf. e.g. XXXIII **2675**). It is sent to the logistes, Flavius Leucadius, by the systates, Aurelius Eustochius, and others. It names a man who will perform the duty of guarding the temple of Hadrian for a period of one year. Although liturgies are known in connection with other temples in Oxyrhynchus, this particular one probably differs slightly from the other examples because in the fourth century the temple of Hadrian is known to have been used as a prison (see 12 n.).

Of greater interest is the fact that this text supplies more evidence to disprove the theory of Mertens (*Les Services de l'état civil*, 41–3) that the systates could be reappointed every third year. The present systates, Aurelius Eustochius, is now known to have been in office in A.D. 317/18 (XXXIII **2675**), 326/7 (this text) and 337/8 (I. **86** 10–11 cf. VIII **1116** 5 note). It is even doubtful whether a minimum of two clear years between appointments (cf. XXXIV **2715** introd.) is still possible, see XLIII **3137** 3–4 n. It must be admitted that our knowledge of the functioning of the liturgical system in the fourth century is still scanty and the evidence so far has not brought to light any significant regularities in this period (cf. A. K. Bowman, *The Town Councils of Roman Egypt*, Appendix II).

→ ὑπατείας τῶν δεσποτῶν ἡμ[ῶν Κωνσταντίνου
   Ἀγούστου τὸ ζϛ καὶ Κωνσταντίου τοῦ [ἐπιφανεστάτου
   (vac.)   Καίσαρος τὸ αϛ.
   Φλαουίῳ Λευκαδίῳ λογιστῇ [᾽Οξυρυγχίτου
5   παρὰ Αὐρηλίου Εὐστοχίου Κοπ[ρέως συστάτου
   τῆς νυνὶ λιτουργούσης φυλῆς [. . . . .
   καὶ ἄλλων ἀμφόδων καὶ Παρίο[νος.]. . . .[. . . .
   χωτου Θεοδώρου ῾καὶ Τι⟦μο⟧᾽μοθέου Εὐλ[ογ]ίου καὶ Θων[ίου
   Φιλαίου καὶ Πτολεμαίου Σιλβανοῦ καὶ . . . . .[. . . .
10   Θεοδώρου τῶν πάντων ἀπὸ τῆς λαμ(πρᾶς) καὶ λαμ(προτάτης)
   ᾽Οξυρυγχειτῶν πόλεως. δίδομεν εἰς λειτο[υργίαν
   πρὸς θύραις δημοσίου Ἀδριανίου ἐφ᾽ ἐνια[υτὸν
   ἕνα ἔτι ἀπὸ νεωμηνίας Θὼθ [ἕως Μεσορὴ
   ἐπαγομένων πέμπτης καὶ α[ὐτῆς πέμπτης
15   τοῦ ἐνεστῶτος ἔτους κα′ ια[′ γ′ τὸν
   ἐνγεγραμμένον ὄντα ἐπιτ[ήδειον πρὸς τὴν
   χρείαν. (vac.) ἔστι δὲ Αὐρ[ήλιος

    ·   ·   ·   ·   ·   ·   ·   ·

2 l. Αὐγούστου   κωνσταντ᾽ιου   10 λαμϛ και λαμϛ   12 l. ἐπ᾽ ἐνια[υτόν   13 l. νεομηνίας

'In the consulship of our lords Constantinus Augustus for the seventh time and Constantius the most illustrious Caesar for the first time. To Flavius Leucadius, curator of the Oxyrhynchite, from Aurelius Eustochius son of Copreus, systates of the tribe . . . and other quarters currently performing liturgies and Parion . . . son of Theodorus and Timotheus son of Eulogius and Thonius son of Philaeus and Ptolemaeus son of Silvanus and [Terentius] son of Theodorus, all from the glorious and most glorious city of the Oxyrhynchites. We present for liturgy at the doors of the public Hadrianeum for a period of one year now from the beginning of the month of Thoth until the fifth epagomenal day of Mesore and including that fifth day of the present year 21, 11, 3, the man herein named who is fit for service. And he is Aurelius . . .'

2–3 The consulship of Constantine Augustus (VII) and Constantius Caesar (I) fell in A.D. 326. The regnal year in line 15 is A.D. 326–7 (cf. note).

4 This attestation extends the term of office of Flavius Leucadius from A.D. 325 (I 52) into the autumn of A.D. 326. His name can now be restored in **3265** (inv. 3 1B.77/B(3)b). Flavius Thennyras was in office in 327–8 (I **83**).

5 The restoration of cυcτάτου is guaranteed by name and circumstances. Eustochius is known from XXXIII 2675 and I 86 10–11 (cf. VIII **1116** 5 n.). See introduction.

6 The name of the tribe is lost, cf. XXXIV 2715 5–6.

7–10 I find no other example of a systates associating other people with him in a presentation for a liturgy, but the κοινόν of systatae appears in XLIII 3137 (A.D. 295), cf. the κοινόν of laographi in XXXVIII 2855.

9 The surviving letters at the end of the line are difficult to read. They look like τερην and I propose Τερην[τίου as a variant on Τερεντίου.

12 Whilst it is true that guards are attested for temples of Thoeris, Serapis, and Isis (I **43** verso iv 16, ii 7, 14, XIV **1627** 12), the fact that the temple of Hadrian at Oxyrhynchus appears to have been used as a prison in the fourth century (XVII **2154** 13–14) suggests that we are dealing with a warder. This is confirmed by P. Harr. 65. 8 (cf. *BL*. III, p. 77). We might compare the προcθυραίων λογιcτηρίου Ὀξυρυγχείτου in XLIII **3104** 8–9 (cf. S.P.P. III 84. 1, 77, P. Iand. III 37. 4).

15 Since the consulship is that of A.D. 326 (see 2–3 n.) and the regnal year is A.D. 326–7 the date of the papyrus falls between Thoth and Tybi of 326. The nomination therefore appears to postdate the beginning of the office (cf. XXXIII 2675 n.).

V. PRIVATE DOCUMENTS

3250. FREIGHT CONTRACT

34 4B.74/K(1–2)a   15 × 18·5 cm.   *c.* A.D. 63

The papyrus, blank on the back, is complete except at the foot though there is minor damage along the vertical lines resulting from the original folding. It contains a freight contract, examples of which are rare in the first century of the Roman period. In form it follows the usual pattern, cf. P. Lond. III 948, p. 219 (A.D. 236) = Meyer, *Juristische Papyri*, 43; the abstracts in P. Ross. Georg. II 18 (A.D. 140); II **276** (A.D. 77); P. Lond. II 256, p. 99 (A.D. 15) = W. *Chr.* 443.

The contract is drawn up at Oxyrhynchus between Anoubas, skipper of a ship (under the orders?) of M. Cornelius Torullus, centurion, and Polytimus, slave of C. Norbanus Ptolemaeus. The charter is for the return trip between Oxyrhynchus and Hermopolis, from which 500 artabas of aracus are to be transported to Oxyrhynchus. Anoubas undertakes to do this for a freight charge of 28 dr. per 100 art., the total being 140 dr., and to transport free of charge a further 12½ art. per 100 art., making an extra 62½ art. and a full load of 562½ art. For the legal background see C. H. Brecht, *Zur Haftung der Schiffer in antiken Recht.*

The main point of interest lies in the details. The stipulation of the entire responsibility of the skipper for the safety of the cargo has often been supposed to have come into use after the first century, see 20 n. Similarly the clauses regarding the rules of navigation specified in the contract are of interest (20–4). Some of these clauses were known to us from a later date (P. Ross. Georg. II 18, A.D. 140) and were thought to be peculiar to a period of civil disturbances (A. C. Johnson, *Roman Egypt*, 413). It is perhaps reasonable to suggest that there was an official code of navigation on the Nile, and that the contractors quoted the relevant clauses according to the circumstances. This is at least borne out for the early Ptolemaic period by the royal ordinances (P. Hibeh II 198. 111 seqq.), which prohibit navigation by night and in a storm. These two rulings are closely echoed in the present document (22–3).

The date is suggested by Rea on the probability that C. Norbanus Ptolemaeus is the person who was iuridicus and idiologus in A.D. 63, see P. Fouad 21. 5, BGU V § 50 134, XI 2059 ii 1.

→   ἐναύλωϲεν Ἀν[ο]υβᾶϲ Ἑρμίου τῶν ἀπὸ Ὑφαντῶνοϲ τοῦ Ἑρμοπολείτου
      Πέρϲηϲ τῆϲ ἐπ[ι]γονῆϲ κυβερνήτηϲ τῆϲ Μάρκου Κορνηλίου Το-
      ρούλλου ἑκατοντάρχου ϲκάφηϲ ποταμίαϲ ἀγωγῆϲ ἀρταβῶν
      πεντακοϲίων Πολυτίμῳ Γαΐου Νορβανοῦ Πτολεμαίου
5   τὴν δηλουμένην ϲκάφην ϲὺν τῇ ναυτείᾳ, εἰϲ ἣν καὶ ἐμβαλεῖ-

ται ἀφ' ὧν ἐὰν αἱρῆται τοῦ Ἑρμοπολείτου νομοῦ ὅρμον ἄρακος
μέτρῳ Ἀθηναίου ἀρτάβας πεντακοσίας καὶ τῶν ἑκατὸν
ἀρταβῶν ἀναυλὶ ἀρτάβας δέκα δύο ἥμισυ, ὥστε ἀποκατασ-
τῆσε εἰς Ἀκανθῶνα καὶ Λιλῆ τοῦ Ὀξυρυγχείτου, ναύλου τοῦ

10　διεσταμένου πρὸς ἀλλήλους τῶν ἑκατὸν ἀρταβῶν
ἀργυρίου δραχμῶν εἴκοσι ὀκτό, ὥστ' εἶναι δραχμὰς ἑκατὸν
τεσσεράκοντα, ἀφ' ὧν ὁμολογεῖ ὁ Ἀνουβᾶς ἐσχηκέναι παρὰ
τοῦ Πολυτείμου ἐπὶ τῶν τόπων δραχμὰς ἑβδομήκοντα
δύο. τὰς δὲ λοιπὰς τοῦ ναύλου δραχμὰς ἑξήκοντα ὀκτὼ

15　ἀποδότω αὐτῷ ἐπὶ τῆς ἐγβολῆς τοῦ ἄρακος. παραστησάτω
οὖν τὴν σκάφην ἑτοίμην πρὸς τὸν ἀνάπλουν τῇ μιᾷ καὶ εἰκά-
δι τοῦ ἐνεστῶτος μηνὸς Σεβαστοῦ, καὶ γενόμενος
ἐπὶ τῶν τοῦ Ἑρμοπολείτου ὅρμων καὶ ἀναλαβὼν καὶ πα-
ραλαβὼν τὸν ἄρακα ἀποπλευσάτω ἀνυπερθέτως

20　μετὰ πάσης ἀσφαλείας, ἑαυτῷ παρεχόμενος ἐν τῷ ἀνά-
πλῳ καὶ κατάπλῳ τὴν τῆς σκάφης χορηγίαν πᾶσαν ἐντελῆ
καὶ ναύτας ἱκανούς, καὶ μὴ ἐξέστω αὐτῷ νυγτοπλοεῖν μηδὲ
χειμῶνος ὄντος. ἀνορμίτω καθ' ἑκάστην ἡμέραν
ἐπὶ τῶν ἀσφαλεστάτων ὅρμων, τῶν διεραμάτων τοῦ

25　Ἑρμοπολείτου ὄντων πρὸς τὸν Ἀνουβᾶν, τῶν δὲ τοῦ Ὀξυρυγχείτου ὄντων πρὸς τὸν Πολύτιμον. τὸν δὲ ἄρακα παρα-
δότω τῷ Πολυτίμῳ ἢ τοῖς παρ' αὐτοῦ ἐπὶ τοῦ τῆς Λιλῆ καὶ
Ἀγανθῶνος ὅρμο⟨υ⟩ μέτρῳ ᾧ ἐὰν παραλάβῃ, τοῦ ἐγβησομέ-
νου ἐκ τῆς κοίλης ὄντος τοῦ Πολυτίμου ἢ ἀποτισάτω

30　αὐτῷ τιμὴ[ν] ἑκάστη[ς　　　　　　c. 25
.............].. [　　　　　　c. 25

6 l. ὅρμων　　8–9 l. ἀποκαταστῆσαι　　11 l. ὀκτώ　　15 l. ἐκβολῆς　　22 l. νυκτο-
πλοεῖν　　23 l. ἀνορμείτω? (see n.)　　28 l. Ἀκανθῶνος, ἐκβησομένου

'Anoubas son of Hermias, from Hyphanton in the Hermopolite nome, Persian of the *epigone*,
skipper of the river boat of 500 artabas burden of Marcus Cornelius Torullus, centurion, has chartered
to Polytimus, slave of Gaius Norbanus Ptolemaeus, the aforesaid boat with her equipment(?), on
which he will load, from whichever harbours of the Hermopolite nome he may choose, 500 artabas of
aracus according to the measure of the temple of Athena, and for every 100 artabas 12½ artabas free
of freight charge, so as to deliver (the cargo) to Acanthon and Lile in the Oxyrhynchite nome, at the
freight charge agreed upon between them of 28 dr. of silver per 100 art., so that the total is 140 dr;
of which Anoubas acknowledges that he has received from Polytimus on the spot 72 dr., but the
remaining 68 dr. of the freight charge Polytimus is to pay to Anoubas on the unloading of the aracus.

Therefore Anoubas is to provide the boat ready for sailing up the river on the 21st of the present month of Sebastus, and having arrived at the harbours of the Hermopolite nome, and after having embarked and received the aracus, he is to sail away without delay, with all security, supplying for himself on the journeys up and down the river full and complete supplies for the ship and sufficient crew. He is not to be permitted to sail by night nor (to weigh anchor?) in foul weather (and?) he is to lay up daily at the safest harbours, the tenders at Hermopolis being at the expense of Anoubas, but those at Oxyrhynchus at the expense of Polytimus. Let Anoubas deliver the aracus to Polytimus or his representatives at the harbour of Lile and Acanthon, using whatever measure he receives by. Whatever shall emerge from the hold is to belong to Polytimus or Anoubas shall pay to him as the price of each (artaba) . . . .'

1 On Hyphanton see P. Sarap. 80 (= P. Amh. I 131) 12 n. Delete from LSJ, therefore, the common noun ὑφαντῶν.

2 Πέρϲηϲ τῆϲ ἐπιγονῆϲ. For different views of this designation see *Aegyptus* 43 (1963) 15–53, *YCS* 18 (1963) 1–129.

2–3 Τορούλλου. Strict transliteration produces a Roman cognomen Torullus, not to be found in PIR¹ or in Schulze, *Zur Gesch. lat. Eigennamen*. It may be a new name or there may be some aberration in the Greek version.

4 Πολυτίμῳ, κτλ. It is probable that this form of words indicates that Polytimus was the slave of C. Norbanus Ptolemaeus, not his freedman, see H. Chantraine, *Freigelassene u. Sklaven im Dienst d. röm. Kaiser*, 170, cf. *BICS* 17 (1970) 140.

At the end of 4 there is a horizontal filler sign, as also in 10. At other line ends the finials are prolonged to fill out the space.

5 ϲὺν τῇ ναυτείᾳ. Information on ναυτεία is scarce, see P. Rev. (Bingen) 85 6, SB V 8299 17, P. Mil. Vogl. III 189 16. The present case may indicate, as Turner suggests, that it means the equipment necessary for a ship to sail.

6 On ἄρακοϲ or ἄραξ see M. Schnebel, *Landwirtschaft*, 185–9, Papyrologica Lugd. Bat. XI 8. 11 n.

8 ἀναυλί is explained in Suidas—ἀναυλεὶ χωρὶϲ ναύλου—but is otherwise, seemingly, new. It is noteworthy that the additional unpaid load brings the total to 562½ art., while the stated burden of the boat is only 500 art. No instance of the actual load exceeding the stated burden is remarked in Merzagora, *Aegyptus* 10 (1929) 135–40. The artaba is a measure of volume, one important factor in loading a boat. The next most important factor would be weight. Probably the burden was calculated on an ideal load of grain, while aracus as a green leguminous plant would be less dense and less heavy. If space could be found, therefore, it was probably safe to carry a greater volume of it than the official calculation of the burden.

9–11 For rates of transport charges see A. C. Johnson, *Roman Egypt*, 407, O. M. Pearl, *TAPA* 83 (1952) 72 seqq.

12–15 It was usual that the freight charge should be paid partly in advance and partly on delivery, cf. P. Ross. Georg. II 18, P. Lond. III 948.

16 The date is equivalent to 18 September, or 19 September in an Egyptian leap year.

20 μετὰ πάϲηϲ ἀϲφαλείαϲ. This is more evidence to disprove the *argumentum ex absentia* that such clauses were a second-century innovation, Schwartz, *BIFAO* 47 (1947) 188 and n. 4. It is also found in late Ptolemaic documents, SB V 8754 18 (49/8 B.C.).

20–1 ἑαυτῷ παρεχόμενοϲ . . . ἐντελῆ. See also P. Ross. Georg. II 18, P. Lond. III 948.

22–3 ἀνορμίτω. At first sight this appears to represent ἀνορμείτω from ἀνορμεῖν, *addendum lexicis*, but probably the copy is defective here, since something has to be understood with χειμῶνοϲ ὄντοϲ. Perhaps the scribe jumped from one sequence of letters to another similar one, e.g. μηδὲ χειμῶνοϲ ὄντοϲ ἀνορμι⟨ζέτω. καὶ ὁρμεί⟩τω, etc. 'nor is he to weigh anchor in foul weather. And he is to lay up each day in the most secure anchorages.' If genuine, ἀνορμεῖν ought to mean 'to weigh anchor', like ἀνορμίζειν, not 'to drop anchor', in spite of the specious English equivalent 'to lay up'. In that case a jump by the scribe would be even easier—μηδὲ . . . ἀνορμείτω. ⟨καὶ ὁρμείτω⟩ κτλ.

For the rest cf. similar wording in P. Ross. Georg. II 18 vi 33, commentary pp. 108–9.

24 διεραμάτων are small boats, see Cl. Rev. 19 (1969) 91–2, Procopius, *Aed.* VI. 1, 3, with Downey's note in the Loeb edition, p. 363, n. 2. Cf. XXXI 2568 16 n.

3251. Acknowledgement of Indebtedness

22 3B.14/G(7–10)b   14×15 cm.   Second/third century

An acknowledgement of indebtedness in duplicate on the same sheet by the same hand. Only endings of the lines survive in col. i. What is printed is the text of col. ii.

The acknowledged debt is incurred through arrears of farm rents. As in **XXII 2350**, the tenure has now expired, and what we have is in effect a deed of loan in kind and money. Only the name of the lessor—and now creditor—is known from ii 13. He is a certain Theon, who is addressed as a former high priest of the temple of Hadrian at Oxyrhynchus. As in **2350** (see introd.) the debt is free of interest, if paid within a specified term, but if overdue it incurs an interest which serves as a fine (17 n.).

In form it follows the general pattern, e.g. P. Merton III 110, P. Strasb. 143, **2350**, **XXXI 2566**, P. Merton I 36 (for future farming).

The handwriting is closest to R. Seider, *Paläographie*, no. 38 (A.D. 201–2) and M. Norsa, *Scrittura documentaria*, tav. 13 (*c.* A.D. 215). The eleventh year mentioned in ii 12 might be of the reign of Severus, A.D. 202/3. Other possible years are 11 Marcus (= A.D. 170/1), and 11 Severus Alexander (= A.D. 231/2). Even 11 Gallienus (= A.D. 263/4) is not ruled out. The back is blank.

·   ·   ·   ·

$\rightarrow$ ......].ιϛ.[.............]..[
     .....].του....θε.[..].εω.[..ἀ]πὸ Ὀ-
     ξυρ[ύ]γχων πόλεως ἀρχιερατεύσαν[τ]ι
     τοῦ ἐν τῇ αὐτῇ πόλει σεβασμιωτάτου
5   Ἁδριανείου χαίρειν. ὁμολογοῦμεν ὀ-
     φίλειν σοι ἀπό τε φόρων καὶ ἐκφορίων
     ὧν ἐγεωργοῦμέν σου ἐδαφῶν πυροῦ
     ἀρτάβας ἐννέα καὶ φακοῦ ἀρτάβας
     πέντε καὶ ἀργυρίου δραχμὰς ἑκατὸν
10 δώδεκα, [ἅ]περ πάντα ἀποδώσομέν
     σοι μέχρι τριακάδος Μεσορὴ τοῦ ἐνεστῶ-
     τος ἐνδεκάτου ἔτους, τὰ δὲ γένη μέτρῳ
     σοῦ τοῦ Θέωνος παραλημφθικῷ. ἐὰν
     δὲ μὴ ἀποδῶμεν τῇ δηλουμένῃ προ-

3 -σαν[τ]ι confirmed by col. i   4 At the end is a wedge-shaped filler sign, also to be seen twice in col. i   13 l. παραλημπτικῷ

15 θεσμίᾳ, ταξόμεθά coι τοῦ ὑπερπεcό(ν)-
τος χρόνου διάφορον τῶν μὲν γενῶ(ν)
ἐκ τετάρτου, τοῦ δὲ ἀργυρίου δραχμιαῖ-
ον τόκον, γεινομένης coι τῆς πράξεως ἔκ τε ἡμῶν ἀλληλενγύων ὄν-
20 των εἰς ἔκτειcιν ἢ ἐξ οὗ ἐὰν ἡμῶν
αἱρῇ. κύρια τὰ γράμματα διccὰ γραφέντα πανταχῇ ἐπιφερόμενα καὶ
. . . .] . . . .
. . . . . .

15 ὑπερπεcō   16 γενῶ

'(. . . to Theon . . .) of the city of the Oxyrhynchi, ex-high-priest of the most august temple of Hadrian in the same city, greetings. We acknowledge that we owe you from the money rent and rent in kind of your lands, which we used to farm, nine artabas of wheat, five artabas of lentils and 112 drachmas of silver, all of which we shall pay back to you by Mesore 30th of the current eleventh year. The debt in kind (will be paid) according to the measure used for payments to you, Theon. But if we fail to make restitution in the appointed time, we shall pay you for the time overdue a supplement in kind of one quarter and on the money interest at the rate of 1 dr. per mina. You have the right of execution either from us acting mutually as sureties for the payment or from any one of us whom you may choose. This deed is valid, written in duplicate, wherever it may be produced and . . .'.

2 Possible would be Θέω[νι] Θέωγ[ος.

5 Hadrian's temple in Oxyrhynchus is known from VIII **1113** 5–6 (A.D. 203) and XVII **2154**, of the fourth century, when the building was apparently used as a prison.[1] See also XXXI **2552**, introd.

6 On φόρος and ἐκφόριον see J. Herrmann, *Bodenpacht*, 98 seqq.

16–17 The term διάφορον is usually used for interest on loans in kind, while τόκος refers to money. The 25 per cent rate of interest is rare (XXXI **2566** ii 15). The usual interest on loans in kind was 50 per cent, see N. Lewis, *TAPA* 76 (1945) 126 seqq. The 25 per cent interest does not figure in his lists.

3252. DEED OF SURETY

31 4B.12/0(1–2)a   5·1 × 16·4 cm.   A.D. 257/8

This narrow piece of papyrus contains a deed of surety of no special significance. The papyrus is broken off at the foot. The back is blank except for an ink-mark. The content may be compared with M. *Chr.* 354–5 and P. Mich. IX 535, where further references are given.

The deed is addressed to Aurelius Sarapion also called Didymus, a former or current gymnasiarch of Oxyrhynchus, by Aurelius Hatres son of Petearpocrates from the Aphroditopolite nome. The latter agrees to provide surety for a slave named Eudaemon who belongs to Sarapion.

[1] Add **3249** 12 above.

→   Αὐρηλίῳ Cαραπίωνι
        τῷ καὶ Διδύμῳ
        γυμνασιαρχ( ) τῆс
        Ὀξυρυγχειτῶν πόλ(εωс)
5   Αὐρήλιος Ἀτρῆс
        Πετεαρποκράτου
        μητρὸς Τάννειτος
        ἀπὸ κώμης Τμου-
        νειψὴ τοῦ Ἀφροδει-
10   τοπολείτου νομοῦ.
        ὁμολογῶ ἑκουсίωс
        καὶ αὐθαιρέτωс
        ἐγγυᾶсθαί сοι
        δοῦλόν сου Εὐδαί-
15   μονα ὃν καὶ παρα-
        стήсω μεχρὶ
        Ἀθὺρ ʽιʼ τοῦ ἰсιόντος ϛ (ἔτουс),
        εἰ δὲ μὴ ἐκτείсειν сοι
        ὑπὲρ αὐτοῦ ἀργυρίου
20   δραχμὰс χειλίαс
        ἑπτακοсίαс ὡс ἐстά-
        θη. καὶ περὶ τού-
        του ἐπερωτηθεὶс
        ὑπὸ сοῦ ὡμολόγηсα.
25   (ἔτουс) εʺ Αὐτοκρατόρω(ν)
        Καιсάρων Πουπλίου
        Λικιννίου Οὐαλεριανοῦ
        καὶ Πο[υπλ]ί[ο]υ [Λικι-

              .   .   .   .   .   .

3 γυμνασιαρ^χ   4 οξυρυγʼχειτων πο^λ   17 ἰсιοντος ϛ§, l. εἰсιόντος   19 ϋπερ
20 l. χιλίας   24 ϋπο   25 ∠ εʺ αυτοκρατορω

'To Aurelius Sarapion also called Didymus (ex-?) gymnasiarch of the city of the Oxyrhynchites, Aurelius Hatres son of Petearpocrates whose mother is Tanneis, from the village of Tmounepse in the Aphroditopolite nome. I agree voluntarily and of my own free will to stand surety to you for your slave Eudaemon whom I will produce up to Hathyr 10 of the coming 6th year, and otherwise I will pay to you for him one thousand seven hundred drachmas cash as was agreed. And in answer to the formal question put by you about this I gave my assent. Year 5 of Imperatores Caesares Publius Licinius Valerianus and Publius [Licinius Valerianus Gallienus . . .]'

8–10 This village does not appear in the *Wörterbuch* or its Supplement or in the index to P. Lond. IV. On the status of the Aphroditopolite in this period see P. Beatty Panop. p. xxxiv.

28 The only example I have found of a papyrus of this year without a Caesar following **Gallienus** is P. Lond. III 1284 (descr.), so the name of a Caesar will almost certainly have followed here. The matter is more complex than this because there are two Caesars in this reign, Valerian the younger and Saloninus, whom P. Bureth, *Les Titulatures Impériales*, pp. 117–18 conflates. The latest certain dating by Valerian the younger is Choiak of year 5 (XIV 1649 3), the first certain one by Saloninus in Mesore year 5 (XXXI 2560 23). Since the month name here is missing we cannot tell which it will have been. (I am indebted to Mr. P. J. Parsons for the substance of this note.)

3253. LETTER OF ZOILUS TO HORION

36 4B.98/D(3–5)a   11·9 × 32·6 cm.   Third/fourth century

A business letter from Zoilus to his agent Horion concerned with action on information received from 'little' Pagenes. It is written across the fibres in a large and fluent late third- or early fourth-century hand. It is tempting to connect this letter with XVII **2142** and **2143** (A.D. 293), two orders for payment from a Zoilus to a Horion, and also possibly XII **1573**, a tax-list of the late third or early fourth century which has the entry at line 13 μερ(ιcμοῦ) Ζωίλου δι(ὰ) Ὡρίωνος.

On the back is the twenty-sixth column or sheet of accounts, of Phamenoth of an unspecified year. The edges were trimmed before the letter was written.

↓   Ζωίλος Ὡρίωνι τῷ φιλ(τάτῳ) χαίριν.
       Παγένης ὁ μεικρὸς λογαρίδιόν μοι
       ἤνεγκεν τῆς περιcυνῆ[c] κατα-
       cπορᾶς ὅπερ co[ι ἔ]πεμψα. μετοξὺ
5   οὖν αὐτῶν γενοῦ καὶ ὅπερ ἐὰν κατα-
       λάβῃς cύνφωνον ἀπ[ὸ] τοῦ λογα-
       ριδίου τοῦτο ἀπόλαβε καὶ ἄφες παρὰ
       cεαυτῷ ἔcτ' ἂν δοκιμάcωμεν τί ὀφί-
       λει αὐτῷ τῷ μεικρῷ Παγένι δο-
10   θῆναι καὶ τί εἰc λόγον τῶν ὀφι-
       λομένων ὑπ' αὐτοῦ. ἀλλὰ καὶ
       τὸν οἶνον ὃν λαμβάνι ὁ ἀγροφύ-
       λαξ cυνάξαc ἄφες παρ[ὰ] cεαυτῷ
       ἔcτ' ἄν τι κρίνωμεν. [κ]αὶ περὶ τού-
15   του η..ατο ὁ μεικρὸc Π[α]γένηc

1 l. χαίρειν   2 l. μικρός   3 ηνεγ'κεν, l. περυcινῆ[c]   8 l. ὀφείλει   9 l. μικρῷ
Παγένει   10 f. l. ὀφει|λομένων   12 l. λαμβάνει   15 l. μικρός

ὡς τινων πινώντων ἐν τῷ
ἐποικίῳ μάλιϲτα Λου[. .]υ. μάθε
οὖν καὶ ποίηϲον α[ὐτο]ῖϲ δοθῆ-
ναι ὑπὸ Βηϲαρίωνοϲ εἰϲ διατρο-
20   φὰϲ ὀλίγα ϲιτάρια ἐπιδείξαϲ
αὐτῷ τὰ γράμματά μου.
(m. 2)   ἐρρῶϲθαί ϲε εὔχομαι

16 l. πεινώντων

'Zoilus to Horion his dear colleague(?) greetings. Little Pagenes brought me the account of the last year's sowing, which I sent you. Mediate between them and what, if anything, you find agreed from the account, take it and keep it with you until we decide what ought to be given little Pagenes himself and what to the account of his debts. Furthermore, the wine which the field guard receives, collect it and keep it with you until we decide something. Also about this little Pagenes . . . that some were going hungry, especially in the settlement of Lu . . s. Find out and see to it that a little grain is given them for food by Besarion, showing him my letters.'
(2nd hand) 'I hope you are well.'

1 φιλ is written without any mark of abbreviation. The likely expansion is φιλ(τάτῳ), which is commonly used in letters between colleagues; φίλ(ῳ), also possible, would imply a social rather than a business relationship. In XVII 2142 and 2143 the opening is Ζωΐλοϲ Ὠρίωνι χαίρειν.

2 Παγένηϲ. The name is not very common, cf. *NB* and Foraboschi *Onomasticon* and none of those examples can be connected with this man. PSI VIII 890 mentions both a Pagenes who is an ἀμπελουργόϲ and a Horion, but is probably too early.

12–13 Most mentions of agrophylakes are of Byzantine date. Then they were both public officials and private employees, see E. R. Hardy, *The Large Estates of Byzantine Egypt* (New York, 1931), 64. However, they are mentioned at earlier dates in P. Lugd. Bat. XIII 6. 2 (first century A.D.), XVII 2122 11 (second/third century A.D.) and P. Princ. III 174 iii 6 (A.D. 260).

15 η . . ατο should mean said, told, reported, wrote.

16 πινώντων; l. πεινώντων. I have found no evidence for a general famine at the end of the third or beginning of the fourth centuries but no doubt there were local shortages, as at Oxyrhynchus in the mid-third century (XLII 3048 introd.).

17 Λου[. .]υ: Λού[πο]υ or Λου[κίο]υ will fit. It seems better to translate 'some were going hungry, especially in the settlement of L', than 'some were going hungry in the settlement, especially L.' For the place name see perhaps P. Warren 10. 9 ὁρμώμεν[οι ἀπὸ ἐποικίο]υ Λουκίου, cf. 23, VI 922 25, 998. All three are of the late Byzantine period.

19 Βηϲαρίωνοϲ. The name is not uncommon, but none can be connected with this document.

VI. DOCUMENTS FROM THE ARCHIVE OF LEONIDES

3254–3262

Pliny describes an important and lucrative flax industry in Egypt, yet papyri have furnished very little information about flax or its cultivation beyond an occasional lease or inclusion of cτιππεῖον (tow) or λινοκαλάμη (flax) in accounts and bills of lading. One reason for this is that the most famous flax came from the area of the Delta, in which papyri have rarely survived. The following documents which give the first extensive evidence for flax production outside this area are the business transactions of one Leonides and his occasional partner Dioscorus whose activity near the villages of Antipera Pela and Ision Panga in the Oxyrhynchite nome spanned some twenty years (A.D. 315–334). The archive consists of nine new texts, six of which are leases, and three documents already published:

Although the majority of the texts are leases, it does appear that business was not limited to the growing of flax. The purchase of an already harvested crop by Leonides (**3262**), various references to stages in the processing of flax, and the address of **103** which gives Leonides and Dioscorus the title cτιπποτιμητ(αί) all indicate that the men were merchants engaged in the preparation and marketing of linen fibre, tow, and perhaps linseed. Leonides himself was meniarch of a tow guild in 324 and 328, and if guild officials were selected like other officials at this time on their ability to assume financial burdens, then Leonides may have been a man of some affluence.

K

Processing:

The processing technique to which there are a number of references in these documents is essentially that which Pliny describes (*N.H.* XIX 16–17). The flax is harvested and allowed to dry, after which the seeds are removed and it is submerged in water until the stalks are sufficiently macerated to permit the inner fibres (linen) to be separated from the outer (tow). This softening process, known as water-retting, is mentioned in three documents: in **103** 18 the rent will be paid in water-retted tow (τεταρι-χευμένης); so also in **3255** 22 (cεcυνβροχιcμένης); and in **3256** the lessees contract to pay all the expenses up to and including the water-retting (cυμβροχιcμοῦ) of the flax. Finally, the rent in PSI 469. 19 is to be paid in tow.

The over-all economic picture of early Byzantine Egypt which these documents present is in substantial accord with what is already known about the period. For example, a comparison of the rent prices of these leases with a flax lease from 306 (**I 102**) shows a rapid and inflationary increase. Further, all of the leases are short-term and most of them are contracted on the basis of rent-in-kind, a device which provided at least some protection against sudden inflation.

On flax growing in Egypt, see I. Kalleris, αἱ πρῶται ὕλαι, 177 ff. and M. Schnebel, *Landwirtschaft*, 203 ff.[1]

3254. SALE OF FLAX

12 1B.143/K(31)a   9·8 × 24·6 cm.   312–15

Only the left-hand portion of this document remains, in two pieces which seem to join without loss of text in line 12. The lower part is much abraded, so that only the formulaic parts of the text can be recovered; the foot, with the subscription, is completely lost. The back is blank.

Aurelius Evangelus has sold the flax crop of one aroura to Leonides for a sum of 7 (or between 7 and 8) talents. The document is not the usual 'sale-in-advance', which acknowledges receipt of the price against a promise of future delivery, for example P. Hamb. 21 (see F. Pringsheim, *Greek Law of Sale*, 278). It states that the sale has been completed, and the price paid over. Comparable texts are P. Tebt. II 379 (A.D. 128: grass crop), P. Osl. II 45 (A.D. 135: acacia trees), VI **909** (A.D. 225: acacia trees), BGU II 456 (A.D. 348: palm trees); a similar transaction is implied in P. Osl. III 133 (second century: garlic). In at least three of these the purchaser is to harvest the crop himself (P. Tebt. 379. 8 f., **909** 24 ff., P. Osl. 133. 14); similar conditions were made in **3254** 16 ff., though the details are now lost. In this form, purchasing the produce is not very different from leasing the land: see Pringsheim 303 f. and 523 f. (note P).

[1] A list of published flax leases is given in *Collectanea Papyrologica*. Texts published in honor of H. C. Youtie, by A. E. Hanson. Part II (= PTA 20) No. 68 introd.

→ ὑπατίας τῶν δεσπ[οτῶν ἡμῶν Κωνσταντίνου καὶ
  Λικινίου Cεβας[τῶν τὸ
  Αὐρήλιος Εὐάγγ[ελος   ἀπὸ
  κώμης Τήεως η′ [πάγου τοῦ Ὀξυρυγχίτου νομοῦ
5 Αὐρηλίῳ Λεων[ίδῃ Θέωνος ἀπὸ τῆς λαμ(πρᾶς) καὶ
  λαμ(προτάτης) Ὀξυρυγχιτῶ[ν πόλεως χαίρειν. ὁμολογῶ
  πεπρακέναι cοι ἐντ[εῦθεν   τὸν
  καρπὸν λινοκαλάμ[ης
  ἐνάτου καὶ ̣′ [ ] ̣ ̣[
10 κοινωνίᾳ ἐμοῦ κ[αὶ
  τιμ]ῆς τῆς cυμπεφ[ωνημένης πρὸς ἀλλήλους
  . . . .] . . . .[
  Cεβας]τῶν νομίcμ[ατος
  ἅπερ [. . . . .] . .[
15 περὶ ἧς ἀριθ[μήcεως
  ἐφ’ ᾧτε . . . .[
  . . .]ωντο . . . . μ[
  .[εἰc τὸ
  ἴδιον τελοῦν[τα   δημόcια τε-
20 λέcματα καὶ ἐπικλαcμοὺ[c καὶ ἐπιμεριcμοὺc τοῦ ἐνεcτῶτος
  ἔτουc καὶ παντοίων χρ[γρα-
  φεῖcα καὶ ἐπερωτηθ(εὶc) ὡμ[ολόγηcα.
  (m. 2) Αὐρήλιος Εὐά[γγε]λος[πέπρακα τὸν καρπὸν ἀρούρης μιᾶc λινοκαλάμης καὶ ἀπέ[cχον
25 τά]λαντα ἑπτὰ καὶ . . .[
  . .] . . . . . τελέcματα[

1 ϋπατιας   3 ευαγ’γ[6 λαμ϶″   19 ϊδιον   22 επερωτηθ^θ

'In the consulship of our masters Constantinus and Licinius Augusti for the . . . time.

'Aurelius Evangelus . . . from the village of Teis in the 8th pagus of the Oxyrhynchite nome:

'To Aurelius Leonides, son of Theon, from the glorious and most glorious city of the Oxyrhynchites, greetings.

'I acknowledge that I have sold to you henceforth . . . the produce in flax . . . ninth and . . . year (?) . . . held in partnership by me and . . . at the price agreed on . . . of the coinage of the Emperors . . . which (I have received from you in full), as to which payment (when the formal question was put I made acknowledgement) . . . on condition that . . . (taking the crop) for your own use, paying . . . the public taxes, and requisitions, and assessments of the current year. . . . The sale is incontestable, written in . . . copies, and in answer to the formal question I have made acknowledgement.

(2nd hand) 'I, Aurelius Evangelus, have sold the produce of one aroura of flax and I have received . . . seven talents and . . .'

1–2 Licinius Augustus appears as junior consul, always with Constantinus, in 312, 313, and 315; the iteration figure must be supplemented accordingly as τὸ β΄, τὸ γ΄, or τὸ δ΄.

4 η΄ [πάγου: for the location of Teis in the 8th pagus, see P. Giss. 115 introd.

7 Supplement, for example, ἐντ[εῦθεν εἰς τὸν ἀεὶ χρόνον, as at BGU II 456. 9.

9 ἐνάτου καὶ ˙΄: the final dash suggests that a numeral precedes, but I cannot read it with any certainty. After the dash, a short space which may originally have contained one letter but was more probably blank; then alpha, or the left half of pi or eta; then phi or rho. ἀρ[ούρης μιᾶς might be supplied from 23 f., so that 9–10 describe the land on which the flax is grown, owned, or leased in common by Evangelus and a partner (10 ἐπὶ] κοινωνίᾳ as, e.g., SB IV 7474. 3). If this is correct, there is no space for further numerals after ἐνάτου καὶ ˙΄.

The numerals are likely to represent a regnal year. They may refer to the separate years of two or more emperors (there is room for a third numeral at the end of 8); or they might be combined as ἐνάτου καὶ ι΄ = 19 (rare but possible, see XXXVI 2765 2, ZPE 8 (1971) 230). The year may be that of the crop (as, e.g., P. Hamb. 21. 7); or possibly that of the original lease or purchase of the land. In theory the following years are available:

(a) δεκάτου καὶ] ἐνάτου καὶ β΄ = 293/4
(b) ἐνάτου καὶ ι΄ = 310/11 (19 Galerius, omitting colleagues)
(c) ἐνάτου καὶ ζ΄ = 312/13 (Maximinus and Constantine, omitting Licinius)
(d) ἐνάτου καὶ ζ΄ = 314/15 (Constantine and Licinius)
(e) ἐνδεκάτου καὶ] ἐνάτου καὶ α΄ = 316/17

Of these, (c) and (d) have to be eliminated, although they overlap conveniently the possible consular dates in 1–2. The scribe did not write ζ. Otherwise I judge that ις΄ would be a good reading; α is possible, β (open-topped) conceivable. If we eliminate (e) on the ground that this sale of 315 or earlier is not likely to involve the crop of 316/17, (a) and (b) remain; if either is right, it must be taken as the date of Evangelus' purchase or lease.

14 e.g. τάλαντα x]‖ ἅπερ [ἀπ' ἐντεῦθεν ἀ]πέ[σχον ἐκ πλήρους διὰ χειρός, cf. BGU II 456. 16 f., XIV 1705 9 f.

15 e.g. ἐπερωτηθεὶς ὑπὸ σοῦ ὡμολόγησα, cf. XIV 1705 10 f.

16 Perhaps ἐφ' ᾧτε σὲ τὸν Αὐρήλ[ιον Λεωνίδην.

18–19 Supplement on the pattern of, for example, XIV 1704 13 ff. καὶ ἀποφέρεσθαι [πάντα τὰ ἀπ' αὐτῶν περιε]σόμενα εἰς τὸ ἴδιον, τελούσας τὰ ὑπὲρ τῶν σιτικῶν ἀρουρῶν δημόσια [τελέσματα καὶ ἐπικλασμοὺς] καὶ ἐπιμερισμοὺς παντοίους.

21 παντοίων χρ[: I have found no real parallel to this phrase. In the context, παντοῖος would be expected to apply to one item in the list of charges to be paid, as at 1704 15. Perhaps something like παντοίων χρ[υσικῶν ἐπιβολήν (but this use of χρυσικά does not appear before the fifth century).

21–2 Supplement κυρία ἡ πρᾶσις ἁπλῆ (δισσή, etc.) γραφεῖσα.

25 Perhaps καὶ τες[or καὶ τετ[.

26 Perhaps δη]μόσια.

3255. APPLICATION FOR LEASE

12 1B.143/K(26)a   16·2 × 25 cm.   6 November 315

An *epidoche* in which Dioscorus, an occasional partner of Leonides (see I **103** and **3256**), undertakes to lease 6⅔ arouras to be sown with flax. The rent on half of the acreage was to be paid in cash, the rent on the other half in kind. There is an interesting reference to the technical process of 'water-retting' in 22 σεσυνβροχισμένης (cf. I **103** 18 τεταριχευμένης).

This text was first published, with commentary, in *Collectanea Papyrologica*. Texts published in honor of H. C. Youtie, by A. E. Hanson. Part II (= PTA 20) No. 80.

→ ὑπατείας τῶν δεσποτῶν [ἡμῶν Κωνσταντίνου καὶ Λικιννίου
    (vac.)   Cεβα[cτῶν τὸ δ
Αὐρηλίᾳ Εὐτροπίῃ θυγατρὶ [Θ]εοδώρου τοῦ καὶ Χαιρ[ήμο-
νος γυμ(νασιαρχήσαντος) πρυ(τανεύσαντος) γενομ(ένου) βουλ(ευτοῦ)
    τῆς [λ]αμ(πρᾶς) καὶ λαμ(προτάτης) Ὀξυρυγχιτ[ῶν
5 πόλεως   (vac.)
παρὰ Αὐρηλίου Διοσκόρου Ἀμμωνίου ἀπὸ τῆς αὐτῆ[ς πόλ(εως).
ἑκουσίω[ς] ἐπιδέχομαι μισθώσασθαι πρὸς μόν[ον τὸ
ἐνεστὸς ι΄ [κ]αὶ ηϚ΄ ἔτος ἀπὸ τῶν ὑπαρχόντων σοι περὶ τὸ Ἰ[cῖον
Παγγᾶ ἐν περιχώματι Πέκτυ ἐν τόπῳ Τέλκε καλουμ[ένῳ
10 ἀρουρῶν δεκαέπτα κοινωνίας Πανάρους κατὰ τὸ τ[έταρτον
ὄγδοον μέρος ὅ ἐστι ἄρουραι ἐξ τέταρτον ὄγδοον [ἐκ γεωμε-
τρίας εἰς[πορ]ὰν [λι]νοκαλάμης καὶ τελέσιν ὑπὲρ φόρου τῆς μὲ[ν ἡμισείας
ἑκάστη[ς ἀρούρης] ἀνὰ ἀργυρίου τάλαντα τέσσαρ.ς ἀν[τὶ δὲ φόρου [τῆς λοιπῆ]ς ἡμ[ισεία]ς ἥ[μ]ισοι μέρος τῆς ἐκβησομέ[νης
15 .ης λιν[οκαλάμ]ης, κἀμὲ δ[ὲ] τ[ὸν] μεμισθωμένον ἀνθ᾽ [ὧν παρέχω
σπερμ[άτων κα]ὶ ἧς ποιοῦμα[ι γεωρ]γίας τὸ λοιπὸν ἥμισο[ι μέρος
καὶ ἐξ ὁ[λοκλήρου τ]ὸ λινόσπε[ρμον ἀ]κίνδυνα πάντα παντὸς [κινδύνου,
τῶν τῆς [γῆς δη]μοσίων ὄ[ντω]ν πρὸς σὲ τὴν γεοῦχον κυριεύ[ουσαν
τῶν κα[ρπῶν] ἕως τὰ [ὀφ]ειλόμενα ἀπολάβῃ[ς]· βεβαιουμ[έ-
20 νης δέ [μοι τῆς ἐ]πιδοχῆς ἐπάναγκες ἀποδόσω τοὺς φόρους
καὶ τὰ ἐκφόρια [τ]ὸν μὲν ἀργυρικὸν φόρον τῷ Παῦνι μηνὶ τὸ δὲ
ἐκφό[ριον τῆς λι]νοκαλάμης ἐπὶ τῆς λίμνου σεσυνβρ[ο]χι[σμένης
τα........ ἐνεστῶτος ἔτους ἀνυπερθέτως, γεινομένης σοι
τῆς πράξεως παρά τε ἐμοῦ ὡς καθήκει. κυρία ἡ ἐπιδοχὴ
25 καὶ ἐπερ[ωτ]ηθεὶς ὡμολόγησα.
ὑπατεία[ς τ]ῆς προκειμένης   (m. 2) Ἀθὺρ ι.
Αὐρηλία Εὐτρόπιον δι᾽ ἐμοῦ Πτολ[
ἔσχον τούτου τὸ ἴσον.

3 ευτροπιη corr. from ευτροπιον   4 γυμϚ πρῡ γενομϚ βουλ, λαμϚ, λαμϚ   8–9 ἴ[cιον] παγ᾽γα
12 l. εἰς σποράν, τελέσειν   13 l. τέσσαρα   14 l. ἥμιcυ   16 l. ἥμιcυ   20 l. ἀποδώσω
24 ως καθ- overwritten on something now illegible

'The 4th consulship of our lords Constantinus and Licinius, Augusti.
'To Aurelia Eutropion, daughter of Theodorus, also styled Chaeremon, ex-gymnasiarch, ex-prytanis, former senator of the glorious and most glorious city of the Oxyrhynchites:
'From Aurelius Dioscorus, son of Ammonius, from the same city:

'Of my own free will I undertake to lease for the current 10th and 8th year only, from your possessions around the village of Ision Panga in the embankment of Pekty in the *topos* called Telke, a three-eighths portion from the seventeen arouras held in partnership with Panares, which is six and three-eighths arouras by survey, for sowing flax, and to pay as rent on half (of the land) four talents of silver per aroura and instead of rent on the remaining half a half share of the crop that is produced: and I, the tenant, in exchange for the seed I provide and the work I do (take) the remaining half share and all the seed; the whole being guaranteed without risk, the taxes to devolve upon you the landowner who retain possession of the harvest until you receive your due. If the undertaking is confirmed to me, I shall necessarily pay the money rents and the rents-in-kind—the cash rent in the month Payni and the rent-in-kind from the flax that has been water-retted in the basin . . . of the current year, without delay. You have the right of execution on me as is proper. The undertaking is incontestable and in answer to the formal question, I have given assent.'

'The aforesaid consulship (2nd hand) 'Hathyr 10. I, Aurelia Eutropion, have received the duplicate of this through me, Ptol. . . .'

3256. APPLICATION FOR LEASE

12 1B.143/K(25)a   12·1 × 16·2 cm.   A.D. 317/18

An *epidoche* written along the fibres of a medium-brown sheet of papyrus; a small portion of the upper and left margin is preserved, but the document breaks off after the terms of the agreement are set out. Leonides in partnership with Dioscorus (see **I 103, 3255**) wishes to lease 13 arouras from Aurelius Heron to sow flax. The rent is a half share of the resulting crop.

→   Αὐρηλίῳ ῞Ηρων[ι] τῷ καὶ Cαρ[α]πίωνι απ[. .]λο.[
      γυμ(νασιαρχήσαντι) πρυτ(ανεύσαντι) τῆς λαμ(πρᾶς) [καὶ
      λαμ](προτάτης) ᾿Οξυρυγχειτῶ[ν πόλ(εως)
      παρὰ Αὐρηλίων Διοσκόρ[ου Ἀμ]μωνίου καὶ Λ[ε]ωνίδ[ου
      Θέωνος ἀμφοτ[έ]ρω[ν ἀπ]ὸ τῆς αὐτῆς πόλεως.
5   ἑκο[υ]cίως ἐπιδεχόμεθα μισθώcαcθαι πρὸς μ[ό-
      νον τὸ ἐνεστὸc ιβϚ'' καὶ [ιϚ'' κ]αὶ βϚ'' ἀπὸ τῶν ὑπαρ-
      χόντων cοι περὶ Ἀντιπέρα Πέλα ἐκ τοῦ Νικοβίου
      κλήρου ἀπὸ ἀρουρῶν εἴκοςι ἓξ τὰς ἐν ἀ⟨να⟩παύcι οὔcαc
      ἀρούρας δεκατρὶc εἰcπορὰν λινοκαλάμηc, ἐφ' ᾧ ἀντὶ
10   φόρου cὲ τὸν γεοῦχον ἔχει[ν ἐν] ἐξερέτῳ λινοκαλάμηc
      ἄρουραν μίαν· τῶν ἑτέρων ἀρουρῶν δώδεκα ἔχει(ν)
      cὲ τὸν [α]ὐτὸν γεοῦχον ἥμιcυ τῆc ἀπ' αὐτῶν περι-
      γινομένηc λινοκαλάμηc, καὶ ἡμᾶc τοὺc μεμιc-
      θωμένουc ἀνθ' ἧc ποιούμεθα γεωργίαc καὶ ὧν
15   παρέχομεν cπερμάτων καὶ ἀναλωμάτων πάντων

2 γυμϚ πρυʳ, λαμϚ, λαμ]Ϛ   6 ὑπαρ-   8 l. ἐν ἀναπαύcει   9 l. εἰc cπορὰν   10 l. ἐξαι-
ρέτῳ   11 εχεῑ   14 θ of ανθ corr. from τ

μ]έχρις κερου̂ cυνβροχιcμου̂ τη̂c λινοκαλάμηc καὶ

αὐτου̂ του̂ cυμβροχιcμου̂ τὸ λο[ι]πὸν ἥμιcυ μέρος

μετὰ καὶ του̂ περιγινομένου cπέρματος ἐξ ὁλοκ[λή(ρου)

ἀκίν]δυνα πάντα παντὸc κινδύν[ου, τω̂ν] τη̂[c γη̂c

20   ]..[...]..[

      .   .   .   .

16 l. καιρου̂ cυμβροχιcμου̂

'To Aurelius Heron also called Sarapion, (former *logistes*?), ex-gymnasiarch, ex-prytanis of the glorious and most glorious city of the Oxyrhynchites:

'From Aurelius Dioscorus, son of Ammonius, and Aurelius Leonides, son of Theon, both from the said city:

'Of our own free will we undertake to lease for the current 12th, 10th, and 2nd year only, from your property around Antipera Pela, being part of the allotment of Nicobius, of twenty-six arouras the thirteen arouras which are lying fallow, to be sown with flax; on condition that, in lieu of money rent, you the landlord receive one aroura of flax as a special payment; of the other twelve arouras you the said landlord receive half of the resulting crop and we the tenants, in compensation for the work we do and the seed and all the other expenses we incur up to the time of the retting of the flax and during the retting itself, receive the remaining half-portion along with the resulting seed complete, the whole being guaranteed without risk . . .'

1 απ[..]λο.[: in theory a patronymic might be read, e.g. Ἀπ[ολ]λογ[ένουc. But there are more attractions in ἀπ[ὸ] λογ[ιcτω̂ν. We might then identify Aurelius Heron-Sarapion with Valerius Heron-Sarapion, *logistes* in 308–9 (XXXIII **2666** 1 n.). J. G. Keenan has plausibly suggested that holders of the *logisteia* in this period took the name Valerius as a tribute to the imperial house (*ZPE* 11 (1973) 44–6). If the identification is correct, we must assume that Heron's new name was surrendered or forgotten when he left office.

7 Ἀντιπέρα Πέλα: XXVII **2473** 16 n.

10 ἐξερέτῳ: J. Herrmann, *Bodenpacht*, 115.

16 μ]έχρις suits the spacing better than ἄχρις; χωρίc suits neither traces nor sense. P. Cairo Isid. 74. 6 [τὰ τω̂ν ἀρουρω̂ν] ἔργα πάντα μέχρι τη̂c {τε} cυνκομιδη̂c κτλ.

cυνβροχιcμου̂ refers to the process of 'water-retting', see general introd. p. 130.

20 The small traces can be fitted to the normal formula: write, for example, δημοcί]ῳν [ὄντ]ῳ[ν πρὸc cὲ τὸν γεου̂χον.

3257. APPLICATION FOR LEASE

12 1B.143/K(4)a   15·6 × 24·8 cm.   10 November 318

An *epidoche* written along the fibres of a medium-brown, rather coarse sheet of papyrus. The original vertical folds have occasioned considerable wear and twisting of the fibres. The back is blank.

Leonides together with Ammonius, the son of Copres, wishes to lease 5 arouras of land near Ision Panga. The rate of 3 talents, 1,000 drachmas per aroura is somewhat less than that stipulated in XXXI **2585** (A.D. 315).

→ ὑπατείας τῶ[ν δεσ]ποτῶν ἡμῶν [Λικιν]ίου Σεβαστοῦ τὸ ϛ″ καὶ Κρίσπου
    [τοῦ ἐπι]φανεστάτου [Καίσαρ]ος τὸ αϛ″
κληρονόμοις [....].ως Οὐαλερίου δ[ιὰ Μ]ατρίν[ου] κηδεμόνος
παρὰ Αὐρηλίων [Λεω]ν[ί]δου Θέωνος καὶ Ἀμμωνίο[υ] Κοπρέ[ω]ς ἀμφ[οτέ]ρω(ν)
5 ἀπὸ τῆ[ς] λαμ(πρᾶς) καὶ λαμ(προτάτης) Ὀξυρυγχειτῶν πόλεως. ἑκουσίως ἐπιδεχό-
                               μεθα
μισθώσα[σ]θαι πρὸς μόνον τὸ ἐνε[στὸ]ς ιγ″ιαϛ″[γ]ϛ″ ἀπὸ τῶν ὑπαρχόντω(ν)
αὐτοῖς περὶ τὸ Ἰσίον Παγγᾶ ἐν περιχ[ώ]ματι Νέσλα ἐκ γεωμετρία[ς] ἀρού-
ρας πέντε οὔσας πρότερον Θωνίου Νέου καλουμένο[υ] εἰσπορὰν λινοκαλάμης καὶ τελέσιν σοι ὑπὲρ φόρου ἑ[κά]στης ἀρούρης [ἀ]νὰ ἀργυρίου ταλάν-
10 των τρίων καὶ δραχμῶν χιλίων [ἀ]κίνδυνα πάντ[α] παντὸς κινδύ-
νου τῶν τῆς γῆς δημοσίων καὶ [ἀννω]νῶν ὄντ[ων π]ρὸς ὑμᾶς το[ὺ]ς
γεούχους κυριεύοντας τῶν καρπ[ῶν ἕ]ως τὰ ὀφι[λόμε]να ἀπολάβη[τε.
β[ε]βαιουμε[....].[.]ης δὲ ἡμῖ[ν τ]ῆς ἐπιδοχῆ[ς ἐπ]άναγκε[ς
ἀ[π]οδώσωμ[εν τὸ]ν ἀργυρικὸν φ[ό]ρ[ο]ν ἐν δυσὶ μη[σ]ὶ Ἐπεὶφ καὶ ....[
15 τοῦ αὐτοῦ ἔτους ἀνυπερθέτως γινομένης ὑμῖν τῆς πράξεως
παρά τε ἡμῶν ἀλληλεγγύων ὄντων εἰς ἔκτισιν ὡς καθήκι. κυρία
ἡ ἐπιδοχὴ καὶ ἐπερωτηθέντες ὡμολογήσαμεν.
       ὑπατείας τῆς προκ(ειμένης) Ἀθὺρ ιδϛ′. (m. 2) [Ο]ὐαλέριος Ματρῖνος
       δι' ἐμοῦ Διονυσί[ου] ἔ⟨σ⟩χον το[ύτου] τὸ ἴσον.

1 ὑπατειας	4 αμφ[οτε]ρῶ	5 λαμ″, λαμ″	6 ὑπαρχοντῶ	7 ἰσιον παγ᾽γα
8 l. εἰς σπορὰν	9 l. τελέσειν ὑπερ	9–10 l. τάλαντα τρία, δραχμὰς χιλίας		11 ὑμας
14 l. ἀποδώσομεν	15 ανϋπερθετως, ὑμιν	16 αλληλεγ᾽γυων	l. καθήκει	18 προᵏ
19 ἰσον				

'In the consulship of our masters Licinius Augustus for the 5th time and Crispus the most noble Caesar for the 1st time.

'To the heirs of . . ., son of Valerius, through Matrinus the executor:

'From Aurelius Leonides, son of Theon, and Aurelius Ammonius, son of Copres, both of the glorious and most glorious city of the Oxyrhynchites:

'Of our own free will we undertake to lease for the current 13th, 11th, and 3rd year only from their holdings around Ision Panga in the embankment of Nesla five arouras by survey, which formerly belonged to Thonius, called Young, for the sowing of flax; and to pay you as rent three talents and one thousand drachmas of silver per aroura; the whole being guaranteed without risk, the taxes and annonae to devolve upon you the landlords who retain possession of the produce until you shall receive your due. If the undertaking is confirmed to us, we shall of necessity pay over the money rent in the two months Epeiph and . . . of the same year without delay. You have the right of execution upon us who are a mutual surety against payment as is proper. The undertaking is incontestable and in answer to the formal question we have given assent.

'14th day of Hathyr of the aforesaid consulate.' (2nd hand) I, Valerius Matrinus, have received the duplicate of this through me, Dionysius.'

8 Νέου: [.]νεου would also be possible, with space for one narrow letter. Otherwise the reading is certain: not νεω(τέρου).

11 [ἀννω]ρῶν: cf. P. Lond. III 979. 18 f. (p. 234).

13 β[ε]βαιουμε[can be read at the beginning, but there is a gap with space for 7–8 letters before]ηc. Either poor papyrus forced the scribe to leave a space, or he has (for example) written μενηc twice. No other variation of the *bebaiosis*-clause will account for the letters which remain or the position of δέ.

14 Ἐπεὶφ καὶ .....[: the last word should be a month-name, but the writing is difficult and perhaps in part a correction. Payni and Epeiph are normally specified, see D. Hennig, *Untersuchungen z. Bodenpacht*, 22–4. Here, however, Παῦνι is not an acceptable reading, nor indeed did the scribe have any reason to reverse the usual order. Within the one year of the lease only Mesore and Epagomenai remain. Of these, Μεϲορ[ή might perhaps be read (the initial mu is very plausible); but I should have expected to see more of the tail of rho.

15 f. γινομένης ὑμῖν τῆς πράξεως παρά τε ἡμῶν: the formula is similarly shortened in XXXI 2585 18 f. (see the note) and 3255 24.

16 κυρία: see Hässler, *Die Bedeutung d. Kyria-Klausels*, 28 ff. The clause 'will der Urkunde *absolute Beweiskraft* verleihen' (Wolff, *SZ* (RA) 90 (1973) 373, who discusses possible English translations of κυρία).

18 Ἀθὺρ ιδ: 10 November 318.

3258. APPLICATION FOR LEASE

12 1B.143/K(27)a   13·2 × 7·0 cm.   A.D. 319

The document is an *epidoche* in which Leonides leases an unknown quantity of land from Aurelius Dius for the current year. The land is near Antipera Pela (see **3259**, **3256**). The back is blank.

→   ὑπατείας τῶν δεσποτῶν ἡμῶν Κωνσταντίνου Αὐτοκράτορ[ο]c
       τὸ εϛ'' καὶ Λικινίου τοῦ ἐπιφανεστάτου Καίϲαρος τὸ [αϛ]''
       Αὐρηλίῳ Δίῳ Ζωΐλου ἀπὸ τῆς λαμ(πρᾶς) καὶ λα[μ(προτάτης)] Ὀξυρυγχ(ιτῶν)
            (vac.)   πόλεωϲ   (vac.)
5   παρὰ Αὐρηλίου Λεωνίδου Θέωνοϲ ἀπὸ τῆς αὐτῆς πόλεωϲ.
       ἑκου[cί]ωϲ ἐπιδ[έχ]ομ[αι μιcθ]ώϲα[c]θαι πρὸ[c] μόνον τὸ ἐνε-
       cτ[ὸc ιδϛ''ιβϛ''δϛ]'' [τὰς ὑπαρχούϲα]c coι πε[ρὶ Ἀντ]ιπέρα [Πέλα
                  .   .   .   .   .

1 ὑπατειαc   3 ζωΐλου, λαμϛ', οξυρυγχ'

'In the consulship of our masters Constantinus Imperator for the 5th time and Licinius the most noble Caesar for the 1st time.

'To Aurelius Dius, the son of Zoilus, from the glorious and most glorious city of the Oxyrhynchites, from Aurelius Leonides, son of Theon, from the same city: Of my own free will I undertake to lease for the current 14th, 12th, and 4th year only from your holdings around Antipera Pela . . .'

7 [ιδϛ'' ιβϛ'' δϛ]'': the space will permit three dates or two dates linked with καί; the former is more probable (see **3257** 6). There is not room for ἔτοc to be written out. I have restored the year as ιδ–ιβ–δ, since these leases are usually drawn up within the first four months of the Egyptian year, i.e. near to the end of the consular year.

3259. LEASE OF LAND

12 1B.143/K(23)a   13·6 × 8·5 cm.   A.D. 319

The beginning of a *misthosis* written along the fibres of a papyrus that has been folded twice vertically and endorsed on the back. Aurelius Apollonius also styled Serenus agrees to lease land near Antipera Pela to Leonides. The terms are missing.

→ ὑπατείας τῶν δεσποτῶν ἡμῶν Κωνσταντίνου
Cεβαστοῦ τὸ ε″ [κ]αὶ [Λικ]ινίου τοῦ ἐπιφανεστάτου
Καίcαρ[ο]c τ[ὸ α]″.
ἐμίcθωcεν Αὐρήλιοc Ἀπολλώνιοc ὁ καὶ Cερῆνοc
5   υἱὸc Ἀπολλωνίου απ . . . . . οξ ἀπὸ τῆc λαμπρᾶc
καὶ λαμπροτάτηc Ὀξ(υρυγχιτῶν) πόλεωc
Αὐρηλίῳ Λεωνίδῃ Θέωνοc ἀπὸ τῆc αὐτῆc πόλεωc
πρὸc μόνον τὸ ἐν[εcτὸc ιδ″ ιβ]″ δ (ἔτοc) τὰc ὑπαρχούcαc
coι περὶ [Ἀν]τιπέρα ʽΠέλαʼ ἐν . [. . . .] . ι Πρωτολε . . λεγομένου
10   α[. . .] . [. . . . .]ει . [. . .] . [. . . . .] . . [. . . .] . . [. . .] . [. .] . .

Back → μίcθωcιc[

1 ὑπατειας′   5 υἱος   6 οξ′   8 ιδ″ ιβ]″ δ″

'In the consulship of our masters Constantinus Augustus, for the fifth time, and Licinius the most noble Caesar, for the first time.

'Aurelius Apollonius alias Serenus son of Apollonius . . . from the glorious and most glorious city of the Oxyrhynchites leased to Aurelius Leonides son of Theon from the same city for the current 14th, 12th, and 4th year only the (so many arouras) which belong to you near Antipera Pela in . . .'
Back. 'Lease . . .'.

2 It would be palaeographically possible to read ϛ (= A.D. 320) instead of ε (= A.D. 319), but the traces later in the line, though doubtfully assigned to individual letters of the name of Licinius Caesar, cannot be made to conform with that of Constantine Caesar, the junior consul of A.D. 320, and the date in 8 denotes the Egyptian year A.D. 319/320, which makes it virtually certain that the date of this lease is some time in autumn A.D. 319.

5 απ . . . . . οξ : either another name or a title. The initial letters are like απ in the ἀπό which occurs later in this line: next a high curved stroke as if an abbreviation or possibly a tiny omicron ligatured to the preceding letter; then a pi-shaped letter (or letters) with the initial descender curving up sharply at the foot, followed by an abraded spot in which high traces and the tail of rho or iota can be seen. The next letter appears to be lambda or delta, followed by -οξω.

J. C. Shelton suggests reading the last seven letters as παρ[α]δοξω in error for παραδόξου (for the title see, e.g., P. Hamb. 21. 2–3), though παρα- seems rather too long for the space.

E. G. Turner suggests perhaps ἀπὸ παρ[α]δόξω⟨ν⟩ on the analogy of ἀπὸ λογιcτῶν, etc.

J. R. Rea tentatively suggests ἀπὸ cτρ(ατηγῶν) Ὀξ(υρυγχίτου); (cτρ′ οξ′ pap?). The ο of ἀπό, if right, is curiously, but not incredibly, misshapen. The next group would naturally be taken as cι, but τ is sometimes written here with the known ductus which puts the first half of the crossbar and the upright first and adds the second half of the crossbar separately. To read τ assumes that the second half of the crossbar is here lost in the damage. After οξ the impression of ω is chiefly produced by the hook on the foot of the ι of Ἀπολλώνιοc above in 4. The title of ex-strategus of Oxyrhynchus would apply to the father rather than the son. The known candidates would be the strategi of A.D. 287 (XIV **1690**), A.D. 292 (I **59**), and A.D. 316 (XVII **2113, 2114**).

8 τὸ ἐν[εϲτὸϲ ιδ″ ιβ]″ δ″: there is room to restore two regnal year numbers, cf. **3257** 6.

9 ϲοι. **3260** displays the same carelessness in pronouns.

ἐν.[....].ι Πρωτολε.. λεγομένου. After ἐν there is a trace somewhat below the base line; likeliest possibilities are α, γ, ι, κ, λ, μ, ρ, τ, χ. After the gap there is a little round loop and some traces below to the right which may belong to the line below; ο, ρ?, ω possible. The pattern may be ἐν τόπῳ... λεγομένου (l. -ῳ), cf. **3255** 9. The place name seems to be new. At the end of Πρωτολε.. (or -ε.[.].) the last trace is the end of a horizontal, ϲ best, υ possible. After ε there is a small rounded trace.

10 ἀ[π' ἀρουρῶν] ϲίκ[οϲι *vel sim.*?

3260. SUB-LEASE OF LAND

12 1B.143/K(29)a   10·2 × 25·2 cm.   A.D. 323

A fairly well-preserved contract written along the fibres of a thick, dirt-encrusted papyrus, in which Gaianus sub-leases 6 arouras to Leonides for a one-third share of the resulting crop. This lease, like **3259**, also a *misthosis*, quickly and bewilderingly shifts into the subjective style of the *epidoche*. The back is blank.

→   το]ῖ[ϲ ἀ]ποδιχθηϲομένοιϲ ὑπάτοιϲ τὸ γ′
       ἐμίϲθωϲεν Γαιανὸϲ Ἀμμωνίου ἀπὸ
       ἐποικίου Χουτῆ ϛ πάγου τοῦ Ὀξ(υρυγχίτου) νομοῦ
       Λεωνίδη Θέωνοϲ ἀπὸ τῆϲ λαμ(πρᾶϲ) καὶ λαμ(προτάτηϲ)
5   Ὀξυρυγχειτῶν πόλεωϲ πρὸϲ μόνον
       τὸ ἐνεϲτὸϲ ιη ϛ ιϛ ϛ″ η ϛ″ ἔτοϲ
       ἀφ' ὧν ἔχομεν ἐν μισθώϲει περὶ κώ-
       μην Ἀντιπέρα Πέλα ἀρούραϲ ἐξ (γίνονται) (ἄρουραι) ϛ
       εἰϲ ϲπορὰν λινοκαλάμηϲ ἐφ' ᾧ
10   ἀντὶ φόρου ἔχειν ϲὲ τὸν μεμιϲθωκό-
       τα τὸ τρίτον μέροϲ τῆϲ περιγινομέ-
       νηϲ λινοκαλάμηϲ κἀμὲ δὲ τὸν μεμι-
       ϲθωμένον τὸ λοιπ[ὸν μέροϲ ἔχειν,
       ἐμοῦ τοῦ Λεωνίδου [*c.* 10
15   τὰ ϲπέρματα ἀκίνδυνα [παντὸϲ
       κινδύνου τῶν τῆϲ γῆϲ δ[ημοϲίων
       ὄντων πρὸϲ τὸν μεμιϲθ[ωκότα
       κυριεύοντα τῶν καρπῶ[ν ἕωϲ τὸ
       τρίτο[ν] μέροϲ ἀπολάβῃϲ. β[εβαιου-
20   μέν]ηϲ δὲ τῆϲ μιϲθώϲεωϲ [ἐπάναγ-
       κ]εϲ ἀποδώϲω [τὸ τρίτο]ν μέρ[οϲ ἐν τῷ
       κ]αιρῷ ἀνυπερθέτωϲ γινο[μένηϲ ϲοι

1 ὑπατοιϲ   2, 28 γαϊανοϲ   8 ϛ—ϛ

τ]ῆс πράξεωс παρά τε ἐμοῦ [ὡс καθήκει.

ϝαντα δετα . . . . [

25 . . . . [.].[.] . . . . τοс. κυρία [

ἡ μίсθωсιс καὶ ἐπερωτηθ(εὶс) ὡμολ[όγηсεν.

. .επ . . . . . . π . ουτϙαπ . . θ . . [

(m. 2) Γαιανὸс μεμίс[θωκα τὴν

γῆν καὶ ἔсχον τὸ ἴсον [τῆс μι-

30 сθώсεωс. Ἐπίμαχο[с ἔγρα-

ψα ὑπὲρ αὐτοῦ γράμ[ματα

μὴ εἰδότοс.

31 ὕπερ

'Under the consuls to be designated for the 3rd time.

'Gaianus, the son of Ammonius, from the hamlet of Choute in the 6th (?) district of the Oxyrhynchite nome, leased to Leonides, the son of Theon, from the glorious and most glorious city of the
Oxyrhynchites for the current 18th, 16th, and 8th year only from those which we hold on lease around
the village of Antipera Pela, six arouras, that is 6 ar., for the sowing of flax, on condition that, instead
of money rent, you the lessor receive the one-third portion of the resulting flax crop and I the lessee
receive the remaining portion—I, Leonides, [taking] the seed, being guaranteed against risk, the taxes
on the land devolving upon the lessor who retains possession of the crop until you take the one-third
portion. If the lease is confirmed, of necessity I will pay over the one-third portion at the appropriate
time without delay, you having the right of execution upon me as is proper. . . .

'The lease is incontestable and in response to the formal question he has given assent. . . .'

(2nd hand) I, Gaianus, have leased the land and have received a copy of the lease. I, Epimachus,
wrote on his behalf since he is illiterate.'

1 το]ῖ[с ἀ]ποδιχθηсομένοιс ὑπάτοιс τὸ γ´: A.D. 323. Cf. e.g. XLIII **3122** introd.

2 ἐποικίου Χουτῆ ϛ πάγου: Χουτῆ is unattested. The number of the district is broken, but stigma fits
the traces better than epsilon or gamma.

14 ἐμοῦ τοῦ Λεωνίδου[: a participle, e.g. λαμβάνοντος or παρέχοντος, should be supplied. In these
part-share leases the lessees supply as well as retain the seed (see **3255** 16–17, **3256** 15–18).

24–5 πάντα δὲ τὰ κτλ: a further condition? Perhaps about the disposition of labour, since there is
no such clause in the earlier part of the document (cf. the other part-share leases, I **103** 11–12, **3255** 16,
3256 14), possibly on the lines of P. Cair. Isid. 103 15–17: τὰ δὲ τῶν ἀρουρῶν ἔργα πάντα ἡμῖс (ἡμεῖс) οἱ
μιсθούμενοι ποιήсομεν. In any case, this does not appear to be part of the *praxis*-clause.

27 From its place in the document, this should be a date (compare **3255** 26, **3257** 18); it is possible
to read π.ον as προκ(ειμένης) but the traces before this do not really fit ὑπατείαс τῆс, and after, the letters
do not suit a month. The line appears to have been squeezed in after the subscription was written.

3261. CONTRACT CONCERNING RECRUITS

12 1B.143/K(12)a   25·8 × 22·8 cm.   A.D. 324

Four meniarchs, among them Leonides, have provided recruits on behalf of the
signatories, who acknowledge liability for the expense by this contract. Most of the
subscription is missing but part of the right margin, nearly as broad as the document
itself, survives and bears at its top, apparently in the first hand, the acknowledgement
of one of the subscribers.

The document gives no details of the assessment, though it does indicate that the service is compulsory, but it is tempting to conjecture that the guild as a whole has assumed the liability for which certain members were responsible. Compare, for example, XXXI 2579, in which a meniarch of a tow-workers' guild is paying the ἐπικεφάλαιον πόλεως on behalf of two of its members.

On recruiting in general see A. H. M. Jones, *The Later Roman Empire* ii 615 ff., A. C. Johnson and L. C. West, *Byzantine Egypt, Econ. Stud.* 215–18.

Of the two government officials mentioned the *praeses* Sabinianus is well attested, but the *dux* Barba is not otherwise known.

The back is blank.

→   τοῖς ἐσομ[έ]νοις ὑπά[τοις] τὸ δ.
     οἱ ἑξῆς ὑπογράφειν [μ]έλλον[τε]ς
     Λεωνίδῃ καὶ Θέ[ων]ι καὶ Μ.[. . .] καὶ
     Σαρμάτῃ μηνιάρχαις .[c. 5]
5   των χαίρειν. ἐπειδὴ ἐπ[ε-]
     βλήθημεν παρασχεῖν τίρω[νας]
     νεολέκτους κατὰ κέλευσιν το[ῦ δια-]
     σημοτάτου ἡμῶν ἡγε[μ]όνος
     Σαβινιανοῦ κατὰ πρόσταξιν [τ]οῦ διασημοτάτ[ου]
10   δουκὸς Βάρβα καὶ [πα]ρασχόντες
     ὑμεῖς αὐτοὺς ἐνεγυήσασθαι διὰ
     χιρογραφειῶν, κατὰ ταῦτα [ὁμολο-]
     γοῦμεν τὰ πάντα ἁπαξαπλ[ῶς]
     ἀναλώματα ὑποστῆναι, [ἕκα-]
15   στον κατὰ τὰ μέρη, καὶ ἐπὶ τούτοις
     συνευδοκεῖν ἡμᾶς πᾶσι τοῖς
     διαφέρουσι τοῖς αὐτοῖς τίρω[σι]
     διὰ τὸ συνπεπῖσθαι κ[α]ὶ συν-
     ευδοκεῖν ἐπὶ τούτοις. κύρια τὰ
20   γράμματα ἁπλᾶ γραφέντα ἐπὶ ὑπο-
     γραφῇ ἡμῶν καὶ ἐπερωτη-
     θέντες ὡμολογήσαμεν.
     ὑπατείας τῆς προκει[μ]έν[ης, c. 5] ιβ.

      .   .   .   .   .   .

Right margin at top → Διόσκορος [.].ίωνος εὐδοκῶ.

11 l. ἐνεγυήσασθε   14 ὑποστῆναι   18 l. συμπεπεῖσθαι   23 ὑπατείας

'Under the consuls to be designated, for the fourth time.

'Those about to undersign to Leonides and Theon and Matrinus(?) and Sarmates, meniarchs of the . . . greetings.

'Since we were enjoined to furnish newly chosen recruits according to the order of our most perfect *praeses* Sabinianus (issued) in accordance with the command of the most perfect *dux* Barba and you furnished them and guaranteed them by deeds of surety, accordingly we agree to undertake all expenses whatsoever, each proportionately, and on these conditions we consent to everything pertaining to these same recruits, because we have agreed and consent on these conditions. The document, written in one copy over our subscription, is valid and in answer to the formal question we gave our assent.

'In the consulship aforesaid, . . . 12th.

'. . . I, Dioscorus son of . . ., consent.'

1 The date is A.D. 324, cf. e.g. XLIII **3122** introd.

3 Μ . . : Ματ[ρίνῳ? See **3257** 3, 18. Compare also XXXIII **2673** (of A.D. 304), where the names Sarmates and Matrinus occur together. However, other names, e.g. Μέλ[ανι, could also suit the traces.

4 μηνιάρχαις. That all four men are meniarchs of the same guild is almost certain. Cf. VIII **1139** 1–2 and O. Tait II 1986. 2, both documents addressed to several meniarchs of a single guild. The guild name is shorter than the word in **3262** 1, certainly too short for c(τ)ιπποκογχιcτῶν, c(τ)ιπποπραγματευτῶν, c(τ)ιπποτιμητῶν, or c(τ)ιπποχειριcτῶν. Perhaps cιππάτων is possible, if cιππαcδεc implies cιππᾶτεc in XXXI **2579** 9.

9 Cαβινιανοῦ. For collected references see PLRE I 789 s.v. Sabinianus (2).

10 If there was only one *dux* acting at this time in Egypt, see P. Abinn. p. 14, Barba was the *dux Aegypti et Thebaidos*; if not, he may have been *dux Aegypti* only. On Egypt's military commands in the fourth and fifth centuries see R. Rémondon in *CÉ* 40 (1965) 180–97.

24 [.].ιωνοc. [Ἀ]πίωνοc would suit the traces, but [ʹΩ]ρίωνοc would not. No doubt there are other less common possibilities.

3262. RECEIPT?

12 1B.143/K(30)a   24 × 9·4 cm.   A.D. 328

This badly abraded document is included because Leonides has written it himself, styling himself meniarch of a tow-linked guild. While the language suggests that the text may be a receipt for repayment of a loan, the exact nature of the transaction is obscure. The papyrus is of poor quality; the back is blank.

↓ Κόμων[ι] υἱ[ῷ] Θωνίῳ Λεωνίδης μ[η]νιάρχης cιππ . . . . .
   . . [.]. χαίρειν. ἀφ' ὧν . . [. . .] . . ἀπὸ προτέρου λόγου [. . .
   . . . . [. .] . . . [. .] . . . τεccαράκοντα δύο ἥμιcου
   .] . . . . . . καὶ οὐδένα λόγον ἔχ[ε]ι[.] πρὸς οὐδενός. ⟦χιρ⟧ ἔχεις μου χῖρα(ν)
5 κβ καὶ ιβ καὶ δ [ʹΕ]πεὶφ τὸν πρότερον καὶ νῦν ἔcχηκα ταπ . . . νηδε
   γ]είνοντε δὲ τὸν πρότερον λόγον ⟦ . . ⟧ γείνοντέ μου μοδίουc μ . . ʹ.
   (ἔτουc) κβʹ καὶ ιβʹ καὶ δʹ. ὁ αὐτὸc Λεωνίδηc [cε]cη(μείωμαι).

1 υἱ[ω], l. Θωνίου   3 l. ἥμιcυ   4 χιρᾱ; l. χεῖρα   6 μ of μοδίουc corr. from δ
7 [cε]cηʹ

'To Comon son of Thonius, Leonides meniarch of the tow-. . ., greetings. Of those which . . . from the former account . . . forty-two and one-half (modii?) and you (or he) have no claim of any kind. You have my chirograph (of?) the 22nd and 12th and 4th year, the former (account?), and now I (or you) have received . . . . My(?) total for the previous account is forty-. . . Year 22 and 12 and 4. I the same Leonides have signed.'

1 Κόμων[ι]: or Κύμων[ι]. The latter is unattested.

ϲιππ.....: a guild obviously connected with tow. After the first four letters the traces appear to be οϲ or οτ or possibly π, followed by a vertical descender like ι, then a semilunate shape ligatured to the previous vertical. The final letter appears to be omega with a line above which may represent a nu in suspension. These traces cannot be reconciled with the title on the back of I **103** (ϲτιππoτιμηταί) or the guild name from **3261** 4–5. It is just possible that Leonides wrote ϲιππ⟨ο⟩πιοω(ν) for ϲιπποποιῶν, see XXXVI **2799** 4, but the reading of omicron is very doubtful.

2 ..[...]..: at the end λω more likely than λoυ or μoυ. ὀφ[εί]λω, ἔχ[ει] μoυ, ἔχ[ειϲ] μoυ, are all possible readings.

3 τεϲϲαράκοντα: cf. 6.

4 .].......: perhaps πλῆρεϲ or ἐκ πλήρουϲ.

οὐδένα κτλ. This version of the usual phrase is curious. πρὸϲ οὐδενόϲ can be explained as a conflation of e.g. πρὸϲ ϲὲ περὶ οὐδενόϲ, but the normal verb form ἔχω cannot be read. The trace, which extends below the break, is clearly from iota, therefore ἔχ[ε]ι, ἔχ[ε]ι[ϲ], or ἔχ[ε]ι[ν] was written. The most reasonable possibility, ἔχειν, is unlikely because the space is insufficient for a letter the size of nu. See also on ἔϲχηκα in 5 n.

χιρᾶ = χῖρα(ν), l. χεῖρα, in the sense of χειρόγραφον. It is not clear whether Leonides thinks of the present document as the chirograph or is referring to some previous document.

5 κβ καὶ ιβ καὶ δ: 22nd year of Constantine, 12th of Constantine II, 4th of Constantius II.

['E]πείφ: between 25 June and 24 July A.D. 328.

τὸν πρότερον. The punctuation is uncertain; either this goes with the preceding date, presumably as an accusative of respect (see Mayser II 2. 326 ff.), or it belongs with the subsequent καὶ νῦν ἔϲχηκα, though how it fits in is unclear.

ἔϲχηκα: or ἔϲχηκαϲ. The final traces are broken and the bits may belong to alpha or αϲ. If ἔϲχηκα is correct, then Leonides has received a payment and the οὐδένα clause should be phrased in the normal fashion, i.e. οὐδένα λόγον ἔχω κτλ. To read ἔϲχηκαϲ (and with it ἔχ[ε]ι[ϲ] in 4) one must assume that Leonides has written a receipt in the second person for a payment he himself is making.

6 In view of the other textual peculiarities in this receipt, it may be that Leonides has merely repeated himself in this line and that one γίνονται should be deleted.

For μoυ read probably μoι, though since the μ of μoδίουϲ has been corrected from δ, it may be that he wrote μoυδ as a false start for μoδίουϲ and did not correct efficiently.

μ..'. From line 3 one might expect μβ (ἥμιϲυ), and that may be correct. However, the second figure looks most like ϵ and the third figure or symbol has an oblique descender at the left which is not easily reconciled with the usual signs for ½, viz. ϛ and L.

VII. MINOR TEXT

3263. Monthly report of village scribe. 31 4B.16/C(1–3)c. 8 × 17 cm. A.D. 215.
Compare XLIII **3133** for this type of text and the parallels. This one has been referred
to in XXXVIII **2876** 14–16 n. and in XLV **3243** 2 n. for the name of the strategus,
who here as a result of the Constitutio Antoniniana bears the nomen Aurelius in addition to Calpurnius.

→ ¹ Αὐρηλίῳ Καλπουρνί[ῳ Ἰ]ϲιδ[ώ]ρῳ ² τῷ καὶ Ἁρποκρατίων[ι] ϲτρ(ατηγῷ)
Ἀρϲι(νοίτου) ³ Θεμ(ίϲτου) καὶ Πολ(έμωνοϲ) μερίδων ⁴ παρὰ Αὐρηλί[ο]υ Ἑρ.[.].ο( )
⁵ κωμογρ(αμματέωϲ) Ἀπόλ[λω]νοϲ πόλεωϲ ⁶ καὶ Ψιντεώ. (vac.) ⁷ δηλῶ μηδὲν ἔχιν
⁸ ἀνῆκον ϲημᾶναι ⁹ ταῖϲ τοῦ ἰδίου λόγου καὶ ¹⁰ ἀρχιερέωϲ ἐπιτροπαῖϲ ¹¹ τοῦ Μεϲορὴ
μηνὸϲ τοῦ ¹² διεληλυθότοϲ κγ (ἔτουϲ). (vac.)

Back ↓ (m. 2?) ¹³ Απο.[..] Ψιντεώ, ¹⁴ Μεϲορή

| 2 ϲτρ⌐, αρϲ·(?) | 3 θε^μ, πο^λ | 4 ερ.[.].° | 5 κωμογρ⌐ | 7 l. ἔχειν | 12 κγ^L |

'To Aurelius Calpurnius Isidorus alias Harpocration, strategus of the Arsinoite nome, departments of Themistes and Polemon, from Aurelius (Hermaeus?, Hermon?, Hermas?), village scribe of
Apollonopolis and Psinteo. I declare that I have nothing to report relating to the procuratorships of
the *idios logos* and of the high priest for the month of Mesore of the past 23rd year.' Back (2nd hand?)
'Apollonopolis and Psinteo, Mesore.'

4 Obvious, but unconfirmed, possibilities are Ἑρμ[α]ίο(υ), Ἕρμ[ω]νο(ϲ), Ἑρμ[ᾶ]το(ϲ).
5–6 For the village names see P. Tebt. II pp. 368, 412.
9–10 ταῖϲ . . . ἐπιτροπαῖϲ. This supports the view that the departments of the idiologus and the
high priest were not united till a late date, if ever, see P. Swarney, *The Ptolemaic and Roman Idios Logos*,
pp. 133–4.
11–12 The report is for Mesore of 23 Caracalla, otherwise 25 July–29 August A.D. 215. The date
of writing must be after 29 August, the last day of this leap year, but should be within a few days of it.
After 12 there is blank papyrus for a depth of *c.* 5 cm., but the bottom margin is torn. Date clause
and subscription are expected; they may possibly have been written further down.
13 The sense requires something like Ἀπόλ[(λωνοϲ πόλεωϲ) καὶ] Ψ.

3264. Declaration about Bribery. Published by A. K. Bowman in *Collectanea Papyrologica*. Texts published in honor of H. C. Youtie, by A. E. Hanson. Part I (= PTA 19) No. 21. 30 4B.35/L(1–2)a. 9·8 × 16·4 cm. A.D. 80–1

¹ [...].[....].[² Ἑρμοφίλῳ .[........].[......].[..]. ³ παρὰ Ὀρϲε[ν]ο̣ύ̣[φεωϲ] τοῦ
Διοϲκό[ρο]υ̣ καὶ Ψ[ο]ϲ- ⁴ νέωϲ τοῦ Ψεν[μεί]νιοϲ καὶ Πεν[άμ]εωϲ ⁵ τοῦ Ἀμεννέωϲ [τῶ]ν̣ ϲὺν
ἄλλο[ιϲ πρ]εϲβυ- ⁶ τέρων κώμηϲ Πεεννὼ τῆϲ μέϲηϲ το- ⁷ παρχίαϲ. πρὸϲ τ̣ὸ ἐπιδοθὲν
Κλαυδίωι ⁸ Ἡρακλείωι ϲτρατηγῷ ὑπό τε ἡμῶν καὶ ⁹ τῶν ϲυνπρεϲ[β]υτέρων ἀναφόριον κα-
¹⁰ τὰ Διογένου[ϲ] χωματ[[ετ]]επιμελητοῦ ¹¹ περὶ τοῦ εἰληφέναι αὐτὸν παρὰ ἀν- ¹² δρῶν πεντήκοντα ἑνὸϲ ἐκ (δραχμῶν) δ εἰϲ ¹³ τὸ μὴ ἐργάϲαϲθαι αὐτοὺϲ εἰϲ τὰ δημό- ¹⁴ ϲια χώματα τὴν
πενταναυβίαν ¹⁵ καὶ περὶ τοῦ διεϲκεπακ̣έναι αὐτ̣[ὸν] ¹⁶ ἄλλουϲ ἄνδραϲ ἐννέα ὁμοίωϲ ¹⁷ εἰϲ
τὸ μὴ ἀπε̣ργάϲαϲθαι, ἐπιζητή- ¹⁸ ϲαντόϲ ϲου τ̣[ὰ] ὀνόματα τῶν προγε- ¹⁹ γραμμένω[ν]
ἐδηλώϲαμεν ἀπὸ τού- ²⁰ των ὀνόμα̣[τ]α̣ ἀνδρῶν δεκατρι- ²¹ ῶν οἳ καὶ ἐ̣[γ]γράπτωϲ
προϲεφώνη- ²² ϲαν τῷ ϲτρα[τ]ηγῷ μηδὲν δεδωκέ- ²³ ναι αὐτοὺϲ μ[ή]τε τῷ Διογένει μηδὲ
²⁴ τοῖϲ αὐτοῦ μηδ' ἄλλῳ τ[ι]ν̣ὶ̣ ὑπὲρ τοῦ ²⁵ μὴ ἐργάϲα[ϲθαι εἰϲ τὰ χώ]ματα· ἐπι- ²⁶ ζητοῦντος
δέ ϲου τὰ τῶν λοιπῶν ²⁷ ὀνόματα ἀποφαινόμεθα ²⁸ ὀμνύν̣τ̣[εϲ] τὴν Αὐτοκράτοροϲ ²⁹ Τίτου
Καίϲ[αρο]ϲ Οὐεϲπα[ϲ]ι̣ανοῦ ³⁰ Ϲεβαϲτοῦ τύχην μηδὲν δύναϲ- ³¹ θαι ἀποδεῖξαι [[δ]] τῶν
διὰ τοῦ προ- ³² κειμένου ἀναφορίου δεδηλω- ³³ μένων. εὐορκοῦϲ̣ι μ[ὲν] ἡμεῖν ³⁴ εὖ εἴη,
ἐπ̣ι̣ο̣[ρ]κοῦϲι δὲ [τὰ ἐνα]ντία. ³⁵ (ἔτουϲ) γ Αὐτοκράτορ[οϲ Τίτου Καίϲαροϲ ³⁶ Οὐε]ϲπα-
ϲι̣α̣ν̣[οῦ Ϲεβαϲτοῦ...... .

12 ϲ   33 l. ἡμῖν   35 Lγ

'To Hermophilus ... from Orsenouphis, son of Dioscorus, and Psosneus, son of Psenmeinis, and Pennamis, son of Amenneus, the elders, amongst others, of the village of Peenno in the middle toparchy. Further to the petition handed in to Claudius Heracleius the strategus by us and our fellow elders against Diogenes the superintendent of the dykes about his taking from fifty-one men four drachmas each for their non-performance of the five-naubia duty on the public dykes and having covered up similarly for nine other men in respect of their failure to complete their work, in response to your demand for the names of the aforementioned, we presented the names of thirteen men from among them who reported in writing to the strategus that they had not given anything to Diogenes or to his agents or to anyone else to avoid work on the dykes; but in response to your demand for the names of the others we declare on oath by the fortune of Imperator Titus Caesar Vespasianus Augustus that we are unable to produce any of the names indicated in the aforementioned petition. May it be well for us if we swear truly, but the reverse if we swear falsely. Year 3 of Imperator Titus Caesar Vespasianus Augustus (month and day).'

3265. Declaration by Glassworkers. Published by A. K. Bowman in *Collectanea Papyrologica*. Texts published in honor of H. C. Youtie, by A. E. Hanson. Part II (= PTA 20) No. 81. 3 1B.77/B(3)b. 15·3×25·7 cm. June/July A.D. 326

Col. ii

→ (m. 1) Ὑπατείας τῶν δεςπ]οτῶν ἡμῶν Κωνςταν-
τίνου ⟨Αὐγούςτου⟩ τὸ ζ′ καὶ Κω]νςταντίου τοῦ ἐπιφανες-
τάτου Καίςαρ]ος τὸ α′. (vac.)
Φλαουίῳ Λευκαδί]ῳ λογιςτῇ Ὀξυρυγχίτο[υ
5   παρὰ τοῦ κοινοῦ τῶ]ν ὑελουργῶν τῆς λαμ(πρᾶς)
καὶ λαμ(προτάτης) Ὀξ](υρυγχιτῶν) πόλεως δι᾽ ἐμοῦ Αὐρ[η-
λίου Ζωίλου ....].· ἐπιζητοῦν[τί
coι λόγον πά]ντων τῶν ἀν[η-
κόν[τ]ων τῇ ἡμετ[έρᾳ τέ]χνῃ εἰς χρείαν [ἐπι-
10   cκε[υ]ῆς θερμῶν δημοcίου βαλανίου τῆς
πόλεως ἀναγκαίως ἐντάξας ἐπιδίδ[ωμι
ἵν᾽ εἰδέναι ἔχοι cοῦ ἡ ἐμμέλια· ἔcτ[ι δέ·
εἰς χρείαν θερμῶν λουτρῶν (vac.) κεν[τ(ηνάρια) ..·
εἰς χρείαν ξυcτοῦ (vac.) κεντ[(ηνάρια) ..·
15   ὡς τοῦ κεντ(ηναρίου) α (τάλαντα)κβ·
γί(νονται) κεντ(ηνάρια) ξ, γίν(ονται) (τάλαντα) Ἀτκ·
ἅπερ προcφωνοῦμεν. (vac.)
ὑπα]τείας τῆς προκ(ειμένης) (vac.) Ἐπε[ὶφ ..·

(m. 2) Αὐρήλιος] Ζωίλος ἐπιδέδωκα
20   ὡς πρόκει(ται)

4 οξυρυγ᾽χιτο[υ   5 λαμ𝈦   6 οξ]?   11 αναγ᾽καιως   12 ϊν   14 κενᵀ
15 κενᵀ, ⌐   16 γι κενᵀ ξ γιν⁻ ⌐ Ἀτκ   18 προᴷ   20 προκε)

(1st hand) 'In the consulship of our masters Constantinus Augustus for the seventh time and Constantius the most illustrious Caesar for the first time. To Flavius Leucadius logistes of the Oxyrhynchite nome from the guild of glass-workers of the glorious and most glorious city of the Oxyrhynchites through me, Aurelius Zoilus . . . . In response to your demand for an account of all the matters affecting our profession relating to the service of fitting out the warm baths in the public bath of the city, I have perforce drawn it up and submit it in order that your grace may be able to know. It is: for the work needed on the warm baths, x hundred pounds; for the work needed on the gymnasium, x hundred pounds; at a rate of 22 talents per hundred pounds. Total 6000 pounds, total 1320 talents. Which we accordingly report. In the aforementioned consulship, Epeiph . . . (2nd hand) I, Aurelius Zoilus, have presented this as set out above.'

3266. Acknowledgement of a Loan. Published by A. K. Bowman in *Collectanea Papyrologica*. Texts published in honor of H. C. Youtie, by A. E. Hanson. Part II (= PTA 20) No. 82. 31 4B.10/E(1–2)a. 25·3×14·2 cm. 13 August A.D. 337. This contract is written in duplicate on a single sheet of papyrus. The texts are identical with the minor exceptions noted in the apparatus and apart from the fact that the line divisions do not correspond.

Col. i

→   Ὑπατείας Φλαουίου Φιλικιανοῦ καὶ Φαβίου Τιτιανοῦ
    τῶν λαμπροτάτων, Μεσορὴ κ'. (vac.)
    Αὐρήλιος Εὐλόγιος Λεοντέως μητρὸς Εὐσεβίας ἀπὸ
    τῆς λαμ(πρᾶς) καὶ λαμ(προτάτης) Ὀξυρυγχειτῶν πόλεως Φλαουίῳ Ἀννια-
5   νῷ πρωτήκτορι διὰ Αὐρηλίου Ἡρακλήου πραγματευ-
    τοῦ χαίρειν. ὁμολογῶ ἐσχηκέναι παρὰ σοῦ εἰς λόγον
    πραγματίας διὰ χειρὸς ἐξ οἴκου σου ἀργυρίου Σεβαστῶ(ν)
    νομίσματος τάλαντα πεντακόσια, (τάλαντα) φ', κεφαλαίου
    ἐπὶ τῷ με ἀντὶ τοῦ αἱροῦντός σοι μέρους τῆς τού-
10   των ἐπικερδείας τελέσιν σοι καθ' ἕκαστον μῆνα
    ἀπὸ] τοῦ ἑξῆς μηνὸς Θὼθ τοῦ εἰσιόντος λβ' κβ' ιδ' ε γ (ἔτους)·
    ἀργυρ]ίου τάλαντα δέκα καὶ τὸ προκίμενον κεφάλαι-
    ον ἀ]κίνδυνον ὂν παντὸς κινδύνου καὶ ἀνυπόλο-
    γον π]αντὸς ὑπολόγου ἐπάναγκες ἀποδώσω
15   σοι τ]ῷ Φαμενὼθ μηνὶ τοῦ αὐτοῦ εἰσιόντος ἔτους
    ἀνυπερθέτως. εἰ δὲ μή, ἐκτίσω σοι τοῦ ὑπερ-
    πεσόντος χρόνου κατὰ μῆνα ἕκαστον ἀργυρί-
    ου τάλαντα δεκαὲξ καὶ δραχμὰς τετρακισχιλείας
    ἄχρ[ι ἀ]ποδόσεως τοῦ κεφαλαίου, γεινομένης
20   σοι τῆς πράξεως παρά τε ἐμοῦ καὶ ἐκ τῶν ὑπαρ-
    χόντων μου πάντων. κύριον τὸ χιρόγραφον
    δι[σσ]ὸν [γρ]αφὲν κ[α]ὶ ἐπερωτηθεὶς ὡμολόγησα.

. . . .

3 μη‾, ii   4 λαμϛ και λαμϛ οξ', ii   l. Ὀξυρυγχιτῶν   7 l. πραγματείας. σεβαστω‾
σεβαστων, ii   8 Ⳑ   10 l. τελέσειν   11 λβ' κβ' ιδ' ε γ ϛ'   λβ' κβ' ιδ' εϛ γϛ', ii   12 l.
προκείμενον   18 l. τετρακισχιλίας   19 l. γινομένης   21 l. χειρόγραφον

'In the consulship of Flavius Felicianus and Fabius Titianus the most illustrious, Mesore 20. Aurelius Eulogius, son of Leonteus, whose mother is Eusebia, from the glorious and most glorious city of the Oxyrhynchites to Flavius Annianus, *protector*, through Aurelius Heracleus, agent, greetings. I acknowledge that I have received from you from hand to hand out of your house to the account of my business a capital sum of five hundred talents in the coinage of the Augusti, talents 500, on condition that, instead of your proportionate share of the profit from this money, I shall pay to you each month from the next month Thoth of the coming year 32, 22, 14, 5, 3, a sum of ten talents and I shall perforce repay to you without delay in the month of Phamenoth of the same year the aforementioned capital sum free of all risk and not subject to any claims; otherwise, I shall pay to you in each month of the extra time a sum of sixteen talents and four thousand drachmas until the capital is repaid, with you having the right of execution upon me and all my property. The deed, of which two copies are written, is valid and in answer to the formal question I have given my consent. . . .'

INDEXES

Figures in small raised type refer to fragments, small Roman figures to columns. References in square brackets are to words wholly supplied by conjecture or from other sources. References in round brackets are to words represented by a symbol. The asterisk indicates words not to be found in LSJ⁹ or its supplement. The article is not indexed, and καί is indexed in the literary sections only.

I. NEW LITERARY TEXTS

(a) ALCMAN, ETC. (3209–3213)

ἀγέρωχος 3209 ² 7?
αγκα.[3211 ² 5.
ἀγνός 3212 2?
-ακολο]ύθως 3210 ² 11?
ἄκρος 3209 ¹ 9.
Ἀλκμάν (end-title) 3209 ¹ 12.
ἀλλά 3211 ² 1?
ἄλλος 3211 ² 1?
ἀνήρ 3213 6.
ἀνιέναι 3213 2.
ἀοιδά 3212 3.
ἀπαλός 3210 ² 26?
ἀπό 3209 ¹ 8, 9.
ἀρᾶσθαι 3213 5.
Ἀρχίδαμος 3210 ² 3?, 6?
Ἀσκαλαφ[3210 ³ ii 3.
ἄτερ 3210 ² 10? 3212 2?
ἀχώ 3209 ¹ 8.

βαρύς (βαρεῖα) 3210 ² 27?

γᾶ 3212 6.
γαιο[3210 ² 11.
γαμ[3209 ⁴ 3.
-γαμία (-ος) 3211 ² 3?
γάμος 3213 5.
γέρας 3212 7?
γῆ see γᾶ
γλυκύς 3213 3.
γράφεσθαι 3210 ² 10.
γυνή 3213 6.

δαισομ[(δαίνυσθαι?) 3211 ² 3.
δέ 3209 ¹ 8 3212 2 1?, 3? 3213 3.
δείδειν (δέδοικα) 3212 4.
δή 3213 4?
διά 3210 ¹ i 10, 12?
δόμος 3209 ¹ 9.

δύνασθαι 3210 ² 19.
δύο 3210 ¹ i 10 3213 3.

Ἕβρος 3209 ² 1?
εἶναι 3210 ² 11.
εἰς 3210 ¹ i 13?
εἰς 3210 ² 16.
ἐκ 3209 ² 10? 3213 2.
ἐκεῖνος 3210 ⁴ i 2.
ἐλπίς 3211 ² 1.
ἐπί 3212 6.
ἐρατός 3213 [1], 5.
εὐθύς (εὐθεῖα) 3210 ² 23?
εὐθύς (εὐθύ?) 3209 ¹ 6.
εὐνή 3213 7.
ἔχειν 3213 2.
ἔως 3210 ² 25?
ἑωσφο[ρ- 3210 ² 25?

-ζύγιος 3211 ² 4.

ἡμεῖς 3210 ⁴ i 1.
ἠχώ see ἀχώ

θεῖος 3210 ² 23?
θεός 3212 2?
θυμός 3212 4.

καί 3209 ² 7?, 3212 3?, 4 3213 6(bis).
καλλίροος 3213 4.
καλός 3209 ⁴ 5?
(-)κλεϊζ.[3212 8.
κλέος 3209 ¹ 3.
κν[3209 ² 3?
κνῖσα 3210 ¹ i 15?
κουρίδιος see κωρίδιος
κ]υλινδρο[3210 ⁵ 7.
κυν.[3209 ³ 1?

(*b*) Euripides, etc. (3214–3216)

ἔτι 3215 ¹ 12.
εὖ [3215 ¹ 15].
εὐγένεια 3214 14.
εὐλογεῖν 3215 ¹ 15 *marg.*
εὐμαρῶς 3215 ¹ 13.
ἔχειν [3214 3](*bis*) 3215 ¹ 4.

ζοφ- 3216 2?

η 3215 ¹ 12.
ηγεμ[3216 27.
ἥκειν 3216 9?
ἦν 3214 1?

ἴσχειν 3216 19.

καί 3215 ¹ 6 3216 13, 16.
καινός 3214 8 *note.*
κακός 3215 ¹ 5.
καλῶς 3214 3.
κατά [3214 6].
κέαρ 3215 ¹ 14.
κεῖνος 3215 ¹ 3.
κήδευμα 3214 8 *note.*
κῆδος [3214 6].
κοινός [3214 13].
κρατεῖν 3215 ¹ 6.
κρύπτειν 3216 11?
κτᾶσθαι 3214 6.

λέγειν 3215 ¹ 15 3216 4.
λείπειν 3214 8.
λέκτρον 3214 3.
λέχος [3214 13].
λύειν 3216 6.

μεθιέναι 3215 ¹ 8.
μέν 3214 1? 3215 16.
μή 3215 ¹ 8.

νεανίας 3215 ¹ 2.
†νεόποις 3216 18.
νουθετεῖν 3215 ¹ 9.

οἶκος 3215 ¹ 10.
οἷός τ' 3216 20.

ὄμμα 3216 12.
ὅς 3214 3?, 4 3216 18?
ὅστις [3214 11] 3216 18?
οὐ 3215 ¹ 15 3216 20.
οὖν 3214 10? 3215 16.
οὕνεκα 3214 11.
οὕτως 3214 14.

παλαιός [3214 8] *note.*
πανδοκεύς (-εῖν) 3214 12?
πᾶς 3216 26.
πατήρ 3215 ¹ 16.
παύειν 3215 ¹ 15.
πολέμιος 3215 ¹ 10.
πολλάκις 3215 ¹ 9.
πόνος 3215 ¹ 3 3216 6?
ποτε 3215 ¹ 7.
ποῦ 3216 11.
πρός 3216 3?
προσδοκᾶν 3215 ¹ 7.
προσφ- 3216 3?
Πρωτεσίλαος (*play*) 3214 9.
Πύθιος [3216 10].

σκαιός 3214 10.
σός 3216 12.
σοφός 3214 6.
σύ 3215 ¹ 5, 7, 8.
συγγηράσκειν 3214 4.
σύν 3215 ¹ 3.

τις 3215 ¹ 19.
τίς 3215 ¹ 7.
τοι 3214 3?

Φοῖβος 3216 14.
Φοῖνιξ (*play*) 3214 7.
φροντίς 3216 5.
Φρύξ 3216 16.

χρεία 3216 9.
χρεών [3214 6].
χρή 3216 17.
χρη.[3215 ¹ 2 *marg.*
χρῆν 3214 13.
χρησμός 3216 15.

(*c*) MENANDER, ETC. (3217–3218)

ἀδικεῖν 3218 ¹ 3.
αὐτός 3217 2?

βλ[3218 ² 5.

ἐγώ 3218 ¹ 3, ² 5.
εἶναι 3217 3?
εἰσιέναι 3218 ¹ 6.
ἔχειν 3218 ¹ 2.

θεός 3218 ¹ 4.

καταλείπειν 3218 ² 4.
κλαίειν 3218 ¹ 5.

λίθος 3218 ¹ 2.
Λύδιος 3218 ¹ 2.

μά 3218 ¹ 4.
μαρτύρεσθαι 3218 ¹ 3.
]μελλε[3218 ² 6.
Μοσχίων 3218 ¹ 5, ² 3.

(-)νοεῖν 3218 ¹ 4?

ὁρᾶν 3218 ¹ 1.
οὗτος 3218 ¹ 1.

πευ[3218 ¹ 6 *del.*
(-)ποδων 3217 4.
προίεσθαι 3218 ² 2.
Πυρρίας [3217 3].

τε 3218 ¹ 2.

φέρειν 3217 6?

(*d*) ROMANCE (?) (**3218** *back*) and TREATISE ON PLATO (?) (**3219**)

Ἀθηναῖος 3219 ² i 6, 8, 12, 13?, ii (*b*) 7–8?, ⁸ 2?
Ἀλεξαμενός 3219 ¹ 10.
Ἀλεξανδρ- 3218 *back* ¹ 3.
ἀλλά 3219 ² i 9, ¹² 2?
ἀλλήλων 3219 ² ii (*a*) 6, ¹⁰ 7.
ἄλλος 3219 ¹ 12?
ἀνειδωλο[ποιεῖν 3219 ² i 11.
ἀνυπόθετος 3219 ¹⁹ 4?, ²⁰ 1?
ἀνώνυμος 3219 ² i 12?
ἀπάγειν 3219 ⁵ 7?
Ἀπόλλων 3219 ⁵ 5.
ἀποφαίνειν 3219 ² i 4.
Ἀριστοτέλης 3219 ¹ 6.
ἀρχή 3219 ²⁰ 1?
αὐτός 3219 ² i 3, 4, ii (*b*) 9?, ⁸ 6?
αὐτοῦ 3219 ii (*b*) 9?
ἀφικνεῖσθαι 3219 ¹ 11?

βασκανία 3219 ¹ 7.
βε- 3219 ¹⁶ 5.

γ̅ 3219 ² ii (*a*) 9.
γάρ 3219 ¹ 5.
γράφειν 3219 ¹ 9.

δ [3219 ² i 5].
δέ 3219 ² i 3, 7, ii (*b*) 5, 7, 10?, ⁴ 2.
(-)δεικνύναι 3219 ⁹ 4?, ²¹ 2.
(-)δειπνον(-ος) 3219 ⁷ 6?
δεύτερος 3219 ⁴ 3.
διά 3219 ² i 4, 9, ii (*b*) 2, 4, 7.
*διαδραματικός 3219 ² i 9?
διαλεκτικός (-ή) 3219 ¹¹ 5, 7, ¹⁹ 1, ²⁰ 3.
διάλογος 3219 ¹ 5, 10, ² i 10, ii (*b*) 6.
διδόναι 3219 ¹⁹ 3.
διέρχεσθαι 3219 ⁴ 1?
Διόνυσος 3219 ³ 2.
δόγμα 3219 ² ii (*b*) 9?

δοκεῖν 3219 ² i 4, ⁸ 4.
(-)δραμ- 3219 ⁶ 1, ⁷ 2?
δραματικός 3219 ¹ 4, 9, ² i 9?

εἰκών 3219 ² i 11?
εἶναι 3218 *back* ¹ 2? 3219 ² i 7, ii (*b*) 3, ¹¹ 6?, ¹⁶ 5, ¹⁹ 4, ²² ii 4?
εἰς 3219 ¹¹ 4?, ¹⁹ 2?
Ἐλεάτης 3219 ² i 6, 7.
ἐλέγχειν 3219 ² i 3, ii (*a*) 7.
ἐν 3219 ¹ 3, 7.
ἐνάντιος 3219 ² ii (*a*) 6?
ἐξευρίσκειν 3219 ¹⁹ 2?
ἐξουρεῖν 3219 ¹⁹ 2?
ἐπάγειν 3219 ⁵ 7?
ἐπανορθοῦν 3219 ¹⁶ 2.
εὐθύς 3218 *back* ¹ 4?
*(-)εφεικτής 3219 ¹ 11?
ἐφικνεῖσθαι 3219 ¹ 11?

θ 3219 ¹⁶ 4?
θέα (θεά) 3218 *back* ² 2?
Θέσπις 3219 ³ 3.
θεωρητικός 3219 ¹² 5?, ²¹ 3?
θεωρία 3219 ¹¹ 9.

καθό 3219 ¹⁶ 4?
καί 3219 ¹ 3, 8, ² i 8, 11, ii (*a*) 5, ¹⁶ 4?, ¹⁸ 4, ²³ i 3?
κατά 3219 ¹ 4?
κυρι- 3219 ¹¹ 6.

(-)λαμβάνειν 3219 ²¹ 1, ²³ i 2?
λεγ- 3219 ² ii (*a*) 9.
λέγειν 3219 ¹ 7.
(-)λέγειν 3219 ⁵ 6.
(-)λογος 3219 ¹⁰ 4.
λοιπός 3219 ² ii (*a*) 9.

μαθηματικός (-ή) **3219** 19 3.
μέθοδος **3219** 15 2?, 18 3, 20 2.
μετά **3219** 2 ii (a) 10, 4 2.
μικτός **3219** 16 3?
μιμεῖσθαι **3219** 1 3.
μιμογράφος **3219** 1 4.

ξένος **3219** 2 i 6, 7(bis), 8, ii (b) 8.

οἰκονομικός **3219** 16 3.
ὅς **3219** 2 i 9?, 11 6?, 19 2?
οὐ **3219** 1 5.
οὐδέ **3219** 2 ii (a) 8.
οὗτος **3219** 1 3, 2 ii (b) 4, 4 2.

πά[θος **3219** 18 4?
παρά **3219** 2 i 3.
Παρμενίδης **3219** 2 i 9, 8 2?
πᾶς **3219** 2 ii (b) 2, 16 6.
πειστέον **3219** 1 5.
περί **3219** 1 8, 8 5?, 9 3, 16 6?
πῇ **3219** 2 ii (b) 6, 7.
πηροῦν **3218** back 1 4.
Πλάτων **3219** 1 6, 9, 2 i 8, ii (b) 9–10?, 11 3.
Πλατωνικός **3219** 2 ii (b) 3–4?
ποιεῖν **3219** 2 i 10.
ποιητική **3219** 1 8.
ποικίλλειν **3219** 2 ii (b) 5.
ποικίλος **3219** 1 2.
πολιτικός **3219** 11 8, 17 4?

πρᾶξις **3219** 18 4?, 20 2?
πρό **3219** 1 8.
πρός **3219** 1 6.
πρόσωπον **3219** 2 i 5, 6 2?, 9 3?
Πρωταγόρας **3219** 2 i 2.
πρῶτος **3218** back 1 1 **3219** 1 8, 11 4.

ῥεῖν **3219** 19 2?

Σοφοκλῆς **3219** 4 4.
Σωκράτης **3219** 2 i 5.
Σώφρων **3219** 1 3.

τέσσαρες **3219** 8 5?
Τήνιος **3219** 1 10.
Τίμαιος (Τειμ-) **3219** 2 i 5, ii (b) 7.
τις **3219** 1 12?, 2 i 11?, ii (b) 8.
-τομος **3218** back 1 2.
τότε **3218** back 1 1?
τραγῳδία **3219** 5 4.
(-)τραγωδ- **3219** 3 4? 5 3?

ὑπάγειν **3219** 5 7?
ὑπό **3219** 1 6, 10, 2 ii (a) 8?
ὑπο(-) **3219** 2 ii (a) 8, 9 2.
ὑπόθεσις **3219** 19 5?
ὑποκριτής **3219** 3 3, 4 3.

φιλοσοφία **3219** 11 4?, 12 2?

II. SUB-LITERARY TEXTS

(a) DECLAMATIONS (3235–3236)

ἀεί **3235** 3 i 18?, ii 7?
Ἀθη[να- **3235** 3 i 9.
Ἀθῆναι **3236** 2 ii 8?
Ἀθηναῖος **3236** 1 i 19, ii 5, 16, 2 ii 8?
Αἰσχίνης **3236** 1 i 2, 11, 22, ii 11.
Ἀκρόπολις **3236** 1 i 17.
ἀληθής **3235** 1 i 8.
ἀλλά **3235** 1 i 11, 2 ii 14, 4 12? **3236** 1 i 16, ii 9, 10.
ἄλλος **3235** 3 ii 16? **3236** 2 ii 2.
ἀμέλεια **3235** 2 ii 9–10?
ἀμελεῖ **3235** 2 i 3.
Ἀμφίπολις **3235** 2 ii 5, 11 **3236** 1 i 12.
ἄν **3235** 2 ii 14?
ἀναλαμβάνειν **3236** 2 ii 21.
ἀνάλωτος **3236** 2 ii 14.
ἀναμένειν **3236** 1 ii 14.

ἀνήρ **3235** 1 ii 15?, 4 6.
ἀνίστασθαι **3235** 2 ii 14?
ἀντιποιεῖσθαι **3235** 1 i 9.
ἀντιτάττειν **3236** 1 ii 16.
ἀξιοῦν **3236** 1 ii 21.
ἁπλῶς **3235** 1 i 12.
ἀπό **3235** 2 ii 11 **3236** 1 ii 1, 7.
ἀπόλλυσθαι **3235** 2 ii 4.
Ἀπόλλων **3236** 2 ii 11.
ἀποστερεῖν **3235** 1 i 13.
ἀσφαλής **3236** 2 ii 10–11?
αὖ **3236** 1 ii 23.
αὐτός **3236** 1 i 8.
αὐτοῦ **3236** 1 i 6.
ἀφαιρεῖν **3236** 1 i 9.
ἀφιστα- **3235** 3 i 8.

πάλαι **3236** ¹ i 16.
παραχω[ρ- **3235** ³ i 5?
πᾶς **3235** ¹ i 1, 12, ³ ii 6 **3236** ¹ i 4, ii 17, ² i 10?
πάςχειν **3235** ⁴ 11?
πάτριος **3236** ¹ i 19.
πατρίς **3236** ¹ i 9.
πατρῷος **3236** ¹ i 1.
Πειραιεύς **3236** ¹ i 16.
περικοπτ- **3235** ¹ ii 16?
(-)πηδᾶν **3236** ¹ ii 8.
πηλός **3236** ¹ ii 1–2?
ποιεῖν **3235** ² ii 1.
(-)πολεμ- **3235** ¹ ii 9.
πολεμεῖν **3235** ¹ ii 13?
πόλεμος **3235** ¹ ii 13?, ² ii 17.
πολιορκεῖν **3235** ¹ ii 7?
πόλις **3235** ³ ii 9 **3236** ¹ i 4, ² ii 9.
ποτε **3236** ² ii 18?
Ποτίδαια **3235** ² ii 6, ⁴ 3–4.
πρᾶγμα **3236** ¹ ii 5–6?
πρόγονος **3236** ² i 17?, ii 6.
προέρχεςθαι **3235** ² ii 13.
προκινδυνεύειν **3236** ¹ i 5.
προλαμβάνειν **3235** ² ii 10–11?
πρός **3236** ¹ ii [4], 17.
προςεπιςκευάζειν **3236** ² ii 20?
πρώην **3236** ¹ ii 1.
Πύδνα **3235** ² ii 4, ⁴ 3.
Πύθιος **3236** ² ii 12, 14.
Πύλαι **3235** ¹ i 4.

ῥῆμα **3236** ¹ ii 4?

ςιρός **3236** ¹ i 14.
-ςπονδος **3235** ² ii 1.
ςτρατηγεῖν **3236** ¹ i 21.
ςτρατιά **3236** ¹ ii 18.
ςύ **3236** ¹ ii 19.
ςυγγεν- **3235** ¹ ii 7, ⁵ 4.
ςύμμαχος **3236** ¹ ii 14, 21.
ςῴζειν **3236** ¹ i 3.

τειχιςμός **3236** ² ii 13.
τεῖχος **3236** ² ii 2, 10.
τις **3235** ¹ i 6 **3236** ¹ i 13.
τοιοῦτος **3236** ¹ i 13.
τριήρης **3236** ² ii 1.
τρόπαιον **3236** ¹ i 19?

ὑμ- **3235** ¹ ii 12.
ὑμεῖς **3235** ¹ i 16, ² ii 3, ³ i 10, 17, ii 11? **3236** ² ii 6, 10, 16?
ὑμέτερος **3235** ¹ i 1, ² ii 9, ³ i 14, ii 15.
ὑπέρ **3236** ¹ ii 23.
ὑπό **3236** ² i 15.
ὑποβολιμαῖος **3235** ¹ i 5.

Φίλιππος **3235** ¹ i 5, ² ii 10, 15, ³ i 7, 11.
φίλος **3235** ⁴ 5?
φυλάττειν **3235** ¹ i 5.

ὡς **3236** ¹ i 15.

(b) Homeric Glossaries (3237–3238)

(i) Homeric forms glossed

ἀγάννιφον **3238** ¹ i 7.
ἀγέμεν **3237** ¹ ii 33.
ἀείδοντες **3238** ¹ ii 71.
αἰγλήεντος **3238** ¹ iv 131.
αἴθοπα **3238** ¹ ii 45.
αἶψα **3237** ¹ ii 4.
ἆλτο **3238** ¹ iv 131.
ἀμβρόςιαι **3238** ¹ iv 128.
ἀμύμονας **3238** ¹ i 12.
ἀμφιβρότης **3238** ³ ii 6.
ἀνθερεῶνος **3238** ¹ iii 104.
ἀνςτήτην **3237** ¹ ii 11.
ἀντιβίοιςι **3237** ¹ ii 9.
ἄνωγεν **3237** ¹ ii 22.
ἀπατηλόν **3238** ¹ iv 125.
ἀπηύρων **3238** ¹ i 19.

ἀπολυμαίνεςθαι **3237** ¹ ii 21.
ἀπόςτιχε **3238** ¹ iv 118.
ἀπούρας **3238** ¹ iii 109.
ἀργυρόπεζα **3238** ¹ iv 138.
ἄρκιον **3238** ³ ii 17.
ἀςπίδος **3238** ³ ii 5.
ἀτελεύτητον **3238** ¹ iv 126.
ἀτρυγέτοιο **3237** ¹ ii 26.
αὖθι **3238** ¹ iii 94.
ἀϋτήν **3238** ¹ iii 97.
αὔτως **3238** ¹ iv 116.

βῆςεν **3237** ¹ ii 18.

γνώωςι **3237** ¹ ii 3.
γουνάςομαι **3238** ¹ i 17.

cφοῦ **3238** ¹ iv 135.
cχίζης **3238** ¹ ii 44.

τάνυccαν **3238** ¹ iii 89.
τέκμωρ **3238** ¹ iv 121.
τελαμών **3238** ³ ii 4.
τελήέccαc **3237** ¹ ii 25.
τερπικεραύνωι **3238** ¹ i 4.
τιταίνων **3238** ³ ii 14.
τώ **3237** ¹ ii 8.
τῶ **3238** ¹ i 2.

ὑγρὰ (κέλευθα) **3237** ¹ ii 20.

ὑφέντες [**3238** ¹ i 32].
ὑψοῦ **3238** ¹ iii 85.

φθινύθεcκε **3238** ¹ iii 93.

χαῖται **3238** ¹ iv 129.
χαλκοβατές **3238** ¹ i 15.

ψαμάθοιc **3238** ¹ iii 86.

ὠκυμορώτατος **3238** ¹ iii 108.
ὠκυπόροιc **3238** ¹ i 9.
ὠμοθέτηcαν **3238** ¹ ii 39.

(ii) Glosses

ἀγαθόc **3238** ¹ i 12.
ἄγαν **3238** ¹ i 7.
ἄγειν **3237** ¹ ii 33.
ἄγκυρα **3238** ¹ i 34.
ᾄδειν **3238** ¹ ii 72.
ἄκαρποc **3237** ¹ ii 26.
ἀκολουθεῖν **3238** ¹ i 14.
ἄλλεcθαι **3238** ¹ iv 131.
ἄμμοc **3238** ¹ iii 87.
ἀναπείθειν **3238** ¹ iv 113.
ἀνήρ **3238** ¹ iii 91.
ἀνθεῖν **3238** ¹ iii 106.
ἀνίcταcθαι **3237** ¹ ii 11.
ἀπατητικόc **3238** ¹ iv 125.
ἁπλοῦν **3238** ¹ iii 75.
ἀπό **3238** ¹ i 29.
ἀπόγειος **3238** ¹ i 37?
ἀποκαθαίρειν **3237** ¹ ii 21.
ἀποτρέχειν **3238** ¹ iv 118.
ἀριcτερόc **3238** ¹ iii 103.
ἄρμενα **3238** ¹ i 23.
ἀρχή **3238** ¹ ii 49.
ἀτέλεcτοc **3238** ¹ iv 126.
αὐτόc **3238** ¹ i 35.
ἀφαιρεῖν **3238** ¹ i 19.

βαθύc **3238** ¹ i 20.
βαίνειν **3238** ¹ i 15.
βροντή **3238** ¹ iii 102.

γένειον **3238** ¹ iii 104.
γεύειν **3238** ¹ ii 51.
γῆ **3238** ¹ iii 84.
γιγνώcκειν **3237** ¹ ii 3.
γονυπετεῖν **3238** ¹ i 17.

δέχεcθαι **3238** ¹ i 21.
διά **3238** ¹ i 34, ii 69, iii 80, 102, 105.
διαδιδόναι **3238** ¹ ii 67.
διακόπτειν **3238** ¹ ii 52.
διαλύειν **3237** ¹ ii 12.
διαπερᾶν **3238** ¹ iii 83.
διαχωρεῖν **3237** ¹ ii 16.
διό **3238** ¹ i 2.
δραcτικόc **3237** ¹ ii 29.
δῶμα **3238** ¹ i 16.

ἑαυτοῦ **3237** ¹ ii 14 **3238** ¹ iv 133.
ἐγώ **3238** ¹ iv 120.
εἶδος **3238** ¹ ii 74.
εἶναι **3238** ¹ i 6, 28, ii 40, 57, 63, iii 77, 80.
εἰc **3238** ¹ ii 58, iii 85, 95, iv 111.
εἷc **3238** ¹ ii 48.
ἐκ, ἐξ **3237** ¹ ii 9 [**3238** ¹ ii 48].
ἕκαcτος **3238** ¹ ii 59.
ἐκεῖ **3238** ¹ iii 105.
ἐκεῖνοc **3238** ¹ iii 94, 95.
ἐκπληροῦν **3238** ¹ ii 61.
ἕλκειν **3238** ¹ ii 55.
ἐμβιβάζειν **3237** ¹ ii 18.
ἐμπείρωc **3238** ¹ ii 54.
ἐν **3238** ¹ ii 43, iii 91, 94.
ἐνάντιος **3237** ¹ ii 9.
ἐνδεήc **3238** ¹ ii 57.
ἐνεργεῖν **3237** ¹ ii 28.
ἐντολή **3238** ¹ iii 98.
ἐξάπτειν **3238** ¹ i 30.
ἐξέχειν **3238** ¹ iii 77.
ἐπίθετον **3238** ¹ i 6.
ἐπιθυμία **3238** ¹ ii 62.
ἐπικλίνειν **3238** ¹ i 22.

cχίδαξ, cχίδη **3238** I ii 44?
cχοινίον **3238** I i 29, [37].

ταχέως **3237** I ii 4 **3238** I i 26.
ταχυθάνατος [**3238** I iii 108?].
ταχύς **3238** I i 9.
τεκμήριον **3238** I iv 121.
τέλειος **3237** I ii 25.
τέλος **3238** I iv 121.
τέρπειν **3238** I i 4.
τοῖχος **3237** I ii 13?
τόπος **3238** I iii 94, 95, 105.
τότε **3238** I iii 94.
τρέχειν **3238** I iii 82.
τριαινοειδής **3238** I ii 47.
τρόπις **3238** I iii 79.

υἱός **3238** I i 1.

ὑπό [**3238** I iii 104].
ὑπομένειν **3238** I iv 136.
ὑπουργός **3237** I ii 30.
ὑποχωρεῖν **3237** I ii 6.
ὕψος **3238** I iii 85.

φθίνειν **3238** I iii 93.
φυcᾶν **3238** I iii 76.
φωνεῖν **3238** I iii 81.

χειμερινός **3238** I i 8.
χιτών **3238** 2 140?

ψάμαθος **3238** I iii 86.

ᾠδή **3238** I ii 70, [74].
ὥcπερ **3238** 2 139?

(*c*) GLOSSARY (?) (3239)

ἀγαθός **3239** 36.
ἀήρ **3239** 40?
αἰεί **3239** 2.
Ἀλεξάνδρεια **3239** 31.
ἄν **3239** 42.
ἄναξ **3239** 15.
ἀνήρ **3239** 40?
ἄνθος **3239** 6.
*ἀντικύριος **3239** 45?
ἄρουρα **3239** 8.

βάρος **3239** 25.

γεωργία **3239** 3.

δεξιός **3239** 24.
δεῦρο **3239** 43?
διψᾶν **3239** 44.

εἰς **3239** 23.
ἕκαστος **3239** 41.
ἐλάδιον **3239** 28.
ἐλπίς **3239** 21.
ἐργόμωκος **3239** 35.
ἔριον **3239** 23.
ἔσω **3239** 43?

ἤγημα **3239** 5.
ἡδονή **3239** 11, 29?

θέλειν **3239** 42.

θεός **3239** 11, 13.
θερμημερία **3239** 16?

ἱλαρός **3239** 3.
Ἶcιc **3239** 21.
ἰταμός **3239** 22.

κακόν **3239** 1.
κάλαθος **3239** 23.
καλός **3239** 18?, 40.
κοιλιά **3239** 6?
κοcμεῖν **3239** 32.
κυνηγικός **3239** 5.
κύων **3239** 22.

λέcχη **3239** 10.
λύχνος **3239** 24.

μέγαc **3239** 21, 25.
μέθη **3239** 12.
μόλιβος **3239** 25.
μῦc **3239** 26.

ν **3239** 27.

ξεῖνος **3239** 37.
ξύcτρα **3239** 28.

ὁδηγός **3239** 36.
οἰκοδόμος **3239** 30.
οἰνόμελι **3239** 29?

III. EMPERORS AND REGNAL YEARS

VESPASIAN

Οὐεcπαcιανός **3242** 10 (Year 3—retrospective).

TITUS

Αὐτοκράτωρ Τίτος Καῖcαρ Οὐεcπαcιανὸc Cεβαcτόc **3264** 28–30, 35–6 (Year 3).
Τίτος **3242** 11 (Year 1—retrospective).

DOMITIAN

Αὐτοκράτωρ Καῖcαρ Δομιτιανὸc Cεβαcτὸc Γερμανικόc **3240** 6–7 (Year lost), 17 (Year 8).

MARCUS AURELIUS AND VERUS

Αὐτοκράτωρ Καῖcαρ Μάρκος Αὐρήλιος Ἀντωνῖνος Cεβαcτὸc καὶ Αὐτοκράτωρ Καῖcαρ Λούκιος Αὐρήλιος
　　Οὐῆρος Cεβαcτόc **3241** 12–15, 26–9 (Year 3).

CARACALLA

ὁ κύριος ἡμῶν Αὐτοκράτωρ Cεουῆρος Ἀντωνῖνος Εὐτυχήc, Εὐcεβήc, Cεβαcτόc **3243** 1 7–8 (Year 22).

SEVERUS ALEXANDER

Μάρκος Αὐρήλιος Cεουῆρος Ἀλέξανδρος Καῖcαρ ὁ κύριος 3244 9–12.

Αὐτοκράτωρ Καῖcαρ Μάρκος Αὐρήλιος Cεουῆρος Ἀλέξανδρος Εὐcεβὴς Εὐτυχὴς Cεβαcτός 3244 28–32 (Year 8).

VALERIAN, GALLIENUS, (AND VALERIAN OR SALONINUS CAESAR)

Αὐτοκράτορες Καίcαρες Πούπλιος Λικίννιος Οὐαλεριανὸς καὶ Πούπλιος Λικίννιος . . . 3252 25–8 (Year 5).

DIOCLETIAN AND MAXIMIAN, CONSTANTIUS, AND GALERIUS

οἱ κύριοι ἡμῶν Διοκλητιανὸς καὶ Μαξιμιανὸς Cεβαcτοὶ καὶ οἱ κύριοι ἡμῶν Κωνcτάντιος καὶ Μαξιμιανὸς οἱ ἐπιφανέcτατοι Καίcαρες 3245 18–20 (Year 13, 12, and 5).

οἱ κύριοι ἡμῶν Διοκλητιανὸς καὶ Μαξιμιανὸς Cεβαcτοὶ καὶ Κωνcτάντιος καὶ Μαξιμιανὸς οἱ ἐπιφανέcτατοι Καίcαρες 3246 2–3 (Year 14, 13, and 6).

]Διοκλητιανοῦ καὶ Μαξιμιανοῦ C[εβαcτῶν . . .] Καιcάρων 3247 22–3 (Year lost).

IV. CONSULS

ἐπὶ ὑπάτων τῶν κυρίων ἡμῶν Αὐτοκράτορος Μαξιμιανοῦ Cεβαcτοῦ τὸ ε′ καὶ Μαξιμιανοῦ ἐπιφανεcτάτου Καίcαρος τὸ β′ (A.D. 297) 3245 1–2, [22?].

ὑπατείας τῶν δεcπ[οτῶν ἡμῶν Κωνcταντίνου καὶ] Λικινίου Cεβαc[τῶν τὸ . . . (A.D. 312–15) 3254 1–2.

ὑπατείας τῶν δεcποτῶν [ἡμῶν Κωνcταντίνου καὶ Λικιννίου] Cεβα[cτῶν τὸ δ′ (A.D. 315) 3255 1–2.

ὑπατείας τῆς προκειμένης 3255 26.

ὑπατείας τῶν δεcποτῶν ἡμῶν Λικιννίου Cεβαcτοῦ τὸ ε′ καὶ Κρίcπου τοῦ ἐπιφανεcτάτου Καίcαρος τὸ α′ (A.D. 318) 3257 1–2.

ὑπατείας τῆς προκειμένης 3257 18.

ὑπατείας τῶν δεcποτῶν ἡμῶν Κωνcταντίνου Αὐτοκράτορος τὸ ε′ καὶ Λικινίου τοῦ ἐπιφανεcτάτου Καίcαρος τὸ α′ (A.D. 319) 3258 1–2.

ὑπατείας τῶν δεcποτῶν ἡμῶν Κωνcταντίνου Cεβαcτοῦ τὸ ε′ καὶ Λικινίου τοῦ ἐπιφανεcτάτου Καίcαρος τὸ α′ (A.D. 319) 3259 1–3.

τοῖς ἀποδειχθηcομένοις ὑπάτοις τὸ γ′ (A.D. 323) 3260 1

τοῖς ἐcομένοις ὑπάτοις τὸ δ′ (A.D. 324) 3261 1.

ὑπατείας τῆς προκειμένης 3261 23.

ὑπατείας τῶν δεcποτῶν ἡμῶν Κωνcταντίνου Ἀγούcτου τὸ ζ′ καὶ Κωνcταντίου τοῦ ἐπιφανεcτάτου Καίcαρος τὸ α′ (A.D. 326) 3249 1–3.

[ὑπατείας τῶν δεcπ]οτῶν ἡμῶν Κωνcταν[τίνου ⟨Αὐγούcτου⟩ τὸ ζ′ καὶ Κω]νcταντίου τοῦ ἐπιφανεc[τάτου Καίcαρ]ος τὸ α′ (A.D. 326) 3265 1–3.

ὑπατείας τῆς προκειμένης 3265 18.

ὑπατείας Φλαουίου Φιλικιανοῦ καὶ Φαβίου Τιτιανοῦ τῶν λαμπροτάτων (A.D. 337) 3266 1–2.

V. MONTHS

Ἀθύρ 3252 17 3255 26 3257 18.

ἐπαγόμεναι 3249 14.

Ἐπείφ 3257 14 3262 5 3265 18.

Θώθ 3249 13 3266 11.

Μεcορή 3247 23 [3249 13] 3251 11 3263 11, 14 3266 2.

Μεχείρ 3241 15, 30.

Παῦνι 3255 21.

Cεβαcτός 3250 17.

Φαμενώθ [3240 7] 3266 15.

Φαῶφι 3248 12.

Χοιάκ 3244 16, 32.

M

VI. PERSONAL NAMES

Ἄγοῦϲτοϲ *see* Index IV (A.D. 326).

Αἰλουρίων, Aur., alias Hesychius, former hypomnematographus, councillor of Alexandria, (ex-?) gymnasiarch, councillor, prytanis in office of Oxyrhynchus **3245** 3–5.

Ἀκόντιοϲ **3247** 5.

Ἀλέξανδροϲ *see* Index III s.v. Severus Alexander.

Ἀμεννεύϲ, f. of Pennamis **3264** 5.

Ἀμμώνιοϲ **3247** 7.

Ἀμμώνιοϲ, Aur., s. of Copreus **3257** 4.

Ἀμμώνιοϲ, f. of Aur. Dioscorus **3255** 6 **3256** 3.

Ἀμμώνιοϲ, f. of Gaianus **3260** 2.

Ἀνδρόνικοϲ, f. of Sarapion **3242** 19.

Ἀννιανόϲ, Flavius, *protector* **3266** 4.

Ἀνουβᾶϲ, s. of Hermias, Persian of the *epigone*, shipmaster **3250** 1, 12, 25.

Ἀντίοχοϲ, Aur., ἐγκυκλιώνηϲ **3241** 3, [18].

Ἀντωνῖνοϲ *see* Index III s.vv. Marcus Aurelius and Verus, Caracalla.

Ἀπολλώνιοϲ, Aur., alias Serenus, s. of Apollonius **3259** 4–5.

Ἀπολλώνιοϲ, f. of Aur. Apollonius alias Serenus **3259** 5.

Ἀπολλώνιοϲ, f. of Ϲαραπίων φροντιϲτήϲ **3241** 2, 10, [17], 24.

Ἀπολλώνιοϲ *see* Index VII(*c*) s.v. Ἀπολλωνίου κλῆροϲ.

Ἁρποκρατίων, (Aur.) Calpurnius Isidorus alias, strategus (Arsinoite; departments of Themistes and Polemon) **3243** I 2 **3263** 1–3.

Ἁρποκρατίων, royal scribe **3242** 1.

Ἀρτεμίδωροϲ **3247** 2.

Ἀρτεμίδωροϲ, Dionysius alias, f. of Aur. Ptolemaeus **3245** 10.

Ἀτρῆϲ, Aur., s. of Peteharpocrates, m. Tanneis **3252** 5–7.

Αὐγοῦϲτοϲ *see* Index IV (A.D. 326).

Αὐρηλία *see* Εὐτροπία.

Αὐρήλιοϲ . . . **3245** 23 **3249** 17.

Αὐρήλιοϲ Ϲεπτίμιοϲ Ἡράκλειτοϲ, *praef. Aeg.* **3243** I 1.

Αὐρήλιοϲ *see* Αἰλουρίων, Ἀμμώνιοϲ, Ἀντίοχοϲ, Ἀπολλώνιοϲ, Ἁρποκρατίων, Ἀτρῆϲ, Δίδυμοϲ, Δῖοϲ, Διόϲκοροϲ, Εἰρηναῖοϲ, Ἑρ . . ., Εὐάγγελοϲ, Εὐλόγιοϲ, Εὐϲτόχιοϲ, Ζηναγένηϲ, Ζωίλοϲ, Ἡράκληοϲ, Ἥρων, Ἡϲύχιοϲ, Θεογένηϲ, Θέων, Θῶνιϲ, Ἰϲίδωροϲ, Καλπούρνιοϲ, Λεωνίδηϲ, Μάξιμοϲ, Πτολεμαῖοϲ, Ϲαραπίων, Ϲερῆνοϲ, Ϲεύθηϲ, Ὠρίων.

Αὐρήλιοϲ *see also* Index III s.vv. Marcus Aurelius and Verus, Severus Alexander.

Ἀχιλλεύϲ, f. of Aur. Sarapion, h. of Dieus **3244** 5, 34.

Βάρβαϲ, *dux* **3261** 10.

Βηϲαρίων **3253** 19.

Γαιανόϲ, s. of Ammonius **3260** 2, 28.

Γάϊοϲ *see* Νορβανόϲ.

Δίδυμοϲ alias Eudaemon, (ex-?) gymnasiarch, councillor, f. of Techosus alias Eudaemonis **3246** 8.

Δίδυμοϲ, Aur. **3245** 9.

Δίδυμοϲ, Aur. Sarapion alias, (ex-?) gymnasiarch **3252** 1–4.

Διεῦϲ, m. of Aur. Sarapion, w. of Achilles **3244** 6.

Διογένηϲ, χωματεπιμελητήϲ **3264** 10, 23.

Διογενίϲ, m. of Aur. Theon, w. of Theon **3244** 25.

Διοκλητιανόϲ *see* Index III s.v. Diocletian and Maximian, Constantius, and Galerius.

Διονυϲία, d. of Sarapias alias Thamunion, Antinoite **3242** 2.

Διονύϲιοϲ **3257** 19.

Διονύϲιοϲ alias Artemidorus, f. of Aur. Ptolemaeus **3245** 10.

Διονύϲιοϲ, f. of Dionysius **3240** 9.

Διονύϲιοϲ, f. of . . . oe **3245** 26.

Διονύϲιοϲ, s. of Dionysius **3240** 9.

Δῖοϲ, Aur., s. of Zoilus **3258** 3.

Διόϲκοροϲ, Aur., s. of Ammonius **3255** 6 **3256** 3.

Διόϲκοροϲ, f. of Orsenuphis **3264** 3.

Διόϲκοροϲ, s. of . . . ion **3261** 24.

Διοφάνηϲ, strategus **3242** 1.

Δομιτιανόϲ *see* Index III s.v. Domitian.

Εἰρηναῖοϲ, Aur., assistant to the prytanis **3245** 7–8.

Ἐπίμαχοϲ **3260** 30.

Ἑρ . . ., Aur., village scribe **3263** 4.

Ἑρμίαϲ, f. of Anubas **3250** 1.

Ἑρμόφιλοϲ **3264** 2.

Ἑϲταῖοϲ *see* Ἰούνιοϲ Ἑ.

Εὐάγγελοϲ, Aur. **3254** 3, 23.

Εὐδαιμονίϲ, Techosus alias, d. of Didymus (ex-?) gymnasiarch, councillor **3246** 8.

Εὐδαίμων, Didymus alias, (ex-?) gymnasiarch, councillor, f. of Techosus alias Eudaemonis **3246** 9.

Εὐδαίμων, slave **3252** 14.

Εὐλόγιοϲ, Aur., s. of Leonteus, m. Eusebia **3266** 3.

Εὐλόγιος, f. of Timotheus **3249** 8.
Εὐσεβία, m. of Aur. Eulogius, w. of Leonteus **3266** 3.
Εὐστόχιος, Flavius, s. of Copreus, systates **3249** 5.
Εὐτροπία, Aurelia, d. of Theodorus alias Chaeremon, late gymnasiarch, prytanis, and councillor **3255** 3, 27 (ευτροπιον).
Εὐτρόπιον see Εὐτροπία.

Ζηναγένης, Aur., strategus **3246** 4 **3247** 1.
Ζωίλος **3253** 1.
Ζωίλος, Aur., **3265** 6–7, 19.
Ζωίλος, f. of Aur. Dius **3258** 3.

Ἡλιοδώρα, Claudia, d. of Canopion, former hypomnematographus, ἀπὸ στεφάνου **3246** 7.
Ἡρακλείδης, ἐγκυκλιώνης **3241** 3, [18].
Ἡρακλείδης, Flavius, ex-strategus **3240** 10.
Ἡράκλειος, Claudius, strategus **3264** 7–8.
Ἡράκλειτος see Αὐρήλιος Σεπτίμιος Ἡράκλειτος.
Ἡράκληος, Aur., πραγματευτής **3266** 5.
Ἥρων, Aur., alias Sarapion, ex-logistes, former gymnasiarch and prytanis **3256** 1–2.
Ἡσύχιος, Aur. Aelurion alias, former hypomnematographus, councillor of Alexandria, (ex-?) gymnasiarch, councillor, prytanis in office of Oxyrhynchus, **3245** 3–5.

Θαμούνιον, Sarapias alias, m. of Dionysia, Antinoite **3242** 2.
Θεα...., s. of Sarapion **3241** [1], 16.
Θεμίστης see Index VII(a) s.v. Θεμίστου μερίς.
Θεογένης, Aur. Thonius alias, exegetes **3246** 6.
Θεόδωρος, alias Chaeremon, late gymnasiarch, prytanis, and councillor, f. of Aurelian Eutropia **3255** 3.
Θεόδωρος, f. of ... **3249** 10.
Θεόδωρος, f. of ... chotes **3249** 8.
Θέων **3251** 13.
Θέων, Aur., alias Maximus, prytanis **3244** 1–3.
Θέων, Aur., s. of Theon, m. Diogenis **3244** 23–5, 38–9.
Θέων, f. of Aur. Leonides [**3254** 5] **3256** 4 **3257** 4 **3258** 5 **3259** 7 **3260** 4.
Θέων, f. of Aur. Theon, h. of Diogenis **3244** 24.
Θέων, μηνιάρχης **3261** 3.
Θώνιος, Aur., alias Theogenes, exegetes **3246** 6.
Θώνιος, Aur., public doctor **3245** 6.
Θώνιος, f. of Comon **3262** 1.
Θώνιος, s. of Philaeus **3249** 8.
Θώνιος Νέος καλούμενος **3257** 8.

Ἰούνιος Ἑστιαῖος, strategus **3240** 8.
Ἰσίδωρος, (Aur.) Calpurnius, alias Harpocration,

strategus (Arsinoite; departments of Themistes and Polemon) **3243** 1 2 **3263** 1–3.

Καῖσαρ see Index III, Index IV (A.D. 297); (A.D. 318); (A.D. 319); (A.D. 326).
Καλλιόπη, m. (or alias) of Πρειμ[, slave [**3241** 21–2?].
Καλπούρνιος Ἰσίδωρος ὁ καὶ Ἁρποκρατίων, strategus (Arsinoite, departments of Themistes and Polemon) **3243** 1 2 **3263** 1–3 (+ Aur.).
Κανωπίων, f. of Claudia Heliodora, former hypomnematographus ἀπὸ στεφάνου **3246** 7.
Κλαυδι[**3247** 8.
Κλαυδία Ἡλιοδώρα, d. of Canopion, former hypomnematographus ἀπὸ στεφάνου **3246** 7.
Κλαύδιος Ἡράκλειος, strategus **3264** 7–8.
Κόμων, s. of Thonius **3262** 1.
Κοπρεύς, f. of Aur. Ammonius **3257** 4.
Κοπρεύς, f. of Aur. Eustochius, systates **3249** 5.
Κορνήλιος; M. Cornelius Torullus, centurion **3250** 2.
Κρίσπος see Index IV (A.D. 318).
Κωνσταντῖνος see Index IV (A.D. 312–15); (A.D. 315); (A.D. 319); (A.D. 326).
Κωνστάντιος see Index III s.v. Diocletian and Maximian, Constantius, and Galerius; Index IV (A.D. 326).

Λεοντεύς, f. of Aur. Eulogius, h. of Eusebia **3266** 3.
Λευκάδιος, Flavius, logistes **3249** 4 [**3265** 4].
Λεωνίδης, Aur., s. of Theon **3254** 5 **3256** 3 **3257** 4 **3258** 5 **3259** 7 **3260** 4, 14 **3261** 3 **3262** 1, 7.
Λικίνιος see Index IV (A.D. 312–15); (A.D. 315); (A.D. 319).
Λικίννιος see Index III s.v. Valerian, Gallienus, (and Valerian or Saloninus Caesar); Index IV (A.D. 318).
Λογγεῖνος, f. of Sarapion **3242** 3.
Λούκιος see Index III s.v. Marcus Aurelius and Verus.
Λου[..]υ (gen.) **3253** 17.

Μ..., μηνιάρχης **3261** 3.
Μαξιμιανός see Index III s.v. Diocletian and Maximian, Constantius, and Galerius; Index IV (A.D. 297).
Μάξιμος, Aur. Theon alias, prytanis **3244** 1–3.
Μάρκος see Κορνήλιος; see also Index III s.vv. Marcus Aurelius and Verus, Severus Alexander.
Ματρῖνος, Valerius **3257** 3, 18.
Μέττιος Ῥοῦφος praef. Aeg. **3240** 8.
Μόνιμος see Index VII(b) s.v. Μονίμου.

VII. GEOGRAPHICAL

(a) Countries, Nomes, Toparchies, Cities, etc.

Ἀλεξάνδρεια [3241 23].
Ἀλεξανδρεύς, ἡ λαμπροτάτη πόλις τῶν Ἀλεξαν-
δρέων 3245 4.
Ἀντινοΐς 3242 2.
ἄνω τοπαρχία 3242 6.
Ἀρσινοΐτης (nome) 3243 ¹ 3 3263 2.
Ἀφροδιτοπολίτης (nome) 3252 9–10.
Γερμανικός see Index III s.v. Domitian.
Ἑρμοπολίτης (nome) 3250 1, 6, 18, 25.
Θεμίστου μερίς 3243 ¹ 3–4 3263 3.
Θηβαΐς 3243 ¹ 12, [² 7?] 3247 19.

μέση τοπαρχία 3264 6.
Ὀξυρυγχίτης (nome) 3240 8 3246 4 [3249 4]
3250 9, 25 [3254 4] 3259 5? (3260 3) 3265 9.
Ὀξυρυγχιτῶν πόλις 3244 3, 7 3245 5, (11) 3246 9
3249 11 3252 4 3254 6 3255 4 3256 2 3257 5
3258 3 3259 6 3260 5 3265 6 3266 4.
Ὀξυρύγχων (πόλις) 3241 1, [16] 3242 3 3251 2–3.
πάγος [3254 4] (η′) 3260 3 (ϛ′).
Πέρσης (τῆς ἐπιγονῆς) 3250 2.
Πολέμωνος μερίς 3243 ¹ 3–4 3263 3.

(b) Villages, etc.

Ἀγανθών see Ἀκανθών.
Ἀκανθών 3250 9, 28 (Ἀγανθῶνος).
Ἀντιπέρα Πέλα 3256 7 3258 7 3259 9 3260 8.
Ἀπόλλωνος πόλις (Arsinoite) 3263 5, 13.
Ἰσεῖον Παγγᾶ 3255 8 3257 7.
Λιλῆ 3250 9, 27.
Μέρμερθα 3247 5.
Μονίμου (ἐποίκιον) 3242 23 3244 17.

Πεεννώ 3264 6.
Πέλα see Ἀντιπέρα Πέλα.
Σκώ 3242 6, 21.
Τῆις 3254 4.
Τμουνεψή (Aphroditopolite) 3252 8.
Ὑφαντών 3250 1.
Χουτῆ (ἐποίκιον) 3260 3.
Ψιντεώ (Arsinoite) 3263 6, 13.

(c) Miscellaneous

Ἀπολλωνίου κλῆρος 3242 6.
Κλαυδιανὰ μέταλλα 3243 ¹ 14.
Νέςλα (περίχωμα) 3257 7.
Νικοβίου κλῆρος 3256 7.
Πέκτυ (περίχωμα) 3255 9.

Πορφυριτικὰ καὶ Κλαυδιανὰ μέταλλα 3243 ¹ 14.
Ποσειδίππου κλῆρος 3242 21.
Πρωτολε.. 3259 9 (ἐν ... Π. λεγομένου, sic).
Τέλκε (τόπος Τ. καλούμενος) 3255 9.

VIII. RELIGION

Ἀδριανεῖον 3249 12 3251 5.
Ἀθηναῖον see Index XI(a) s.v. μέτρον Ἀθηναίου.
ἀρχιερατεύειν 3251 3.
ἀρχιερεύς 3263 10.
θεωρία 3248 5.
ἱερός 3248 3, 13.

Καπιτωλιακός [3248 4?].
σεβάσμιος 3251 4.
Σεβαστεῖον 3248 2.
Σουχεῖον 3244 40?
τύχη (genius) 3244 12 3264 30.

IX. OFFICIAL AND MILITARY TERMS AND TITLES

X. PROFESSIONS, TRADES, AND OCCUPATIONS

XI. MEASURES

(a) WEIGHTS AND MEASURES

(b) MONEY

XII. TAXES

ἀννῶνα [3257 11].
δημόσια 3255 18 3257 11 [3260 16].
ἐγκυκλιακόν 3241 6.
ἐπικλαςμός 3254 20.

ἐπιμεριςμός [3254 20].
πενταναυβία 3264 14.
προπρατικόν 3241 8.
τέλεςμα, δημόσια τελέςματα 3254 19–20, 26.

XIII. GENERAL INDEX OF WORDS

ἀγαθός see ἄριςτος.
ἀγρόδρυον see ἀκρόδρυον.
ἀγροφύλαξ see Index X.
ἀγωγή 3250 3.
αἱρεῖν 3250 6 3251 21 3266 9.
ἀκίνδυνος 3255 17 [3256 19] 3257 10 3260 15 3266 13.
ἀκρόδρυον 3242 7 (ἀγρ- pap.).
ἁλιεύς see Index X.
ἀλλά 3247 8 3253 11.
ἀλληλέγγυος 3251 19 3257 16.
ἀλλήλων 3250 10 [3254 11].
ἄλλος 3240 8 3249 7 3264 5, 16, 24.
ἄμπελος 3242 7, (12), 19, 20.
ἄμφοδον see Index IX.
ἀμφότερος 3245 10 3246 6 3247 7 3256 4 3257 4.
ἄν see ἔςτ' ἄν.
ἀνά 3255 13 3257 9.
ἀνάγειν 3242 13.
ἀναγκαίως 3265 11.
ἀναγράφειν 3242 17.
ἀναλαμβάνειν 3250 18.
ἀνάλωμα 3256 15 3261 14.
ἀνάπαυςις 3256 8.
ἀνάπλους 3250 16, 20.
ἀναυλί 3250 8.
ἀναφόριον 3240 9 3264 9, 32.
ἀνενδεῶς 3244 14.
ἀνήκειν 3263 8 3265 8–9.
ἀνήρ 3264 11, 16, 20.
ἀννῶνα see Index XII.
ἀνορμεῖν (?) 3250 23.
ἀντί 3255 13, 15 3256 9, 14 3260 10 3266 9.
ἀντίγραφον (3245 25).
ἀνυπερθέτως 3250 19 3255 23 3257 15 3260 22 3266 16.
ἀνυπόλογος 3266 13.
ἄνω see Index VII(a) s.v. ἄνω τοπαρχία.
ἀπαιτεῖν 3247 10, [12], 13.
ἁπαξαπλῶς 3261 13.
ἀπεργάζεςθαι 3264 17.
ἀπέχειν 3254 24.

ἀπηλιώτης (3242 18).
ἁπλοῦς 3261 20.
ἀπό 3241 1, 16 3242 3, 8, 10 3243 1 6, 2 3 3244 7, 15 3245 6, [10] 3249 10, 13 3250 1, 6, 12 3251 2, 6 3252 8 3253 6 [3254 3, 5] 3255 6, 8 3256 1 ?, 4, 6, 8, 12 3257 5, 6 3258 3, 5 3259 5 ?, 5, 7 3260 2, 4, 7 3262 2, 2 3264 19 3266 3, [11].
ἀπογράφεςθαι 3242 3, 20, 23.
ἀποδεικνύναι 3260 1 3264 31.
ἀποδιδόναι 3250 15 3251 10, 14 3255 20 3257 14 3260 21 3266 14.
ἀπόδοςις 3266 19.
ἀποκαθιςτάναι [3240 16] 3247 4 3250 8.
ἀποκεῖςθαι 3243 1 10.
ἀπολαμβάνειν 3253 7 3255 19 3257 12 3260 19.
ἀποπλεῖν 3250 19.
ἀποτίνειν 3250 29.
ἀπουςία 3247 6.
ἀποφαίνειν 3264 27.
*[ἀπο]χιμαῖος? 3247 14.
ἄραξ 3250 6, 15, 19, 26.
ἀργυρικός 3255 21 3257 14.
ἀργύριον 3250 11 3251 9, 17 3252 19 3255 13 3257 9 3266 7, [12], 17.
ἀρίθμηςις 3254 15.
ἀριςτερός 3245 16.
ἄριςτος 3246 10.
ἄρουρα see Index XI(a).
ἁρπάζειν 3240 12.
ἀρτάβη see Index XI(a).
ἀρχαῖος 3242 7.
ἀρχιερατεύειν see Index VIII.
ἀρχιερεύς see Index VIII.
ἀςφάλεια 3240 6, 13 3250 20.
ἀςφαλής 3250 24.
αὐθαιρέτως 3252 12.
Αὐτοκράτωρ see Index III; Index IV (A.D. 297, 319).
αὐτός 3240 11, 12 3241 6, 9, 11, [25] 3244 8 3245 6, 12, 14, 15 [3249 14] 3250 15, 22, 27, 30 3251 4 3252 19 3253 5, 9, 11, [18], 21 3255 6 3256 4, 12, 12, 17 3257 7, 15 3258 5

τέссαρες **3255** 13.

τέταρτος (**3242** 8, 9, 15, [16]) **3251** 17 **3255** [10], 11.

τετρακισχίλιοι **3266** 18.

τέχνη [**3265** 9].

τιμή **3250** 30 [**3254** 11].

τίρων *see* Index IX.

τις **3243** ³ 3 **3253** 14, 16 **3264** 24.

τίς **3253** 8, 10.

τοίνυν **3246** 10.

τόκος **3251** 18.

τοπαρχία *see* Index VII(*a*) s.vv. ἄνω τ., μέςη τ.

τόπος **3240** 15 **3243** ¹ 15 **3250** 13 **3255** 9.

τραῦμα **3245** 16.

τρεῖς **3247** 9 **3257** 10.

τριακάς **3251** 11.

τρίτος **3241** 12, [26] **3260** 11, 19, [21].

τροφή **3243** ¹ 12.

τύχη *see* Index VIII.

ὕδρευμα **3242** 15.

ὑελουργός *see* Index X.

υἱός **3259** 5 **3262** 1.

ὑπάρχειν **3242** 5, 20 **3255** 8 **3256** 6 **3257** 6 [**3258** 7] **3259** 8 **3266** 20.

ὑπατεία *see* Index IV (A.D. 312–15); (A.D. 315); (A.D. 318); (A.D. 319); (A.D. 324); (A.D. 326); (A.D. 337).

ὕπατος *see* Index IV (A.D. 297); (A.D. 323); (A.D. 324).

ὑπέρ **3241** 4 **3247** 8 **3252** 19 **3255** 12 **3257** 9 **3260** 31 **3264** 24.

ὑπερπίπτειν **3251** 15 **3266** 16–17.

ὑπηρ[.].[**3245** 24.

ὑπηρετεῖν **3243** ¹ 13.

ὑπηρέτης *see* Index IX.

ὑπό **3240** 12 **3241** 5 **3242** 4 **3245** 7, 9 **3247** 10 **3252** 24 **3253** 11, 19 **3264** 8.

ὑπογράφειν **3261** 2.

ὑπογραφή **3261** 20.

ὑπόλογος **3266** 14.

ὑπόμνημα [**3241** 25].

ὑπομνηματίζειν [**3248** 8?, 9?].

ὑπομνηματογράφος *see* Index IX.

ὑφιστάναι **3261** 14.

φακός **3251** 8.

φέρειν **3253** 3.

φίλος **3253** 1.

φοῖνιξ **3242** 7.

φόρος **3251** 6 **3255** 12, 13, 20, 21 **3256** 10 **3257** 9, 14 **3260** 10.

φορτίον **3247** 9.

φροντιστής *see* Index X.

φυλή *see* Index IX.

χαίρειν (**3240** 8) **3241** 4, [19] **3243** ¹ 4 **3251** 5 **3253** 1 [**3254** 6] **3261** 5 **3262** 2 **3266** 6.

χειμών **3250** 23.

χείρ **3245** 16 **3262** 4 **3266** 7.

χειρογραφία **3261** 12.

χειρόγραφον (**3244** 41) **3266** 21.

χίλιοι **3247** 12 **3252** 20 **3257** 10.

χίρ *see* χείρ.

χιρογραφεία *see* χειρογραφία.

χορηγεῖν **3244** 12.

χορηγία **3250** 21.

χρ[**3254** 21.

χρεία **3243** ¹ 13 **3249** 17 **3265** 9, 13, 14.

χρόνος **3242** 11, 13 **3251** 16 **3266** 17.

χῶμα **3246** 10 **3264** 14, [25].

χωματεπιμελητής *see* Index IX.

ὡς [**3244** 35] **3247** 4 **3252** 21 **3253** 16 **3255** 24 **3257** 16 [**3260** 23] **3265** 15, 20.

ὥστε **3245** 11 **3250** 8, 11.

PLATE I

fr. 4

fr. 5

fr. 2

fr. 1

fr. 3

fr. 6

3209

PLATE II

fr. 1

fr. 2

fr. 3

fr. 4

fr. 5

fr. 6

fr. 7

fr. 8

fr. 9

fr. 10

3210

PLATE III

3212

3215 fr. 2

fr. 1

fr. 2

3213

3215 fr. 1

PLATE IV

ΑΡΩΣΗΝΗΗΛCΕΝΑΝ
ΑΞΑΝ...ΟΗC
ΛΕΛ...   ΔΙΑ΄ΦΟ
ΙΝΟΙCΙ   ...ΓΧΟC
ΕΞΑΝΤΙΟΠΗC
...ΤΟΝΤΟΝΕΥ΄ΔΟΝΚΙ
ΕΚΦΟΙΝΕΙΟC
...ΩΝΛΕΙΠΕΤΗΚΗΔ
ΕΚΠΙΩΤΕCΙΛΛΟΥ
ΟΥΛΜΙCΚΛΛΟC
ΛΙΚΟCΟΥΝΕΝΑΝ
ΤΟΥ   Λ ΙΛΟΝ...
...ΙΝΛΧΙΗΜ.ΥΗΛ...
ΥΤΟCΟΥΓΕΝΟ..Λ

3214

3216

3217

ΟΙΤΑΥΤΗΝΙΔΩΝ.ΥΘ
ΟΙΛΝΤΕΧΩΝΝΕΟΥ
ΜΑΔΙΚΕΙCΜΑΡΤΥΡΟΝ
ΛΗΓΜΑΤΟΥCΟΟΥC
ΕΛ ΙΚΩΝΙΟCΠΙΩΝ
...ΛΘΕΙΠΕC

ΡΩΗCΟΜΑΛ
ΙΟCΧΙΩΛΗ
ΛΤΕΛΙΠΟΗ
...ΤΩΒΛ
.Ε..Ε

3218

PLATE V

fr. 1

fr. 3

fr. 2

fr. 4

3229

PLATE VI

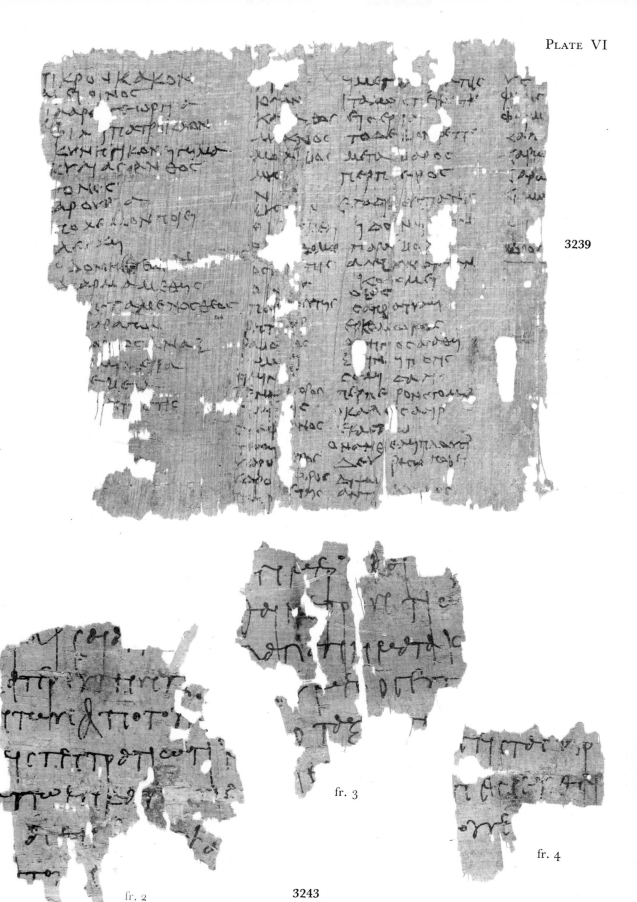

3239

fr. 2

fr. 3

fr. 4

3243

PLATE VII

PLATE VIII